Gretsch® 6120

The History of a Legendary Guitar

Try this fast, easy-playing guitar!

....says Chet Atkins

THE FRED. GRETSCH MFG. CO.

Edward Ball

Schiffer Publishing Ltd®

4880 Lower Valley Road Atglen, Pennsylvania 19310
Printed in China

Dedication

For my Dad, who showed me that this was possible, and my Mom, who helped make it happen.

First writing lesson, spring 1966.

Other Schiffer Books on Related Subjects:

Vintage Electric Guitars: In Praise of Fretted America,
0-7643-1361-4, $29.95

Electric Guitars, 0-7643-0964-1, $39.95

Photo Credits

Previous Page: *Guitar Courtesy of Vintage & Rare Guitars.*

Front Cover: *Guitar Courtesy of Andrew Morrison. Photo by Steve Hovery.*

Page 192: *Photo Courtesy of Ted Broman.*

Back Cover: *Chet Akins Photo by Gordon Gillingham, ©2008 Grand Ole Opry. Brian Setzer Photo Courtesy of Naoaki Toyofuku.*

Cover and book designed by: Bruce Waters
Type set in Humanist 521-Headings, Goudy Oldstyle-Text

ISBN: 978-0-7643-3484-9
Printed in China

Schiffer Books are available at special discounts for bulk purchases for sales promotions or premiums. Special editions, including personalized covers, corporate imprints, and excerpts can be created in large quantities for special needs. For more information contact the publisher:

Acknowledgments

This book would not have been possible without the gracious contribution of images from a lot of wonderful people. They are recognized throughout the book. There are several, however, who have participated to such a large degree that they became integral to the project's success. My heartfelt thanks go to Rick Burda, Nino Fazio, Christopher Guido, Rod McDonald, Daniel Nicolas, Sergio Rivero, Dave Rogers, Fred Stucky, Anne Tangeman, and Steve Wilson.

Published by Schiffer Publishing Ltd.
4880 Lower Valley Road
Atglen, PA 19310
Phone: (610) 593-1777; Fax: (610) 593-2002
E-mail: Info@schifferbooks.com

For the largest selection of fine reference books on this and related subjects, please visit our web site at
www.schifferbooks.com
We are always looking for people to write books on new and related subjects. If you have an idea for a book please contact us at the above address.

This book may be purchased from the publisher.
Include $5.00 for shipping.
Please try your bookstore first.
You may write for a free catalog.

In Europe, Schiffer books are distributed by
Bushwood Books
6 Marksbury Ave.
Kew Gardens
Surrey TW9 4JF England
Phone: 44 (0) 20 8392 8585; Fax: 44 (0) 20 8392 9876
E-mail: info@bushwoodbooks.co.uk
Website: www.bushwoodbooks.co.uk

Contents

Introduction

Most things in life are iterative—not the result of an original and unique occurrence. Music, for example, is highly sensitive to influence, and each new sound evolves from something before. The Beatles' album *Sgt. Pepper's Lonely Heart's Club Band* did not miraculously materialize in June 1967. This landmark was dependent on "I Want to Hold Your Hand" (1964) coming first, which in turn would not have been created without Chuck Berry's musical contributions before it, and T-Bone Walker's before that, and so on and so on, back to the very beginnings of music.

Similarly, the tools used to create music have also evolved over time. There have been times when a new musical direction has served to promote a change in an instrument's design, and other times when an advance in instrument technology has made an impact on the sound of subsequent music.

Even though most things are on a perpetual continuum of evolution, there are instances when, despite the development of a more advanced form of something, a prior manifestation is still deemed desirable. Vintage guitars are an example of this. So refined are the current automated processes of instrument construction, modern materials, and technology of sound, that it is hard for some to accept that a guitar from fifty years ago could possibly be better than a new one. This, of course, represents a matter of taste, and is highly subjective. But using the marketplace as a gauge, some musicians are willing to pay many times over what they would for a brand new modern guitar to posses one from the Golden Era of the 1950s and '60s. It seems there must be something better about them. Granted, some buyers are willing to invest these exorbitant prices to simply pay homage to the guitar heroes of their yesteryear, or to recapture some element of their youth. Regardless, many purists will debate that the sonic qualities of these older versions are superior, and as such are willing to pay a premium to achieve that standard.

The journey through time does not follow a constant trajectory of progress. An era that achieves higher standards can sometimes be followed by a period with lesser advancement, or even degradation. The culture and people of a period dictate this change.

Over time popular music and the instruments used to play it are susceptible to these fluctuations and influences. In a modern context, this would include marketplace conditions, technological advancements, and the fickle artistic trends of the moment. However, in the big picture of things, these influences may not always be positive.

Cultural influences can often lead to missteps in advancement, however, it tends to happen so gradually that they are not perceived and corrected until much later. This is how an antique can be more desirable than a similar contemporary item and is one reason for the popularity of the antiques market. Be it furniture, art, or jewelry, people seem to long for items from the past that represent the epitome of an original form. Vintage American guitars are a prime case study of this phenomenon.

The fact that a 1959 Gretsch Chet Atkins 6120 hollowbody guitar graced the cover of the May 1996 issue of *Art & Antiques* magazine not only illustrates the mainstream appeal that vintage guitars were having at the time, but also the status of this particular model within the collector's community. The fact that it is actually a 1958 model year guitar reinforces the value of the book you are reading!

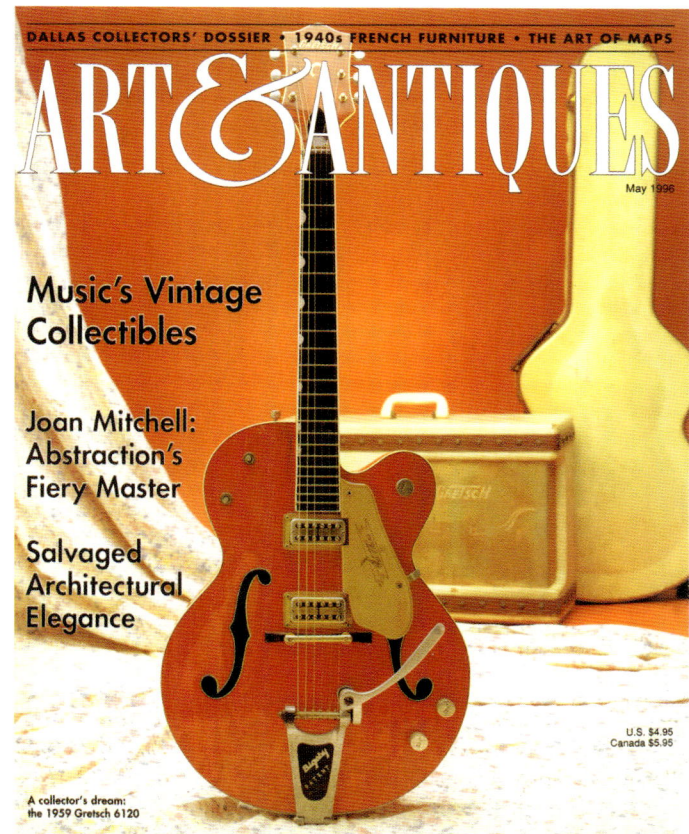

DALLAS COLLECTORS' DOSSIER • 1940s FRENCH FURNITURE • THE ART OF MAPS

ART&ANTIQUES

May 1996

Music's Vintage Collectibles

Joan Mitchell: Abstraction's Fiery Master

Salvaged Architectural Elegance

A collector's dream: the 1959 Gretsch 6120

U.S. $4.95
Canada $5.95

Environmental Influences on Evolution

Evolution can be defined as the change in something over generations. The most notable evolutionary theorist is Charles Darwin, whose 1859 *On the Origin of Species* introduced his fundamental principle of natural selection, which states that the variations which prove advantageous to a plant or animal in its struggle for existence in a changing evironment better enable it to survive. These favorable variations, which are manifested as structural changes to the organism, are then passed on to the offspring of the survivors and spread to successive generations. This is known as descent with modification.

This same general theory can be applied to modern cultural artifacts, including automobiles, fashion, and even guitars. Most of these have an ancestry of more primitive versions of their current state, and tracking the corporate and cultural influences affecting any consumer product line is also an interesting study in evolution.

The questions this book considers are: just what were the changes in the American environment and how did they influence structural changes within the Gretsch guitar product line?

This book identifies and analyzes examples of subtle product line transitions, a few big breakthroughs, and the key environmental shifts that ultimately influenced The Gretsch Company to produce one of the most iconic of musical symbols, the Chet Atkins 6120 Hollowbody guitar.

It is evolution and the idea of common ancestry that explains why this 1850s German parlor model is so alien when compared to the Golden Era guitars that Gretsch made one hundred years later. *Photo Courtesy of Jesse Whiteside, Folkway Music*.

Dyer Style 5 (c.1912). *Photo Courtesy of Jesse Whiteside, Folkway Music*.

Much as the dinosaurs were driven to extinction by an abrupt change in their environment, these amazing acoustic models had pretty much disappeared by the mid-1920s in favor of the more utilitarian acoustic archtop format. (above and opposite)

This 1925 Gibson L-5 is considered one of the most influential guitar designs ever produced. *Photo Courtesy of Jesse Whiteside, Folkway Music.*

Gibson Style-U Harp Guitar (c.1916). *Courtesy of Nino Fazio, Real Vintage Guitars, Italy.*

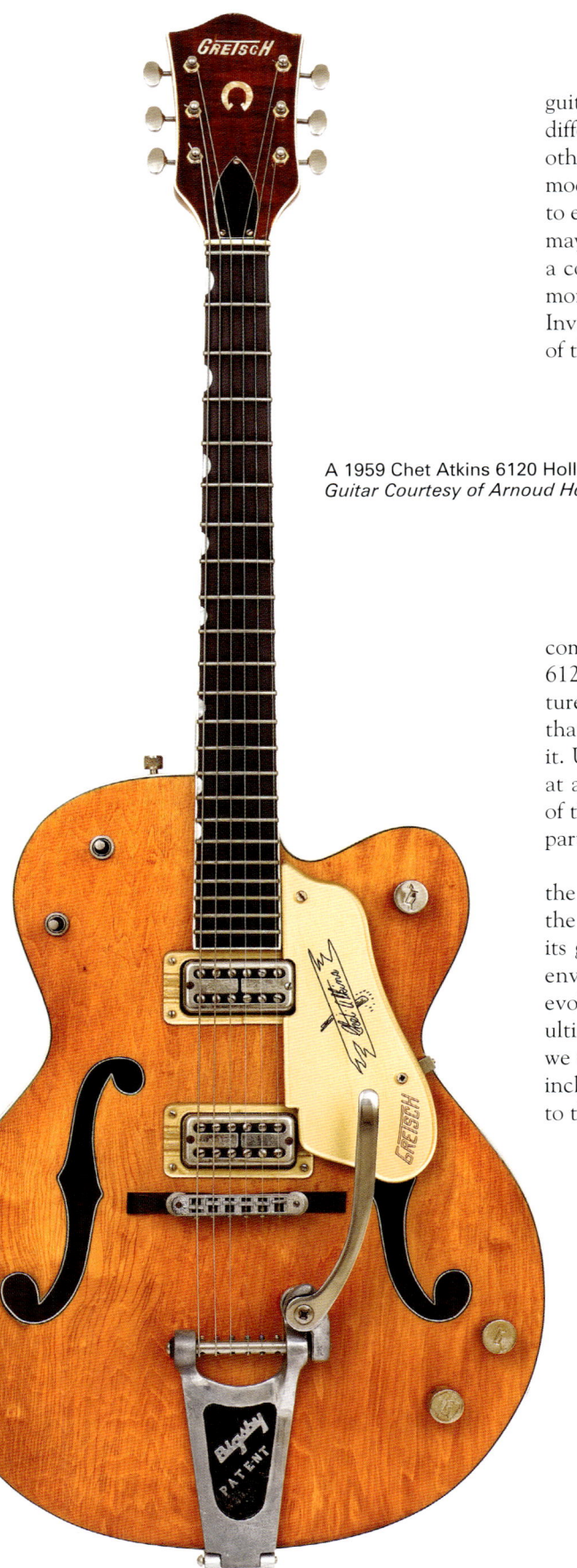

Invariably, some of the changes introduced to Gretsch guitars in the 1950s were motivated by novelty and the need to differentiate from other manufacturers' instruments. But clearly other changes speak to the theory of natural selection. They are modifications that have proven more effective for the musician to execute the desired musical style than previous designs. They may also be an attempt to mimic and benefit from a trait that a competitor has proven successful. Guitars that lacked a new, more effective attribute, did not sell well, and were discontinued. Inversely, a guitar that continued to meet the ever changing needs of the musician remained in demand and survived.

A 1959 Chet Atkins 6120 Hollowbody from the #299xx batch.
Guitar Courtesy of Arnoud Holsboer. Photo by Daniel Nicolas.

Darwin's evidence for evolution depended on data from comparative anatomy. Using the micro example of the Gretsch 6120 model, this book examines the various and respective features of this guitar and carefully documents the transformations that resulted in the several models that proceeded and followed it. Unlike nature, changes to the Gretsch line were engineered at a rapid pace, not only occurring in every annual generation of their product line, but even between and within batches of a particular generation.

To understand the common ancestry of Gretsch guitars from the Golden Era, we will need to delve deeply into the origins of the electric archtop guitar and understand the forces that drove its genesis. From there, a journey forward through the various environmental changes will eventually lead us to the highly evolved late 1950s 6120 model electric archtop guitar, and its ultimate place at the top of the Gretsch guitar species. Finally, we will address the modern day legacy of this influential model, including how, 50 years after its conception, it remains the key to the success of the Gretsch brand.

Gretsch Mania

But why should we care about evolution and the series of events that led up to the manifestation of the Chet Atkins 6120 guitar? As fans of pop-culture and/or vintage guitars, we enjoy immersing ourselves in the minutia of our addiction. It is human nature. The desire to understand where we came from is in all of us, and many of us project that need to know onto the inanimate objects that are near and dear to us. This inquisitiveness is not unique to the vintage guitar enthusiast. Many people have a child-like fascination with the past, especially when new revelations are presented which challenge what we thought we knew.

At our core, humans are hunters and gatherers. We inherently seek and find. This is one of the reasons collecting vintage guitars can be such a compelling interest. The search for these elusive instruments is half the fun. But when we start talking about pricey collectible vintage guitars, sometimes the only thing many of us can afford to hunt and gather is information.

Herein lays the value of the research offered in this book. The hope is that the information on the evolution of the Gretsch electric archtop guitar will serve to feed that hunger for knowledge. Perhaps it will help create more of a connection to this wonderful symbol of American nostalgia, even if you cannot afford the $15,000 price tag for a clean and original vintage 1950s 6120 of your own.

The other obvious question is: why Gretsch? Think of it as the road less traveled. Gibson and Fender have sold many more guitars than The Gretsch Company since the 1950s. They each have their own colorful stories, contributions to music, and tales of product and product line maturation. The histories of these companies have been well and accurately documented.

The Gretsch Company, on the other hand, still retains an air of mystery in many ways. Part of this intrigue is the fact that much of its production history is reported to have been lost to fires in the 1970s. So, where there is annual production data and shipping totals available for most Gibson models going back five or six decades, there is no such archive of the Gretsch manufacturing legacy in the vaults of the current company. This fact, the passage of time, and the dissemination of misinformation through the Internet, has resulted in a fair amount of inaccurate data about the Gretsch product line circulating within today's vintage guitar community.

Limited exposure has also made Gretsch electric archtop guitars less familiar to the general public. Although there were some key associations with celebrity artists, which are thoroughly documented in this book, they tended to be from the 1950s era. In addition, the popular music of the mid-1960s and '70s did not lend itself to the full-sized, hollowbody format. Gretsch began producing different designs, to address the apparent limitations of the Golden Era instruments, which became increasingly less prevalent. And finally, the fact that the Gretsch guitar product line disappeared from the guitar community all together from 1980 to 1989 might have impacted its perceived place in the hierarchy of brands.

This mystique is in part what draws many of us to Gretsch. Musicians and collectors who have grown bored with the endless sea of seemingly identical Fender Stratocasters, and equally pervasive Gibson Les Paul models, as well as the many clones of each, have found uniqueness in the Gretsch guitar product. Perhaps these Gretsch guitars appeal to their rebellious side, which seems to be inherent in many musicians, as they endeavor to not be like everybody else. Or, maybe it is simply the ego trip they enjoy when they go into a club or vintage guitar show and open their case revealing a Gretsch archtop and receive the admiration and compliments of everybody in the room. It is hard to say for sure, but those that have discovered the magic of these instruments seem to fall hard, and typically require more than one. These are the loyal disciples, those who are willing to align their allegiance to a brand whose cool factor remains indisputable.

GRETSCH
INSTRUMENTS

Gretsch

GRETSCH

Gretsch Serial Numbers: Methodology of the Data

Historically there were only a few resources available to assist with dating vintage Gretsch guitars by their serial numbers. The first real attempt at unlocking the secret of the Gretsch chronology and serial numbering system was published 25 years ago in A.R. Duchossoir's *Guitar Identification*. Ten years later Jay Scott provided much more context to those attributions in his wonderful book *The Guitars of the Fred Gretsch Company*. As invaluable as these resources were, they were also fairly non-committal about defining model versus production year and they often dealt in round numbers with generous overlaps of up to 1000 serial numbers (i.e. 1000 guitars) between years. Considering that Gretsch's annual production at the beginning of the 1950s was 1500-2000 guitars, and by the end of the decade had only just exceeded 4000 units, an overlap of 1000 guitars makes for a substantial margin of error. However, these historically accepted parameters are not necessarily incorrect, just imprecise.

Since Gretsch's official production records were reportedly lost to fires in the 1970s, it is not clear how the existing rules of thumb for chronology were developed. Today the concepts of "model year" (feature-based) versus "production year" (calendar-based) can easily become convoluted when discussing Gretsch guitars, particularly the ever changing 6120 Chet Atkins Hollowbody model. This book endeavors to establish exactly how each model year's attributions are determined, and occasionally suggests their relationship to calendar year production. These calculations are based on new serial number research and batch identification, which has been distilled from the analysis and comparison of thousands of vintage Gretsch examples from the company's Golden Era of the 1950s and '60s.

The methodology employed in this book exploits the sequential nature of the Gretsch serial numbering system and cross-references it against the various model year feature changes found from production batch to production batch. Other evidence considered when drawing conclusions on this chronology includes first hand accounts, surviving original bills of sale, dated neck stamps, and documented potentiometer code information.

Research has confirmed that the Gretsch factory manufactured its guitars in batches typically comprised of either 50 or 100 units of a particular model. Throughout this book batches are referenced by the first three digits of the five-digit serial number followed by "xx" (i.e. batch #262xx). This assumes that most 100-unit batches begin at #26200, for instance, and run through #26299. This, however, was not always the case and it is possible that a batch could begin in the middle (at #26250) if it was a smaller 50-unit batch. If a 100-unit group followed a 50-unit batch it would create a scenario like batch #16450-16549. It is probable that there were some exceptions. For example, not every batch was exactly 50 or 100 units in size, but it would appear that most were, so this is the method for their identification within this resource.

One revelation that has become apparent from this research is that the Gretsch serial numbering system was not nearly as haphazard as history has suggested. Admittedly there have been two separate occasions identified where upwards of 1000 consecutive serial numbers were either not used in sequence, or not used at all. Beyond these instances, the company remained fairly consistent with its logical administration throughout the period when the sequential numbering system was in place (late 1940s to early 1966). Furthermore, this research has yielded a new hypothesis for why there seems to exist many Gretsch examples from 1966—the year the company abandoned its customary sequential serial numbering in favor of a date-coded approach—with anomalous serial numbers.

Even with this new wealth of data about Gretsch guitar production, there remains no definitive, Gretsch Company endorsed timeline of events. A certain amount of interpretation and even speculation becomes unavoidable to glean meaning from the raw data. The book attempts to identify those situations throughout the text so as to leave room for alternative theories. There is no doubt that there will be some who disagree with the attribution of one batch or another, or exactly when a certain feature was introduced. History itself may ultimately redefine these parameters as more information inevitably surfaces. This is exactly why the website http://www.6120freak.com was developed—to continue the quest for accuracy beyond what these pages can deliver.

Section I

A Very Brief History of The Gretsch Company

If you are already a Gretsch fanatic, you can probably skip over this brief, but necessary, Gretsch Company history. However, in case this book has lured any of the uninitiated into its pages, there is an obligation to provide you with the basic background information about the brand. With that in mind, the following is an abbreviated account of the company's beginnings and the origin of the 6120.

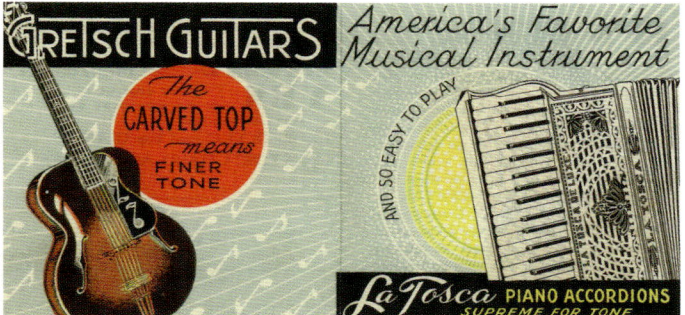

A view of the Brooklyn Gretsch factory building at 60 Broadway from the Brooklyn-Queens expressway. This historic building was converted to luxury condos in 2005. *Photo Courtesy of Larry Lader.*

Before relocating to 60 Broadway in 1916, The Gretsch Company operated from this seven-story building at 104 South 4th Street in Brooklyn, New York. *Courtesy of The Gretsch Company.*

In 1883, the same year the Brooklyn bridge opened, a young German immigrant named Friedrich Gretsch opened a musical instrument shop in Brooklyn, New York. Friedrich passed away in 1895 leaving his teenage son, Fred Sr., to run the business. By 1916 Fred Sr. had established himself as a major American distributor and manufacturer of musical instruments, such as banjos, accordions, and drums at The Gretsch Company's new Brooklyn factory at 60 Broadway.

Gretsch transitioned to making self-branded archtop acoustic guitars in the 1930s, first with a line of mid and lower-end instruments, then with a high quality offering in 1939. After an initial partnership with the Kay Musical Instrument Company in Chicago prior to World War II, Gretsch began manufacturing its own electric archtop guitars in the late 1940s.

In 1942, Fred Jr. took over from his father, but soon joined the Navy and relinquished operations to his brother William (Bill), who died unexpectedly in 1948. Fred Jr. was reinstated as President and oversaw the company through its Golden Era of the 1950s and early 1960s, before selling the Gretsch brand to the Baldwin Piano Company in 1967. Baldwin ultimately moved its manufacturing operation to Booneville, Arkansas, where in the early 1970s they endured several fires. Gretsch branded guitar production was eventually discontinued in the early 1980s.

Fred W. Gretsch with a Brian Setzer Nashville 6120 model guitar. *Courtesy of The Gretsch Company.*

The Gretsch name reemerged when Fred W. Gretsch, great grandson of Fredrick Gretsch, bought back the company in 1985 and began producing guitars again in 1989. In late 2002 an agreement was made with the Fender Musical Instrument Company (FMIC) to oversee all the manufacturing and distribution of the Gretsch guitar line. A decade into the new millennium, the Gretsch brand is strong. Although most production now takes place outside the US, the quality of the instruments is outstanding, and the breadth of the line unprecedented. Much of this success is a result of the effective rebirth of the 6120 model and the many variations that Gretsch/FMIC have spun of the original Chet Atkins-endorsed hollowbody guitar.

The brevity of this historical overview is not intended to minimize or under-appreciate the efforts required to build a successful, privately owned American business and brand through four generations. This is truly an impressive accomplishment and a manifestation of the American Dream. However, other than its mere survival, the events of the first fifty years of The Gretsch Company have little to do with the factors that contributed to the birth of the iconic 6120 model. The following chapters will identify the cultural events, key personalities, and marketplace pressures that influenced both American music and the guitar industry, and ultimately enabled the birth of this classic American symbol. To begin to understand the genesis of all this, we must initially immerse ourselves into the dynamics of American music and culture of the 1930s.

Music and Culture in the 1930s

The guitars we made in the '30s and post war period of the late '40s...they were the preamble to the 6120.

-Fred W. Gretsch, president, The Gretsch Company

History might suggest that the 1930s and the onset of the Great Depression ended the party many enjoyed in the late 1920s. The lavish dance halls with full orchestras pumping endless ragtime and dance music were abruptly silenced when the American stock market crashed.

Despite this dark period in history, the ever resilient American people continued to desire entertainment. As access to electricity expanded, so did the expansion and continued development of the radio. Throughout the 1930s millions of home radios were sold in the United States and suddenly the masses were able to enjoy music in their homes. Other advancements that would soon impact the cultural landscape of American music included the invention of the car radio in 1929 and the development of the jukebox in the 1930s.

Student sheet music holders were used as a marketing device by The Gretsch Company. This one is circa 1935.

Even during the heart of the Great Depression music was alive. Radio City Music Hall opened in 1932—its 6000 seats made it the largest facility of its kind. Then, in 1933, stereo recording first emerged. Many aficionados consider a December 1934 broadcast of NBC Radio's *Let's Dance,* featuring the Benny Goodman Orchestra, to be the birth of swing music. Just a few years later, *Billboard Magazine* published the first "Music Hit Parade" reflecting popular taste in music, which by 1938 included another new musical style called boogie-woogie. Music was really beginning to change as the 1940s loomed, and The Gretsch Company was preparing to make a splash.

The Competitive Environment

There were many manufacturers producing high-end professional quality orchestra-style archtop guitars during this period. The field was comprised of companies and brands, such as Epiphone, Regal, Stromberg, and Paramount, as well as mid-range quality archtop offerings from Harmony, Kay, and Vega. Even Martin had a competitive pre-war acoustic archtop guitar model. But indisputably, the giant of the field was the Gibson Company, which had set the standard for design excellence with the 1922 release of the 16" wide L-5 acoustic archtop model.

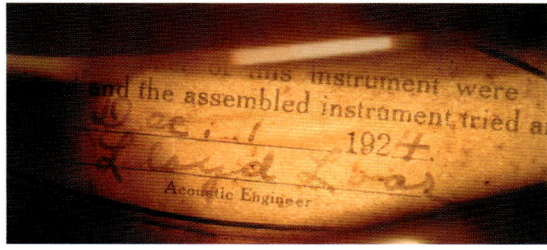

The success of the Gibson L-5 model affected all the musical instrument makers of this period. This 1924 specimen is signed by Lloyd Loar. *Courtesy of Nino Fazio, Real Vintage Guitars, Italy.*

Gibson had enjoyed a majority market share since the 1920s when Lloyd Loar, their famed acoustics engineer, developed high-end acoustic instruments for the Master Model Series. In many people's minds, Loar is considered the architect of the modern stringed instrument. For a period of time he hand-signed the labels of many instruments, taking personal accountability, and probably pride, in their acoustic perfection. Today, a Loar-signed Gibson L-5 is like the Holy Grail for vintage guitar enthusiasts and can fetch upwards of $50,000.

The original Gibson L-5 model was introduced as a f-hole archtop at approximately 16" wide. This guitar set the precedent for this body format, which would then be emulated by most competitors. It is important to note that in this period of time the 16" body format was popular in both the high-end and budget line guitars. However, due to the need for increased volume within the ensemble-based musical environment of the day, many manufacturers were making their premier instruments with wider 17" and 18"-plus formats. This was illustrated by Gibson's decision in the mid-1930s to unveil the Advanced Line of their existing models, which were outfitted with larger body widths. The 1934 Advanced L-5, for example, was 17" wide.

Another important competitor, located close to Gretsch's and Epiphone's New York operations was John D'Angelico (1905-1964). Although D'Angelico never rivaled the shear volume of guitars the others could produce, the company enjoyed a reputation for excellence in design aesthetics second to none. D'Angelico hand built exceptionally fine archtop instruments that reflected the city's art deco architecture of the 1930s and were revered by many of the finest musicians of the day. D'Angelico's earliest archtops possessed specifications very similar to the 16" parallel-braced Gibson L-5.

This 1934 D'Angelico Exel is one of the earliest made. The spelling of the model was changed to Excel soon after. *Courtesy of Nino Fazio, Real Vintage Guitars, Italy.*

D'Angelico's flagship models from the mid-1930s throughout his career were the 17" wide Excel, which originated with a slightly smaller body, and the 18" wide New Yorker, introduced in 1936. Each of these models exploited X-bracing inside their acoustically engineered archtop bodies, which were typically constructed with a spruce top and a highly figured, curly maple back and sides.

Both can be found with Grover Imperial tuning machines, although some Excels display the more pedestrian button style. D'Angelico's early production guitars employed non-adjustable, metal reinforced necks, but by the early 1950s he had adopted the Gibson approach of an adjustable truss rod with access at the headstock.

His guitars are notorious for the lavish mother-of-pearl inlay on the their headstocks. Every appointment was crafted with elegance, including the variety of fretboard marker designs he applied, the classic pickguard shapes, the multi-layered bindings, and the distinctive tailpieces that typically bore the D'Angelico name. In the late 1940s a single-cutaway option was first offered by special request, ultimately becoming the more popular format.

Although his records show that he made less than 1200 guitars, D'Angelico's distinctive style and design sensibilities have made his instruments legendary to musicians and collectors alike. An interesting fact is that at the time Gretsch first approached Chet Atkins in the early 1950s, Atkins' primary and favored guitar was a customized D'Angelico model, which set the standard to which all Atkins' subsequent guitars would be compared.

Despite being marketplace competitors, some of the companies within the instrument making industry were collaborative. In a September 28, 2007 interview for *Modern Guitars Magazine*, Fred W. Gretsch described it as "a time of cooperation among manufacturers…and by the middle 1950s John D'Angelico was just across the bridge and making guitars, so he was a frequent visitor to our factory." In fact he wasn't just a visitor, he was a customer, buying tops, backs, and sides, along with pieces of choice wood from Gretsch stock for his ornate guitar designs.

Gretsch American Orchestra Series (1933)

By 1935 the Gretsch 16" acoustic guitar offering was eight models strong, including six archtops, a tenor model, and a flat top Hawaiian model.

When comparing this mid-1930s Gretsch model 35 to the Gibson L-5, the similarities are obvious, once you get past the violin or multi-burst finish on the Gretsch. *Photo Courtesy of Jesse Whiteside, Folkway Music.*

In its capacity as a jobber, The Gretsch Company marketed some mid-level, and student grade acoustic archtop guitars, which were typically distributed under other brands. In 1933, they launched the American Orchestra Series of archtop and flat top guitars, which bore the Gretsch brand name. The model numbers on these instruments reflected their initial retail price. The Auditorium-Special category, for example, was a 16" wide instrument with a 24.75" scale and three models: 25, 35, and 65. Each of these ascending models displayed increments of ornamentation, such as inlay and binding. All three models shared the violin-style, multi-burst finish surrounding each f-hole.

American Orchestra Artist 150 model headstock (c.1935). *Courtesy of Tony Hendrix.*

In 1935, Gretsch introduced the 50, 100 (Artist model), and 150 (Supreme Artist model). The model 50 and 150 possessed the more traditional shaded brown sunburst finish. Soon to follow would be the apparently short-lived model 250, still 16" wide but with a deeper body, bound f-holes, and distinctive musical clef motif on both its headstock and pickguard. During its short life the model 250 represented the new top-of-the-line. Although Gretsch intended to market this line as a lower cost alternative to Gibson's instruments (Gretsch advertised "savings of 20% to 60%!"), some of these were quite ornate for the day. They featured pearl veneered headstocks, fancy inlaid fret markers, hand-etched pickguards, select curly maple wood, and gold-plated hardware. This line remained the primary guitar offering until 1939, when a significant overhaul took place.

As the country emerged from the Great Depression, The Gretsch Company decided to refocus its sights on the high-end professional orchestra instrument market. They dropped much of the American Orchestra Series, at both the introductory level and the top of their line, only maintaining the 35, 40 (Hawaiian flat top), and 50. They added a new introductory model 30, which seems to be very similar to the former model 25 with the addition of an adjustable bridge and bound top. These additions made this guitar identical to the existing model 35, so Gretsch changed its violin-style finish to the standard sunburst shaded style and added an extra inlay of pearl inside the guitar top's edge binding to set it apart. This was another example where the retail pricing matched the model designation. These changes aside, the real transformation was occurring at the high-end of the Gretsch acoustic archtop line.

Dating Early Gretsch Marketing Material:

Because many of the old Gretsch brochures and catalogs do not have a copyright date on them—or even suggest a production year for the instruments they advertise—dating these materials and the instruments is a challenging part of researching the company. But in the absence of any official Gretsch records explaining exactly when different models were introduced, we are left with these ephemera to piece it all together. For example, these two Gretsch American Orchestra guitar brochures are both from the mid-1930s. A potential source of confusion is that these brochures have similar titles. So, if someone makes reference to the *Oh Man! What a Guitar!* brochure, you cannot be sure which one it is. This is an annoying Gretsch practice that has also misled many enthusiasts investigating the 1950s product line.

Gretsch brochure (c.1934/35)

Gretsch brochure (c.1936)

The brochure with the model 150 on the cover is considered circa 1934-1935 for the following reasons. First, it cannot be from any earlier because upon the release of these guitars in 1933, their retail prices matched their model numbers. In this 1934-1935 brochure the three inaugural models have already experienced a price increase. Secondly, this brochure includes the 50, 100, and 150 models with corresponding retail prices, which were reportedly introduced in the 1935 time frame.

Now, consider the other, slightly later brochure. Using the same slogan, it advertises the same line of guitars with one exception, the addition of the model 250. In fact, it refers to this model as the Supreme Artist model, relegating the model 150, which was formerly referenced as the Supreme Artist model in the earlier brochure, to the lesser standard of simply Artist model. Clearly a change had been made at the top of the line, and thus the need for a marketing device to announce that change. Therefore, this latter brochure was released.

Chapter

2

Gretsch Synchromatic Acoustic Line (1939)

The American Orchestra Series, models 65, 100, 150, and 250 were discontinued because they were not competitive enough in the high-end market. Gretsch then announced their innovative Synchromatic line of acoustic archtop guitars in time to display them at the 1939 World's Fair in New York. There were six new models in the initial Synchromatic launch, with increasing degrees of scale and ornamentation between them.

The most basic of these were models 75 and 100, which were 16" wide and featured traditional f-style sound holes. However, apparently feeling that their previous line was sonically challenged, the new 160, 200, and 300 models were larger guitars with 17" wide Super-Auditorium-sized bodies, 26" scale lengths, and unique cat's eye sound holes, which were purported to project sound more effectively.

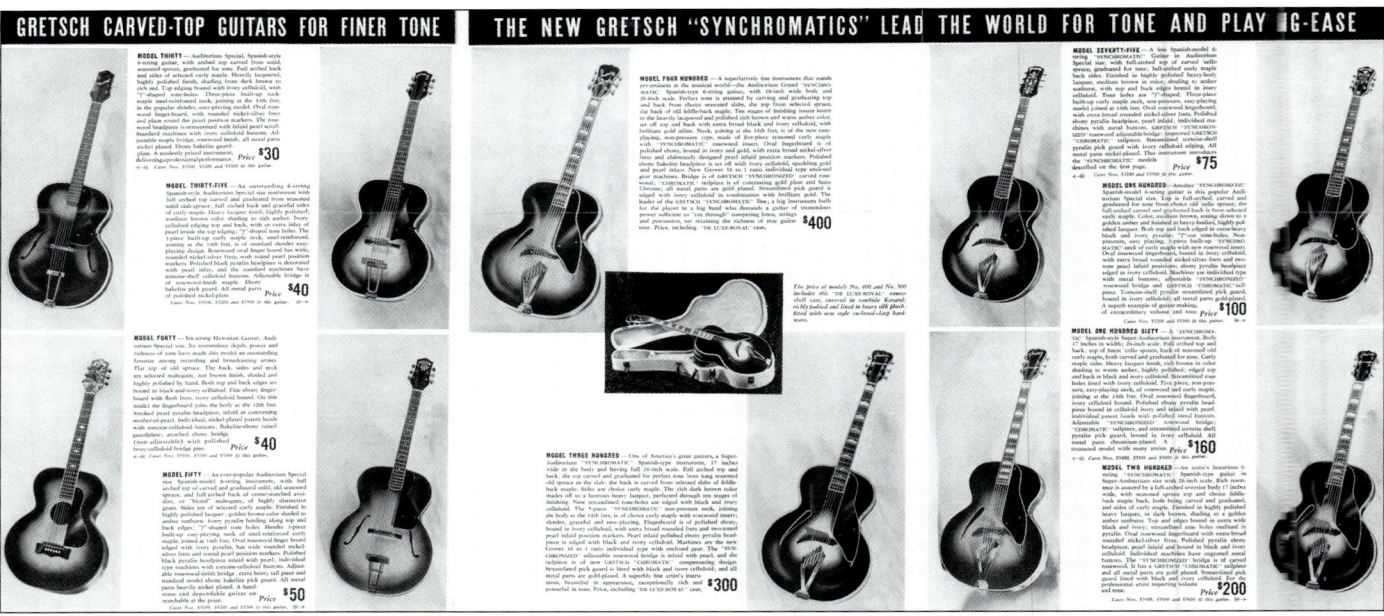

Gretsch brochure (c.1939)

A rarely encountered pre-war version of the Synchromatic 100 model (c.1939/40). *Photo Courtesy of Mass Street Music.*

Completely refurbished with modern hardware and an added pickup, this Synchromatic 400 model (c.1940/41) displays the elegance of The Gretsch Company's top-of-line acoustic model. *Photo Courtesy of Nick Anderson.*

A Synchromatic 200 model (c.1948/49) *Photo Courtesy of Big Jim's Guitars.*

At the top of their line resided the Synchromatic 400, the most ostentatiously decorated of the group. With its 18" wide Auditorium Grand body, it was the one guitar that could compete with industry foes, such as the Gibson Super 400 and the Epiphone Emperor, which were introduced in 1934 and 1936, respectively. The Gretsch Synchromatic line held up admirably against these competitors and sold well enough to erode market share from the two, more established rivals.

The Gretsch brothers, Fred Jr. (left) and William (right), at the 1946 National Association of Music Merchants trade show in Chicago. *Courtesy of The Gretsch Company*

The Gretsch Synchromatic line of guitars also reflected the design sensibilities that defined the art deco movement in American culture. Its most obvious innovation was the bound cat's eye sound holes, which challenged the prevailing industry standard f-hole made so popular by Gibson. Other features included a gold harp-styled chromatic tailpiece and the synchrosonic bridge, fashioned in an elegant stair step form. It is the combination of these two innovations that inspired the Synchromatic name. All edges were bound in decadent white, black, and gold multi-layered binding—sometimes up to 13 layers thick (Synchro 400). The guitars' bodies were often enhanced by the selection of flamed-grained wood, and either a tasteful brown sunburst or natural wood high-gloss finish. The 5-piece maple non-pressure neck was asymmetrically shaped, designed to fit the hand more comfortably. Other ornaments worn proudly included inlaid mother-of-pearl markers contrasting off an ebony fretboard, bound and inlaid headstock reflecting various Synchromatic logos, and gold Grover 16:1 Imperial tuning machines.

In an April 1995 article for the *Vintage Gallery Magazine*, Bianca Soros observed that:

This was the era where designers emphasized simplicity, horizontal attributes, and sheerness of form. Americans craved fresh new products, and a new attitude of materialism emerged in the wake of the great Depression. Fred Gretsch, Sr. understood the vision of this new age. He hired the designers that actualized the dream. Not only are pre-war Synchromatics some of the most visually striking and collectible [acoustic] vintage instruments ever produced, they are also a tribute to American industrial design in the early 20th century.

The cover of the March-April 1947 issue of *Fretted Instrument News* features Django Reinhardt with Harry Volpe and their Gretsch guitars.

The Synchromatic series got a boost from the unofficial endorsement of one of the highest profile musicians of the time, Django Reinhardt (1910-1953), who in 1946 recorded duets with Harry Volpe and often used a Synchromatic 400 while preparing for his United States tour with the Duke Ellington Orchestra. Usually Django Reinhardt is associated with the Selmer Maccaferri flat top acoustic with its characteristic oval sound hole, however, many photographs are available of him playing a Gretsch Synchromatic, and The Gretsch Company did not hesitate to capitalize on that. This, in fact, foreshadowed the future success Gretsch would ultimately experience with unofficial celebrity endorsement.

Gibson ES-150 and Electric Amplification

Unfortunately for The Gretsch Company, at about the same time they were entering the high-end orchestra guitar market with the Synchromatic line, other external forces were changing the music that Americans listened to. Electricity did not just impact the methods by which music was delivered to the masses; it changed the way music was being made. The development of electrical amplification for guitars not only changed how they sounded, but also how they could be played. With the arrival of the magnetic pickup, located on the instrument's top, under the strings, the guitar, typically relegated to providing rhythm accompaniment, was suddenly able to become more of a lead instrument within the big band environment.

The Gibson Company did not invent the electrically amplified guitar. Credit for that important breakthrough is generally bestowed upon the Rickenbacker Company. Gibson, however, was successful at transforming this innovation into a viable consumer product. In 1936, Gibson introduced the Gibson ES-150, a 16.25" wide, hollowbody archtop with a blade-style pickup affixed through the spruce top in the neck position and three adjustment screws between the pickup and the bridge. The ES-150 conformed to the industry standard sunburst finish and non-cutaway body format, but despite their dynamic abilities, these were plain looking instruments with dot inlay fretboard markers, unbound f-holes, a simple trapeze-style tailpiece, and a wooden bridge. To control the pickup's output Bakelite tone and volume knobs were positioned diagonally on the lower treble bout. As the preeminent manufacturer of high quality instruments, Gibson's embrace of what, at the time, was a radical new direction, instantly added credibility to the technology.

A parallel occurrence that helped to feed the fire of this new technologic advancement was the emergence of a young African American guitarist named Charlie Christian, who in 1937 acquired an ES-150. The blade-style pickup used on this model has since been commemorated as the Charlie Christian-style pickup. Hugh Gregory, author of *1000 Great Guitarists*, describes Christian's legacy by proclaiming that "Christian will go down in history as the guitarist chiefly responsible for the early popularization of the electric [archtop] guitar, and his clean, articulated lines were only made possible with the clarity and volume that such an amplified instrument offered." Christian's contribution to the establishment of the guitar as a lead instrument was an early and important influence to the entire industry. The guitar's success in this capacity not only forced the need for subsequent technical innovation, but it also expanded the market by creating greater demand for these instruments. It is for these reasons that Charlie Christian must be a stop on the developmental timeline of any electric guitar.

The Gibson ES-150 employed a single, blade-style pickup in the neck position. *Guitar Courtesy of Dr. William Alpert. Photo by Tyler Roe.*

Influential Personality: Charlie Christian

No analysis of the music scene of the late 1930s would be complete without recognition of the immeasurable contributions of Charlie Christian (1916-1942). Christian was born to musician parents and began to play the guitar at an early age. It has been suggested that his playing may have been positively impacted by his exposure to Lester Young's tenor saxophone style.

This prodigy began his professional music career at 18, when he played with a stomp band out of Oklahoma City that included Bill "Count" Basie. They provided their audience with a danceable form of blues-inspired music based on orchestral riffs. Basie then defected to Kansas City, along with guitarist Eddie Durham, and in 1938 recorded the famous Kansas City 5 and Kansas City 6 sessions with Lester young on horn. Durham was among the first guitarists to establish the guitar as a lead instrument in the big band setting.

Around this time, and even as early as 1927, there were other soloists who tested the boundaries of the traditional acoustic guitar within jazz combos, including Django Reinhardt, Eddie Lang, Paul Whiteman, and Lonnie Johnson. Oscar Moore, who played with the Nat King Cole trio and Lionel Hampton's band, is credited by many for the development of an early style of comping—embracing full, legato chords used in an intermittent manner in place of the traditional percussive chords. But like Durham, they all struggled with the lack of volume available from the conventional acoustic archtop guitars of the day. It was out of this necessity that Durham began pioneering the use of amplification, ultimately enabling the development of the guitar as a solo voice.

So, it was not that Charlie Christian was alone in his fluidly stylistic approach and mastery of diminished and augmented chords. He was also not necessarily considered the father of the electric guitar either, as other musicians, such as Alvino Rey and Les Paul were already experimenting with these early electric models. But it is the convergence of the two, the mastery by which Christian exploited this newfound sonic gift, and his deft approach to the music that arguably makes his work the genesis of the modern electric guitar.

Guitar Player magazine, March 1982.

Through 1938 Christian played his electric guitar with a variety of small combos, building his reputation. In 1939 the legendary jazz producer John Hammond arranged for Christian to join the Benny Goodman Band. Goodman was not keen on the idea of an electric guitar, but recognized Christian's genius immediately. The exposure Christian enjoyed as a result of the Goodman period gave him access to the big city and introductions to many of the top musicians of the day. This provided him the opportunity over the next few years to collaborate with the likes of Count Basie, Hoagy Carmichael, Kenny Clarke, and Dizzy Gillespie, ultimately developing the basis for what would become Bebop, in what history refers to as "the Minton laboratory."

Ironically, this new musical genre was a departure from the characteristic swing music of the Goodman band. It was instead intended to create an environment for listening, not dancing, and for that reason was deemed controversial within the music industry. The music was competitive, elitist, and only the upper echelon of musicians were able to keep up in this environment of abstract chords, legato textures, tight riff figures with flowing lines, and a new focus on the individual.

Charlie Christian died in 1942 at the age of 23. Jazz greats, including Tal Farlow and Wes Montgomery both point to Christian and those early Goodman recordings as a primary impetus to their pursuit of the guitar. In his 1982 book, *The Guitar Players*, James Sallis proposes: "No electric guitarist today, and few of any kind outside sternly classical discipline, is innocent of Christian's influence."

The Gibson ES-150 was the model that Charlie Christian used to help transform the guitar into a lead instrument. *Guitar Courtesy of Dr. William Alpert. Photo by Tyler Roe.*

Gretsch Electromatic Spanish Model (1939)

By 1938 Gibson had introduced two more electric archtop models, the smaller 14.75" wide ES-100 and the ES-250, which had a 17" maple top and fancier ornamentation. Only two years later, however, the ES-250, with its lofty price tag of $150, was discontinued in favor of the wartime price of the model ES-125 (16"), which featured a six-pole-piece pickup unit located toward its bridge. Regardless of this adjustment to their line, it was clear by then that Gibson saw the electric archtop market as a fertile arena for growth.

An Electromatic lap steel (c.1939). *Photo Courtesy of Guitarville.*

Back cover of the 1939 Gretsch brochure.

No doubt feeling pressure to react to the Gibson challenge, The Gretsch Company attempted to capitalize on this new technological advancement with the release of its first electric archtop guitar, the Electromatic Spanish model. These Gretsch branded guitars were included in a 1939 brochure along with matching Hawaiian-style lap steels and amplifiers. Although debuting in the very same brochure as the new Synchromatic acoustic line, these Electromatic Spanish models were not pictured. The model's description was also located on the back cover and easily overlooked. These guitars came in a traditional non-cutaway archtop format with a 16" wide body that was 4.25" deep and featured unbound, segmented f-holes; a simple rosewood bridge; and a trapeze tailpiece. The big difference (for a Gretsch model), however, was the existence of a single-coil pickup with its six pole pieces protruding up through the guitar's top, just below the base of the fretboard.

Unfortunately these guitars lacked the elegance and distinctive design statements that Gretsch featured on their Synchromatic acoustic line. Instead they seemed more akin to the lower-end acoustic archtops of some of their competitors. Obvious attempts to upgrade the appearance and to distinguish it from that of a student model included the addition of multi-colored inlaid dot markers on the fretboard, checkerboard binding around the body and neck, and a brown tortoise shell plastic pickup surround, which allowed only the six magnetic poles to show on the soundboard. A matching tortoise shell pickguard, an art deco-inspired headstock displaying a diagonal pearloid design motif, and the words "Gretsch Electromatic" in a simple hand etched style completed the ornamentation.

One feature of this inaugural offering that would become commonplace with future Gretsch guitar models was the fact that it was made available in both a sunburst and natural, blond finish. Early examples displayed the same six-on-one-side tuner configuration as their cousin Hawaiian lap steel models, but that apparently changed quickly, and later examples would have what would become the more conventional three-per-side arrangement, as well as the more elegant open f-hole design. Another awkward aesthetic decision, considering today's modern sensibilities, was the positioning of the Bakelite control knobs on each of the upper bouts of the guitar. All indications suggest these early Gretsch electric archtops (MSRP $110, with amp) were manufactured by the Kay Musical Instrument Company of Chicago—and they looked like it.

Electromatic Spanish electric archtop (c.1939) displaying coordinating features to the lap steel also offered in this fledgling line of electrically amplified instruments. *Courtesy of the Bachman Gretsch Collection.*

Electromatic Spanish electric archtop (c.1939) in the natural finish. The control knobs are not original. *Courtesy of the Bachman Gretsch Collection.*

There is no evidence of how well these Gretsch Electromatic Spanish models sold. The relative scarcity of surviving examples suggests they may not have done that well. With the pending war, the marketplace may not have been a reliable indicator of the appeal of these instruments. On the other hand, they must have been successful enough to convince the Gretsch decision makers that the electric archtop format was viable. Eventually, Gretsch made plans to manufacture the next generation of electric archtops in their own factory, but the company was delayed as the United States entered World War II.

A wartime, student sheet music holder, dated 1944.

Photo Courtesy of Mike Merisola, Coocoou 20th Century Modern.

Clones by Kay

Interestingly enough, during the same period there was a very similar competitive Electric Spanish guitar being sold by the Oahu Company, which was known for its lap steels (which also resembled the 1939 Gretsch offering). This guitar debuted in the Oahu 1939 No. 23 catalog, retailing for $55, along side their Deluxe amplifier ($110). Although identical in structure, when compared to the Gretsch model's styling, this Oahu guitar appeared to be more of a low-end offering. It had simple white dot markers on its fretboard, white body and fretboard binding, and a more generic trapeze-style tailpiece. Although the exposed six-pole-piece pickup was identical to Gretsch's, the surrounding material, as well as the pickguard, were made of plain black plastic. It appears that this model was introduced with the three-per-side tuner configuration, but it also still maintained the segmented f-holes like the earliest of the Gretsch branded examples. The feature that is the most

Photo Courtesy of Rob Wesley.

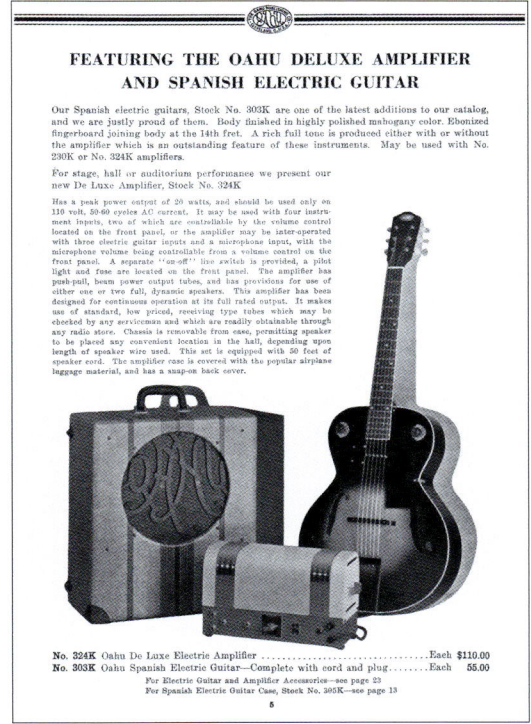

The 1939 Oahu catalog (#23).

obvious link between the two manufacturers' guitars was the identical control knobs on the upper bouts. The headstock of the guitar reflected its brand through a simple oval decal that said "Oahu Publishing Company, Cleveland, Ohio."

Unlike the Gretsch branded model, the Kay Company's involvement in this Oahu guitar was a little more overt. Small blue labels can be found inside the body cavities that read, "Manufactured by the Kay Musical Instrument Company." This confirms that Kay was supplying the Oahu Company with the same basic guitar at the exact same time. Even with the fancier features of its guitars, it is clear that Gretsch was going for the low-cost entry into the market, undercutting the Oahu guitar and amp package by 30 percent.

Gretsch Second Generation: Electromatic Spanish Model 6185 (1949)

As the 1940s progressed and World War II escalated, the United States government put restrictions on certain materials, including most metals. The Gretsch (Kay-made) electric archtop guitars were thus discontinued. It took a few years for The Gretsch Company to regroup after the war ended, but Electromatic Spanish model production started up again at Gretsch's Brooklyn factory in 1948-1949 as model 6185. During the next four years all the Gretsch guitar models would carry a simple four-digit model number as a sole identifier. The numbers #61xx represented electric models and the #60xx series were assigned to acoustic models. Names would eventually accompany most models and this numbering system would continue into the early 1970s.

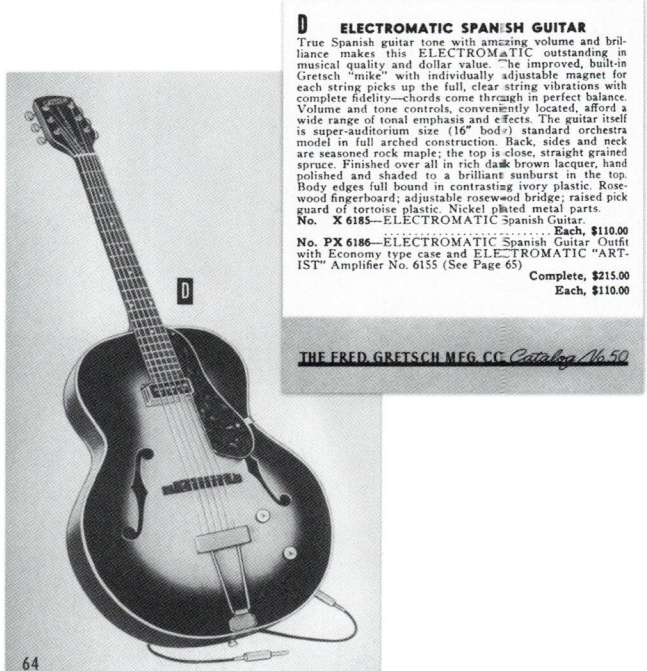

Model 6185 entry from the 1949 *Catalog No. 50*. *Courtesy of Rod McDonald*.

Earlier iterations of *Catalog No. 50* exist that were presumably produced before the 6185 guitar design was actually finalized, as they depict this similar looking guitar with a non-descript pickup, an earlier style trapeze tailpiece, and the volume and tone control knobs curiously located on the pickguard. The "Electromatic" identifier was also missing from the headstock. *Courtesy of Nick Anderson*.

The 6185 model, in a brown sunburst finish, or shaded as it was described, was introduced in the 1948-49 *Catalog No. 50* at a price of $110 (no amp was included this time). The guitar's depth was reduced to 3.375" and the catalog described this 16" wide guitar as a "Super-Auditorium size," a carryover reference from the acoustic product line of the 1930s. Its top was made of spruce, the back and sides of maple, and the hardware was nickel-plated. It displayed simple dot markers on a rosewood fretboard, a cellulous tortoise shell pickguard, adjustable rosewood bridge, and what Gretsch described as a "modernistic fluted" (i.e. trapeze) tailpiece etched with the Gretsch name at its base. Taking a page from the Gibson designers, Gretsch repositioned the volume and tone controls, placing the two clear plastic knobs out of harm's way on the lower treble side bout.

The 6185 model announced its identity with its headstock. A black, pyralin overlay provided a background for a white, etched Gretsch T-roof logo that sat at an angle across the top. The word "Electromatic" ran vertically down the face of the headstock, just above a small zigzag design motif that tapered into the top of the fretboard. Gretsch would employ this basic style of headstock overlay on a variety of models over the next six or seven years with the exception of the highest-end guitars in the line. The earliest 6185 examples (debut batch #41xx) displayed old-fashioned, shorter f-holes and a wide headstock with a rounded silhouette. Future model year examples would see these features evolve into the oversized f-hole variety and a sharper cut outline on the headstock (1951).

Electric amplification enabled the bodies of these guitars to be made more compact and thus more comfortable for some players than the 17" and 18" monster acoustic models. Not having to rely on size and depth to project the sound of the instrument, Gretsch, and others, would again focus on the ergonomically friendly 16" body width as a standard category. However, they also continued to maintain at least one larger option within the line, as many musicians had simply come to expect that the highest-quality guitars came in such a scale. Electric amplification also impacted the depth required on a 16" wide guitar. Deep guitar bodies were no longer essential for volume, and in fact became problematic, contributing to undesirable feedback. Over the next 10 years the Gretsch electric archtop product line became increasingly shallower than the 6185's original depth of 3.375".

This first electric archtop model that Gretsch made in-house looked much more related to its cousins in the acoustic line than the Kay-manufactured model of the late 1930s. Aesthetically the 6185 might be considered nothing more than a Gretsch New Yorker (acoustic model 6050) that employed a single pickup mounted on and through the guitar's soundboard in the rhythm position. This amplification device, which the 1949 catalog referred to as the "Gretsch built-in mike," and a later 1951 brochure referenced as the "Gretsch-DeArmond built-in Fidelatone," would ultimately come to be called the DeArmond Dynasonic pickup. These pickups were designed by Harry DeArmond, who was one of the early inventors of a commercially viable, removable guitar pickup in the mid-1930s.

DeArmond had developed a relationship with Gretsch prior to World War II, as evidenced by a 1940 guitar method brochure that depicts a young Jimmie Webster playing a Synchromatic acoustic archtop outfitted with a DeArmond removable mi-

Although set up to play right-handed, the control knob position and holes on the bass side, which accommodate pickguard bracket screws, verify that this early example of the 6185 is in fact an ultra rare left-handed specimen. The celluloid tortoise pickguard is original but showing extreme shrinkage from age. *Guitar Courtesy of Rivington Guitars. Photo by Rick Burda.*

crophone. Inside there is a pitch for the Synchromatic guitar product, but it also adds that with Webster's new playing style, "the new DeArmond mike must be used, for it is the only mike that eliminates pick and string noises." This 1940 method brochure grants each company equal billing as it presents the basics of a technique they called the Gretsch-DeArmond Method (for Electric Spanish guitar). There is more on this in the Jimmie Webster profile on page 64.

The 1948-49 *Catalog No. 50* offers quite a variety of these removable microphone devices made for all kinds of stringed instruments, including stringed bass, mandolin, banjo, round sound hole guitars, and f-hole archtop guitars. The top-of-the-line was the DeArmond Rhythm Chief ($37.50). Harry DeArmond leveraged the solid business collaboration he enjoyed with Harold Rowe, whose company, Rowe Industries, manufactured the DeArmond line of pickups in their Toledo, Ohio, factory.

What the 1949 Gretsch model 6185 showcased was an early built-in DeArmond pickup technology. This pickup provided six adjustable magnetic poles that enabled fine adjustment of intonation and when engaged through the tone and volume controls would, as *Catalog No. 50* praised, "afford a wide range of tonal emphasis and effects." These pickups delivered a distinctive output and established The Gretsch Company's early sonic signature in the American music consciousness, simultaneously defining "That great Gretsch sound," a slogan coined in later Gretsch marketing literature. The DeArmond Dynasonic would become standard equipment across the Gretsch electric archtop line until 1958, when the in-house manufactured Filter'Tron technology would replace it on most Gretsch models.

As the 1940s ended, The Gretsch Company, influenced by technological developments and the competitive environment, made several adaptations. Like the first fish that ventured on to land, the debut of the 6185 represented the beginning of something new. However unglamorous, as compared to the high-style, pre-war Synchromatic peacocks, the 6185 was clearly a more mature version of its humble Electromatic Spanish electric predecessor. Gone were the weak Kay-inspired attempts at glitz. What remained was a capable, utilitarian instrument and a basic design platform just waiting for refinement. It would not have long to wait.

Throughout the 1940s, developments in musical genres and mass media paved the way for further environmental changes. Big bands continued to be the vehicle for up-tempo, adrenaline-filled dance music, but other genres were evolving at a rapid rate. In 1944 the Bebop era had begun, and by 1947 the cool jazz sounds of Miles Davis and John Coltrane were born.

As the decade ended, the landscape was further changed by developments to mass media. The television age began in 1947 and in 1949 RCA and Columbia introduced the 45 rpm single and 33-1/3 rpm LP record formats, respectively. These environmental changes and paradigm shifts would be critical to delivering popular music to a whole new, and culturally significant, demographic—the teenager.

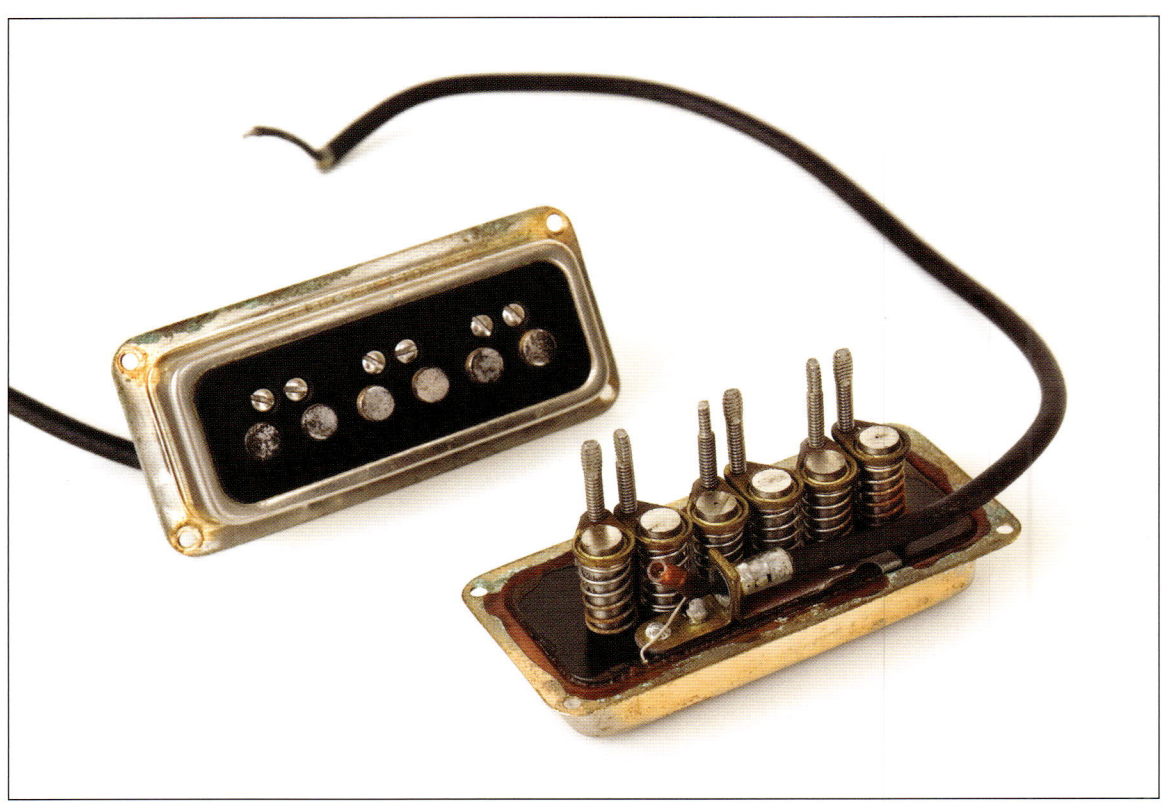

Individual screws under each pole allow for independent height adjustment on each of the DeArmond Dynasonic pickup units. *Photo Courtesy of Daniel Nicolas.*

Section II

Music and Culture in the 1950s

From the minute the war ended, the American economy was on a fast track that lasted throughout the 1950s. When the troops returned, they bought homes, started families, and triggered an unprecedented boom of consumerism. This burgeoning prosperity buoyed Gretsch through their Golden Era (1953-1965) and the company witnessed a growth triggered primarily by the transformation in popular music that took place during this period.

Optimism prevailed throughout American society and this was reflected in the mainstream music of the day. Performers, including Perry Como, Rosemary Clooney, Dinah Shore, and Frank Sinatra delivered an upbeat innocence in the early 1950s.

In other genres the guitar was a driving force. The blues were alive and well with guitarists Muddy Waters, John Lee Hooker, and others producing records for the Chess Record Company. Meanwhile, Les Paul was popularizing his innovative approach to jazz and leveraging his unique recording techniques.

Country and western music was another fertile genre for the guitar. In the mid-1940s Ernest Tubb and his Texas Troubadours featured early electric guitar playing pioneers, such as Jimmie Short, Harold Bradley, and Billy Byrd at the Grand 'Ole Opry. The (Bob) Wills Band also contributed to the advancement of the electric sound and some of the first recordings using an Electric Spanish guitar, played by Jim Boyd, are attributed to them. As the 1950s began, the Nashville-style electric guitar heroes included Merle Travis and Chet Atkins, but out on the West Coast the newly developed solidbody guitars were infiltrating the country sound, courtesy of Joe Maphis, Buck Owens, Jimmy Bryant, and other artists.

Then there was rockabilly, a derivative musical category that combined genres of music and featured an upbeat tempo. It was not quite rock and roll and certainly more aggressive than Country. This new style featured acts like Johnny Cash, Carl Perkins, Buddy Knox, and future rock and roll personalities, such as Eddie Cochran, and even a very young Elvis Presley. Never gaining the wide range appeal of the other genres, this hybrid style of music would nonetheless survive to have an important impact on the Gretsch guitar brand about 30 years later (see Brian Setzer profile on page 162).

It seemed that as the 1950s were getting underway, the guitar's role as a lead instrument was fully established and accepted—the instrument would continue to support these mu-

Good timing. Fender became an industry player in 1950, when they released their Broadcaster and Esquire solidbody models. They changed the name from Broadcaster to Telecaster in 1952, when Gretsch pointed out that they were using a similar name for their drum line. This example falls into the category of no-caster, as it was produced during the name transition. *Guitar Courtesy of Dave Rogers. Photo by Tim Mullally.*

sical categories in much the same way it did in the late 1940s. However, what occurred just a few years into the decade might best be characterized as a reaction to what many American youth considered conservative, idyllic music for grown-ups. It would not be long before the guitar became recognized as a vehicle and voice of this new generation.

Teenagers!

The teenager phenomena seems to have been, in part, a byproduct of the kind of authority that strict parents who had endured the hard times of the Great Depression and World War II exerted. A unique characteristic of this generation, however, was the fact that many had discretionary income. Teenagers became an important new category within the population. Embodied by the likes of James Dean in the movie *Rebel Without a Cause* (1955), teenagers were establishing their own identity—influencing fashion and young attitudes.

The perfect storm of opportunity that existed for the guitar industry in the 1950s was created by a robust post-war economy and this new key demographic of teenage consumers. But the fuel that drove it all was the emergence of a new kind of music called rock and roll.

Rock and roll was the blend of gospel music, Southern blues, and a strong back beat. But it was more than that—it was the beginning of a scene. Rock and roll provided a soundtrack for a generation of young people looking to express themselves. It was an opportunity to emerge from the conforming American middle class mold they perceived their parents to be trapped in. Early artists who exuded this adolescent vitality, and explored this newest direction in music included Elvis Presley, Bill Haley, Chuck Berry, and Jerry Lee Lewis. Chuck Berry sums up this new style quite succinctly in the documentary movie *Hail, Hail, Rock and Roll*, when he says "One thing about rock and roll... it's freedom."

Feeding the fire were celebrity disc jockeys like The Big Bopper and Alan Freed, who was credited with coining the term "rock and roll" in 1952. They controlled the music that the American youth were exposed to. Freed, in particular, influenced a broader young audience when he moved his Cleveland-based radio show to New York in 1954. He continued to feature black R&B music, often broadcasting live performances to his listeners.

Meanwhile, the establishment of the day attempted to combat this radical new genre. In 1955, Pat Boone, a clean-cut, boy-next-door began releasing sanitized renditions of R&B hits originally recorded by black artists, altering what were considered to be inappropriate lyrics and de-energizing the delivery of the material. These futile efforts, however, could not derail the inevitable rise of a more primal brand of music, one that captured the American teenager in an intoxicating way, one that become part of the very fabric of this first teenager generation.

In addition to radio, new, post-war technologies were a primary catalyst to the rise of Elvis and the rest of the pop music phenomenon of the mid-1950s. Teenage fans suddenly had unprecedented access to the rock and roll culture as a direct result of these advancements in entertainment.

Technology

The proliferation of rock and roll was accelerated by the introduction of technologies like the pocket-sized transistor radio, which the Regency company brought to the market in 1954. These devices made it possible to listen to music anywhere. By early 1957 the company that would soon be known as Sony had improved on the original design, and was manufacturing hundreds of thousands of units for export to the US. This particular technology not only provided portability, but was also priced so that many teens could afford to buy it.

Another influence was the increased presence of television sets in living rooms across America. Seeing something on TV made it "real," which was a huge impetus to consumerism—advertising became a priority for corporate America. This was a crucial marketing strategy as variety shows hosted by personalities like Milton Berle, Ed Sullivan, and Jack Parr provided a valuable opportunity for musical acts to showcase their talents, and their guitars to a national audience. This was not lost on guitar companies like Gretsch, Fender, and Gibson, who began producing lighter colored guitar finishes so their products would stand out on black and white transmissions.

With the development of color television, guitars featured more diverse color finishes, first with Gretsch, then with Fender, in an attempt to better exploit this latest visually dynamic medium. Another development called videotaping was introduced in 1956, which would soon revolutionize how television programming would be produced. This was also about the time when music was impacted by the further development of stereophonic recording, which combined two channels of sound to create a sense of space and fuller tone.

Television also made it more important for performers to be attractive, and sometimes talent was sacrificed for "the look." A contributing factor to this trend was born in October 1952, when a local TV station in Philadelphia debuted a daily televised dance party hosted by Bob Horn. The show provided a platform for musical acts and offered its viewers regular access to new music. Dick Clark took over the show in July of 1956 and it was subsequently renamed *American Bandstand* when ABC picked it up. The show debuted nationally on August 5, 1957 and aired on weekday afternoons. The regulars, local teens who frequently appeared as dancers, became as famous as some of the acts. *Bandstand* represented the very heart of pop culture for the mid-1950s teenager. It was a lifeline, a daily diet of music, fashion, and celebrity.

The guitar industry was a major beneficiary of all these developments. Rock and roll was, for the most part, performed by smaller groups of musicians primarily driven by saxophones, but to a growing extent, guitars. Young people were now able to acquire a guitar and imitate the songs that they heard on the radio much more easily than when orchestra and big band ensembles were the rage. With the advent of television, fans were also able to see their musical heroes, who were increasingly singer/songwriter musicians capable of playing the guitar while they performed, further motivating devotees to take up the instrument. It did not take long for young teenage men to figure out that playing guitar was a new way to meet members of the opposite sex. Once the concept of coolness was irrevocably associated with guitars and guitar playing, the race was on.

Gretsch Third Generation: Electromatic Series Models (1951)

With the 1950s looming and the economic indicators all rising, the guitar industry made preparations to provide their market with increased inventories of compelling new products. As is always the case, the marketing experts attempted to anticipate the consumer demand, but in this case there was no way they could have predicted what was ahead for the culture, for music, and for the competitive environment within the musical instrument industry.

The 1949 Gibson catalog specified nine electric archtop options in their ES (Electric Spanish) fleet. Some had multiple pickup configurations; others displayed the newly relevant cutaway on the treble bout, which was pioneered by Gibson on their 1947 ES-350 model. This degree of commitment to the electric archtop category further legitimized the technology and forced would-be competitors to follow.

Gretsch responded to this paradigm shift with their 1951 offering, which was featured in a brochure entitled *Your Album of Gretsch Guitars for 1951*. It presented a modest stable of three electric archtops, augmenting their eight model acoustic line. This lineup included the existing 6185 model—the 16" non-cutaway archtop—and announced the birth of two new dual-pickup models, the Electro II twins (fraternal), each available in two finish options.

These new Electro II models were positioned to take up the battle with Gibson, expanding the Gretsch electric archtop line beyond their lone 6185 model. This group also represented a testing of the waters, with several new feature combinations. Illustrating a textbook example of descent with modification, the new Electromatic Spanish models each displayed slightly different features, but inherited the shared commonality of the Dynasonic pickup technology found in the preceding generation. They also allowed Gretsch, for the first time, to market a range of electric archtop products—the 6185 model represented the entry level and the Electro II models covered the mid-range and higher-end. In his book, *50 years of Gretsch Electrics*, Tony Bacon documents that these new models were first shown to an audience of industry representatives in January 1951 at a special three-day promotional event at the New York Park Sheraton Hotel, where Jimmie Webster demonstrated the new guitars in the line.

Following the individual lineage of the Gretsch electric archtop line beyond these three 1951 models is a confusing endeavor. In some cases, particularly within their budget line, Gretsch introduced new, discrete model numbers for different finish options of the same guitar. In other cases they did not and a single model designation was available in two finish options. Curiously, in an alternate spin on change for change's sake, Gretsch would also discontinue one model, but introduce another with practically the same specifications as the previous one.

Adding to the ambiguity, from late 1951 through 1953 the company used a dual-model stamp for the labels inside many of their guitar models. Regardless of what finish option an instrument possessed, it received the same generic model indicator. Other inconsistencies later surfaced in what was to ultimately become the Clipper model, as Gretsch seemingly neglected altogether to create a unique model indicator between the cutaway and non-cutaway versions of that guitar. It is certain that, at the time, these were expedient decisions made for very practical reasons. It is only now, five decades later that we in the vintage guitar community struggle as a result. Hindsight is 20/20, but if you did not know better, you would almost think Gretsch was actually trying to throw us off the scent.

Your Album of Gretsch Guitars

A primary source of confusion for guitar historians has been the fact that the 1951 brochure, *Your Album of Gretsch Guitars for 1951* (a 12-panel, 6" by 9" publication featuring 11 total models, including the three electric archtops), was very similar to another brochure they published a couple of years later. The second Gretsch brochure, presumably published in 1953, looked very similar to the 1951 brochure, and even had the same title, *Your Album of Gretsch Guitars*. It also featured three electric archtop models as part of an 11-instrument offering. It is clear that this brochure was issued a few years after the 1951 version for two reasons. First, the prices were higher. Second, the latter publication employed the practice of pricing alternate finish options at a slight premium.

The 1951 Gretsch guitar brochure.

The Gretsch 1951 Electromatic lineup.

The Gretsch 1953 Electromatic lineup.

The Gretsch guitar brochure (c.1953).

In recent years it appears that some folks may have mistakenly used the later brochure which omitted the 6185 model, as the basis for surmising that *three* new electric archtops were announced for 1951, when in fact there were only *two*—the Electro II guitars.

The following is an effort to clarify the journey of each of the electric archtop progeny that Gretsch launched in the early 1950s. This is important because these guitars reflect some key features that ultimately emerged as dominant traits within the product line and the industry. These traits eventually converged to create an optimized package, both musically and from a marketing perspective, that assured the success of the company's most notable creation just a few years later.

Model 6185

The 6185 was the original Gretsch-manufactured electric archtop offering. It premiered in 1949 as an unadorned, but functional, 16" wide sunburst non-cutaway body with unbound f-holes and fretboard and a single DeArmond Dynasonic pickup. Subsequently, a variation with Clear Natural finish, identified as 6185N, graced the pages of the 1951 brochure. Beyond its blonde exterior it possessed identical features, specifications, and price ($125) to its "Shaded" (sunburst) alter ego. From late 1951 through much of 1953, both sunburst and natural-finished 6185 guitars were labeled with the model number 6185-6. All of the Electromatic archtop models produced during this timeframe should have the dual-model designation on their label.

The 6185-6 dual-model stamp suggests that at some point the natural finish version of the 6185 was identified as model 6186, but in 1951 it was not. One reason for that may be found back in the fine print of the 1948-1949 *Catalog No. 50*. In its debut, the 6185's designation identified the "Electromatic Spanish Guitar," which retailed for $110. Just below that was another model indicator for a 6186, which identified an "outfit" or package deal that included the guitar, an "economy type case," and an "Electromatic Artist Amplifier No. 6155" for $215. In essence the 6186 was technically established, but it never related to a specific, alternate finish option and was presumably abandoned by 1951. The demise of the 6185 model guitar preceded the end of the dual-model stamp period, which explains why there do not seem to be natural-finished, 6186-labeled examples out there to be found.

GRETSCH ELECTROMATIC ELECTRIC SPANISH GUITAR

Arched 16" body in selected maple and spruce, highly polished. With GRETSCH-DE ARMOND built-in "Fidelatone" pick-up with adjustable magnets.

X6185- Shaded Finish.
X6185N- Clear Natural Finish.
Each $125.00 List.

Model 6185 excerpt from the 1951 *Your Album of Gretsch Guitars.*

The actual model designation stamp that was used on Gretsch labels was applied to a label from a pre-printed roll that already possessed a serial number. These stamped model numbers tend to fade over time. In some cases they have become completely invisible. *Photo Courtesy of Mike Burkoff.*

The latest examples of the 6185 model can be identified by their very narrow headstock, which still maintained the Electromatic designation and features like the zigzag motif. There appears to be no known example of a model 6185 with an adjustable truss rod (and headstock cover), further supporting the fact that in late 1953, when the entire Gretsch electric archtop line received adjustable truss rods, the model 6185 was already discontinued. It was the oldest member of the line by that time and may have been deemed stale.

But Gretsch had a replacement model ready to go to fill the low-end void left by the 6185. Curiously, however, for all intents and purposes it was a clone. Perhaps Gretsch's strategy was to create a splash in the market by introducing a "new" model. In the industry this was often considered good for business. A couple of batches of 6185 model guitars are documented in early 1953, before the model disappeared completely—its last batch was probably #108xx.

In retrospect, the 6185 model, considered a late entry into the industry, was a fine opening act for the burgeoning Gretsch electric archtop line. As with many pioneering forms, it was ultimately proven obsolete as the industry experimented with and adapted modifications. Gretsch seemed to understand this. In what could be analogous to genetic engineering, Gretsch used the 1951 production offering as a test-bed for introducing mutations to the form and new combinations of traits. This process would continue to be the basis of their efforts to develop the optimal electric archtop package.

A 1953 Electromatic model 6185. *Photo Courtesy of Mike Burkoff.*

The last of its kind, this rare tenor model 6185-6 is from late in the final #108xx batch. The block inlay and bound fretboard on this specimen are not consistent with the standard 6-string version of the model. Tenors were made to order not in batches, so whatever tenor necks Gretsch had, they used. *Photo Courtesy of Steve Wilson.*

Model 6187 Electro II

The model 6187 was one of the two, new-for-1951 designs known as Electro II each featuring a dual-pickup configuration—a first for the Gretsch product line. This model was differentiated from the other by its 16" wide non-cutaway body and an Electromatic-style headstock with zigzag motif. In addition to its two DeArmond Dynasonic pickups, it had a few higher-end features, including large inlaid block fretboard markers; an elegant stair step (synchronized) bridge; and the newly patented, steel reinforced Miracle Neck, which, like its no-pressure neck forerunner, featured an asymmetrical profile purported to fit the musician's hand more naturally and improve the ease of play.

Model 6187-8 excerpt from the 1951 *Your Album of Gretsch Guitars* brochure.

Most examples display the dual-model stamp of 6187-8. *Photo Courtesy of Randy Pappenfort.*

Conversely, this model also maintained a few more humble features, including a trapeze-style tailpiece, clear plastic control knobs, white plastic button tuning keys, and tortoiseshell cellulous pickguard, which were inherited from the existing generation (model 6185). This mix of features, in conjunction with its $200 retail price, suggests an attempt to provide a mid-range example within the line. It was also available at the same price in a natural finish (model 6188), which was depicted in the 1951 brochure. Presumably installed for the 1952 model year, Gretsch changed the control knob configuration on this model, adding a master volume knob onto the upper treble bout. In an odd design decision, Gretsch located this knob awkwardly off center. When applying modern aesthetic sensibilities, it tends to look fine on the cutaway Electro II body, but on this 6187-8 Electro II, it looks quite misplaced with its non-cutaway bout.

The 6187 Electro II models were short-lived, disappearing in early 1953 after only four or five batches had been produced. This was about the same time the 6185 model was discontinued. It is not known whether this was merely a result of poor sales or if this could also have been a conscious effort to better define the product line, relegating the non-cutaway body style exclusively to the budget models. If that was the case, the 6187 Electro II could not overcome the perceived limitations of its non-cutaway body—an attribute that was suddenly out of favor within mid-range instruments—and became extinct.

A 1953 Electro II model 6187-8. *Guitar Courtesy of Monster Pawn. Photo by Fish Carpenter.*

An interesting fact about the Electro II 6187 model is that its viability within the Gretsch line may have been affected by the fact that Gretsch licensed what is basically the exact same guitar to be sold through Montgomery Ward's mail order catalog under the Bacon Belmont brand. These guitars were also 16" wide non-cutaway archtops with a 3.25" body depth, available in natural finish only. Their hardware consisted of two Dynasonic pickups, a trapeze tailpiece, a rosewood bridge, and that same oddly placed master volume knob on the upper bout. The black pyralin headstock overlay displayed the word "Bacon" along with a decorative design motif where the horizontal Gretsch T-roof logo usually resided. The word "Belmont" was displayed in a large script style vertically, where the "Electromatic" designation was located on the 6187 model. Otherwise, these two differently branded guitars were identical. The early Bacon Belmont guitars utilized a three-digit serial numbering scheme unrelated to the Gretsch models. These numbers were typically hand written in pencil in the body cavity.

In today's vintage guitar market, these Bacon Belmont models seem to appear as frequently as the Electro II 6187 examples do. Speculation into the 6187's premature demise within the line, suggests that Gretsch may have realized that they were eroding their own sales. In the 1952-1953 *Montgomery Ward Fall-Winter Catalog*, the sole Bacon Belmont branded guitar, one of five Electronic Spanish models offered, retailed at $129.95, making it their highest priced option. In comparison, a year earlier, the Gretsch 1951 brochure listed the Electro II 6187-8 at $200. Clearly the Bacon Belmont was the better deal.

Since Bacon Belmont examples exist both with and without the oddly placed master volume knob, it appears that these guitars were offered simultaneously with the Gretsch version. Two years later this 6187-8 clone was still featured in the 1954-1955 *Montgomery Ward Fall-Winter Catalog* ($159.95), along with another Gretsch clone, which was identical to the Town and Country flat top acoustic. This supports speculation that Gretsch was using the Bacon Belmont brand and the Montgomery Ward catalog as an avenue to continue marketing the former Electro II 6187-8 guitar, which had already been discontinued from the Gretsch electric archtop line.

Photo Courtesy of Dr. James S. Brown.

P BACON BELMONT ELECTRONIC SPANISH GUITAR. Super Auditorium size, 41x16 in. 2 De Armond built-in magnetic pick-ups; one accentuates high tones, the other low tones. Magnets adjust individually for each string. Dual pick-ups make it possible to obtain contrasting tone timbres. Adjust lower pick-up for variety of combinations. 4 tone and volume controls. Natural Blonde finish, hand-rubbed, polished. Fully arched. Spruce top; Curly Maple back, sides, celluloid bound. Rosewood fingerboard, inlaid position markers. Adj. bridge. Heavy celluloid guard plate. Instructions, pick, 12-ft. detachable cord. Shipped Express from Chicago. Order from, pay charges from nearest Mail Order House.

Catalog No.	Item	Ship.Wt.	Down	Cash
53 B 8390RT	Guitar Only	13 lbs.	$13.00	$129.95
53 B 8391RT	Guitar; Case (2)	22 lbs.	15.00	149.95
53 B 8392RT	Guitar; Amplifier(W)	37 lbs.	23.00	229.50

Excerpts from 1952-1953 Montgomery Ward Fall-Winter Catalog.

Model 6192 Electro II

The second of the Electro II guitars, model 6192, was designed specifically to compete with the Gibson 1951 lineup, which consisted of the L-5CES and Super 400CES, electric single-cutaway versions of their stalwart acoustic line. As such, this Electro II was given a larger 17" wide body and a single-cutaway on the treble side to go with its dual-pickup configuration. The combination of these latter two traits proved to be dominant in the Gretsch line and sealed future success for subsequent models. Also available in a natural finish option (model 6193), and priced at $325, these Miracle Neck-equipped guitars became capable competitors to the Gibson opposition. They represented the top of Gretsch's fledgling line.

The Electro II 6192 model was not just the bigger, single-cutaway brother of the Electro II 6187, it was actually a very different guitar. It was as much a descendant of the Gretsch Synchromatic acoustic line as it was the inaugural model 6185 electric archtop. The most obvious indicator of this influence was the Synchromatic-style script logo headstock design, making it the only member of this generation of electric archtop offspring not to carry the Electromatic-style headstock overlay. The 6192 model also featured other Synchromatic traits, including the art deco-inspired harp (chromatic) tailpiece, bound fretboard, stair step (synchronized) bridge, the unique opulence of bound f-holes, and 24-karat gold-plated hardware, which neither of its 1951 Gretsch brethren shared.

Model 6192-3 excerpt from the 1951 *Your Album of Gretsch Guitars* brochure.

Large and in charge. The 17" wide Electro II 6192 model topped the modest Gretsch electric archtop line upon its introduction for the 1951 model year. *Courtesy of Teddy Rasch.*

This first batch specimen might be considered the missing link between the Electro II 6192-3 model and the Country Club. Note the Synchromatic-style fretboard with its missing first fret block inlay. Other early features include the plain top control knobs and early Melita bridge with Bakelite components. Newer Country Club features include the "G" cutout tailpiece, bullet-style truss rod cover, and inlaid T-roof logo on the headstock. This example establishes that the upgrade to Country Club features and the addition of the 6196 model in Cadillac Green happened simultaneously. Only a few other specimens of this model have been found to have this Synchromatic-style fretboard. They seem to be sprinkled into the early serial numbers from the debut batch of Country Clubs (#12550–12650). *Guitar Courtesy of Dave Rogers. Photo by Tim Mullally.*

1953 model year Electro II 6192-3. *Guitar Courtesy of Dave Rogers. Photo by Tim Mullally.*

In this Gretsch ad for the Country Club model, guitarist Jimmy Cannady is shown playing a guitar from a very early first batch of the model with a tell-tale missing block inlay on the first fret.

It appears that the highly adjustable Melita bridge was adopted by the 6192 model during the 1952 model year and the aforementioned fourth control knob was positioned on the cutaway bout. In late 1953, an adjustable truss rod with bullet-style truss rod cover was incorporated, the T-roof logo was introduced onto the headstock, and the "G" cutout tailpiece added. At this time the model was re-named the Country Club and a third finish option was added—the distinctive Cadillac Green (model 6196). Midway into 1954, as Gretsch upgraded much of the archtop product line with new cosmetic features, the Country Club received hump block markers on the fretboard, fancy Grover Imperial tuners, and arrow motif control knobs, which replaced the transitional plain-topped version.

In 1955 the Country Club's 17" body format continued to be the successful representative at the high-end of Gretsch's stable. The sunburst 6192 model retailed for $385, the Cadillac green 6196 for $395, and the natural 6193 for $400. Just like the expensive Synchromatic acoustics from years earlier, Gretsch apparently continued to equate body size with pre-eminence. This perception and the ongoing success of the format in the marketplace no doubt encouraged Gretsch to introduce other 17" models, including the Convertible (model 6199) and the even flashier White Falcon (model 6136), which were released in early 1955.

A 1956 model year 6192.
Courtesy of Teddy Rasch.

In late 1957, in part a response to Gibson's humbucking pickup, but also as a byproduct of the influence Chet Atkins was wielding within Gretsch at the time, Gretsch retooled the Country Club models and the rest of the Gretsch electric line with the new Filter'Tron pickup technology for the 1958 model year offering. In addition, neoclassic fretboard markers were adopted, a tone switch appeared on the upper bout, and a space control bridge ultimately replaced the Melita bridge. The Country Club model went on to become the longest surviving model in the Gretsch line, evolving along the way, acquiring features such as a thinner body depth, zero fret, string mutes, and several aesthetic modifications. It made a final appearance in the 1978 catalog before finally being discontinued. Rising from its ashes, the Country Club (G6192) was reincarnated in the mid-1990s when the newly revived Gretsch Company began its modern production. It continues to a have place in the Professional Series electric archtop family today.

Blessed with the good fortune to possess two highly successful adaptations, the single-cutaway body and the dual-pickup configuration, a combination that would go on to become de facto standards across the industry, the Electro II 6192 model lacked one attribute that might have arguably made it the optimal design for the masses. That missing element was a more ergonomic 16" wide body. Even so, the Electro II 6192 would be the only model of the 1951 offering to survive into the next generation of the Gretsch electric archtop line. Always frugal, Gretsch used the same illustration of this model for their 1953 brochure, maybe not realizing (or caring) that it failed to show the new master volume control knob position on the cutaway or the Melita bridge referenced in the text.

These three pioneering models, 6185, 6187 Electro II, and 6192 Electro II, comprised the maiden Gretsch electric archtop line in the 1951 model year. As feedback from the marketplace and influence from competitors was quickly internalized, Gretsch was motivated to make some quick lineup changes not too much later. Apparently the jury was in on their initial electric archtop offering and modifications were deemed necessary to remain competitive. As a result, when the 1953 version of *Your Album of Gretsch Guitars* brochure was released, it still displayed three electric archtops in their line of 11 total guitars. However, some faces had changed.

A 1958 model year 6192. *Photo Courtesy of Mass Street Music.*

Gretsch Fourth Generation: Electromatic Series Models (1953)

Debuting in the 1953 version of the *Your Album of Gretsch Guitars* brochure, the 6182 model could have easily been confused with the existing 6185 design. A 16" wide by 3.375" deep non-cutaway, single-pickup archtop with clear control knobs, utilitarian trapeze tailpiece, and an Electromatic headstock design, the new 6182 model was basically the same guitar as the 6185 model. The 6182 came in a standard sunburst finish and retailed for $137.50. A natural finish option (model 6183) was also available for $10 more. The absence of the 6185 model in this catalog signaled its demise and was proof that Gretsch intended to eliminate it. Perhaps in an example of designed obsolescence, the company needed something that at least sounded fresh and new, even if it was not. Gretsch appears to have waited until the last batches of 6185 guitars were all shipped, before beginning the production of the 6182 model, not that this necessitated much more than a label change.

Model 6182-3

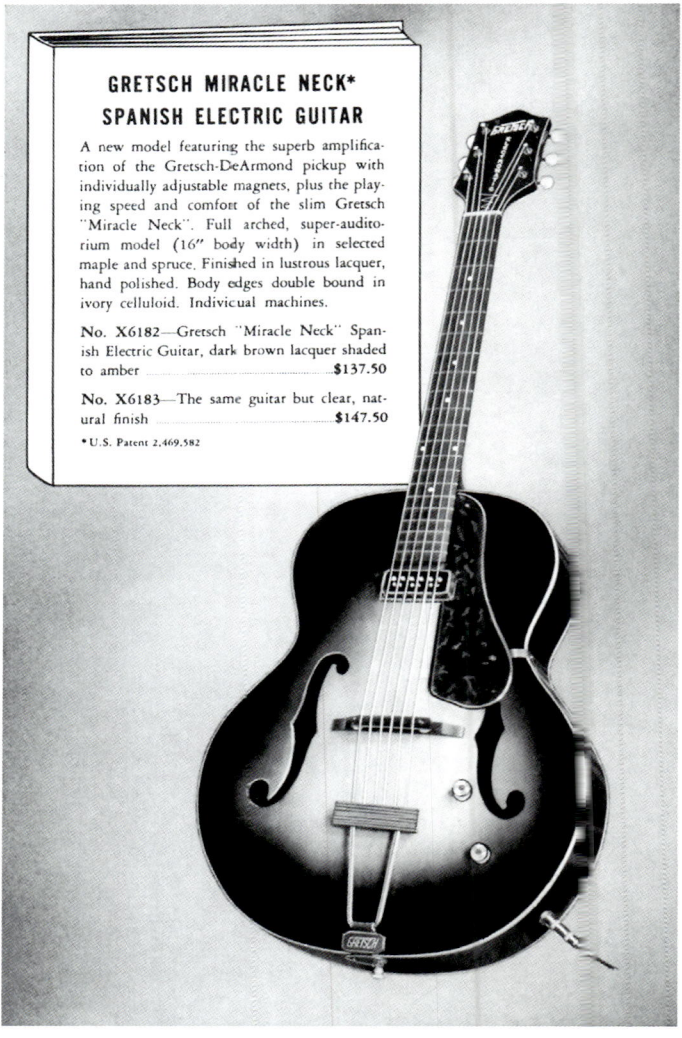

Model 6182 excerpt from the 1953 *Your Album of Gretsch Guitars* brochure.

The 6182 models are documented to have hit the market as Gretsch's new non-cutaway budget instrument sometime around mid-1953—at batch #113xx. In addition to its introduction in the 1953 *Your Album of Gretsch Guitars* brochure, it was also included in a subsequent company pricelist dated March 10, 1954, which provided the first indication that Gretsch was making a move towards adding model names, as the 6182 and 6183 are identified as the "Corvette" models. It was not long after its introduction that the Corvette model was honored by being one of the highlighted guitars on the back cover of Gretsch's now famous 1955 *Guitars for Moderns* catalog.

The dual-model label stamps were discontinued for the 1954 model year, perhaps because some Gretsch models (i.e. Country Club) now had three color options. Another identifier of the 1954 produced Corvettes is the introduction of an adjustable truss rod (mid-batch #126xx) and bullet shaped truss rod cover at the base of the Electromatic headstock. Interestingly, in another illustration of Gretsch's practice of not wasting materials, there are many examples from the 1954 model year Electromatic guitars where this truss rod cover fails to completely conceal the zigzag motif that was prevalent on the previous generation of guitars. Small white lines can be found peeking out from behind these covers.

Another rare, tenor configuration, this time applied to the model 6182-3. *Photo Courtesy of Steve Wilson.*

A 1953 model year 6182-3, or pre-Corvette, missing its tortoiseshell celluloid pickguard. *Photo Courtesy of Mark Hoebeke.*

A 1956 model year example of the Corvette 6184 in Jaguar Tan finish. *Courtesy of the Bachman Gretsch Collection.*

A gorgeous, late batch example of a 1955 model year 6183 Corvette. It was unusual for Gretsch to invest this type of flamed grain wood into this model. *Courtesy of Mike Gillentine.*

The 1955 Gretsch catalog revealed the newest of the Corvette models, the 6184 model ($157.50), in a slightly metallic Jaguar Tan finish, an option that was not yet listed for this model in the March 1954 pricelist. Sharp eyes will note that the 6184 example on the back cover of the 1955 catalog displays a silver Lucite pickguard, which was more contemporary than the celluloid tortoiseshell of the other Corvette models. Another unique feature the 6184 model possessed that its sibling models, 6182 and 6183, did not, was the adoption of the arrow (only) chrome control knobs, evident from the very first batch. The sunburst and natural examples continued to feature the standard Gretsch clear plastic knob throughout the 1955 model year.

In the second half of the year (batch #184xx) and in anticipation of the pending 1956 model year, the larger style truss rod covers began to appear—a change that seems to be largely aesthetic in nature. Another unexplained oddity of this batch is the fact that many of its Corvette specimens display a significant narrowing of their Electromatic headstock. Curiously, this feature seems inexplicably intermittent, regularly occurring between and within many of the batches throughout the period. Specimens possessing the wider headstock are just as common.

The Corvette model guitars only really got started in mid-1953. They demonstrated that even the budget models within the Gretsch line could have some flash. Unfortunately, these came to somewhat of an abrupt end early in 1956, when Gretsch banished the models from the line. Because the Corvette is so commonly confused with its predecessor the 6185 model, as well as its replacement, the 6186 Clipper, it is hard to get a fix on just how common vintage examples are in today's marketplace. Recent research has uncovered 13 batches of Corvettes documented between serial #113xx and #201xx, which probably means no more than 1300 guitars were produced. The most coveted of these are the 6184 model examples in Jaguar Tan finish. Because these were only produced during a portion of the Corvette's short lifespan, they are considered rare indeed.

In retrospect, the discontinuation of the Corvette model seems to have been a curious tactic. If it was simply that the marketplace had spoken, and non-cutaway body styles were being considered obsolete, then the last thing Gretsch should have done is replace this model with another non-cutaway guitar, but that is exactly what they did. Perhaps fueled by the continuous need to have new and improved products in the rapidly changing, and highly competitive, marketplace of the mid-1950s, Gretsch once again replaced a discontinued model with a near mirror image. The sunburst-finished Clipper (model 6186) and two-tone 6187 option debuted at batch #206xx. Flying in the face of Gretsch convention, however, it seems the company did not make a model (presumably 6188) with the natural finish.

Over the years the Clipper model would endure significant transformations, including the introduction of a single-cutaway in 1957 and being downgraded to a thinner body, HiLo'Tron pickup-equipped, sunburst-finished base model in 1959. Ultimately it would survive into the mid-1970s.

Model 6190-1

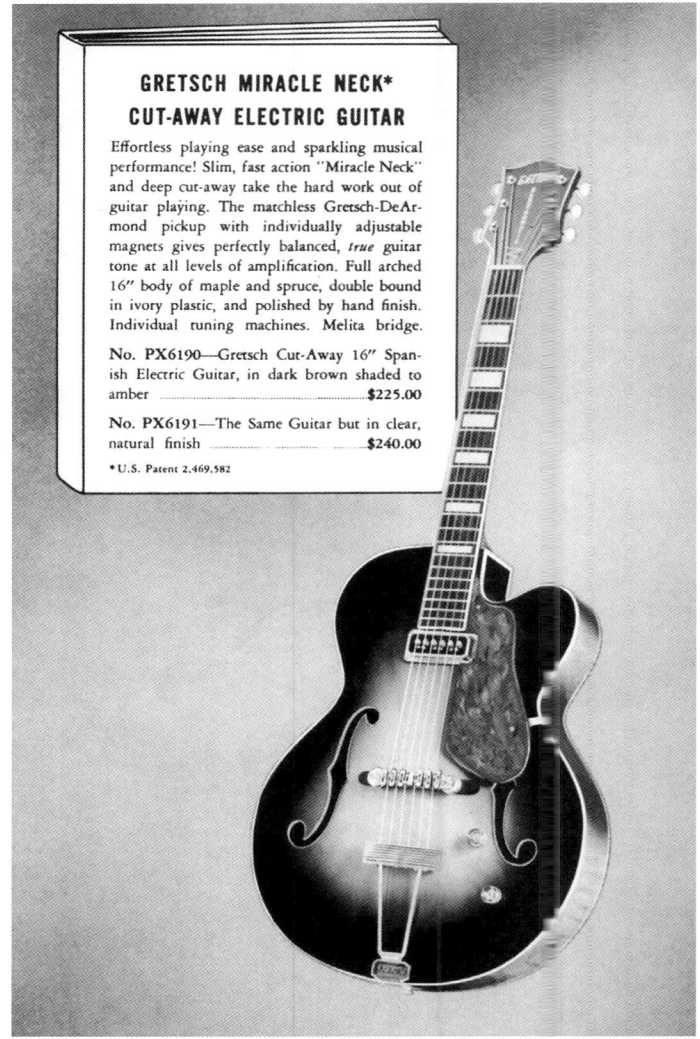

Model 6190-1 excerpt from the 1953 *Your Album of Gretsch Guitars* brochure.

The other new model that debuted in the 1953 version of the *Your Album of Gretsch Guitars* brochure, was the sunburst-finished model 6190. From this generation of electric archtop guitars, it might just be the most important to the Gretsch bloodline. Vintage examples of this initial offering are identified by their dual-model 6190-1 designation and spruce tops.

Historically there have been reports that state the 6190-1 model was introduced in 1951, but this misinformation is most likely a result of the aforementioned confusion related to the two different, but similarly titled Gretsch brochures. Evidence now confirms that the 6190-1 was not offered until 1953 though the initial batch could have been produced at the very end of 1952 in preparation for the new model year. In addition to its absence from the 1951 brochure, research can document only three batches of 6190-1 guitars produced before the upgrade to the official Streamliner model in early 1954. The earliest examples documented have the serial numbers #99xx.

Clearly a direct descendant of the seminal model 6185 design, and presumably the replacement for the soon to be discontinued Electro II 6187, the 16" wide sunburst 6190 model and natural 6191 version were truly mid-range examples—retailing for $225.00 and $240.00, respectively. Looking at its features, this 6190-1 variation on the Gretsch electric archtop theme seems to have been the 16" format best suited for survival. At least that is the body dimension category the Gretsch catalog put it in. Oddly enough, the 6190-1 was closer to 15.5" wide throughout its production—an idiosyncratic trait that it would pass along to future generations of the Gretsch electric archtop species.

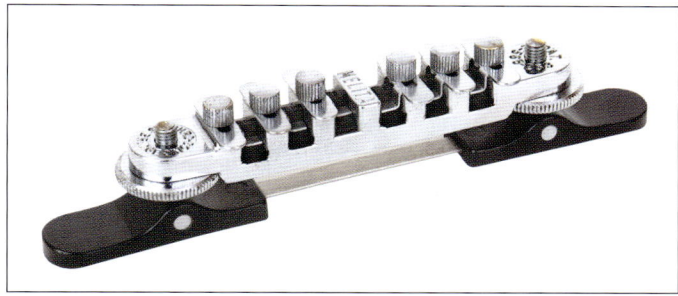

The Melita adjustable bridge. *Photo Courtesy of Daniel Nicolas.*

The 6190-1 model, in essence a pre-Streamliner, was born with some slightly more ornate features than its 6185 parent, including inlaid pearloid block markers and a bound, rosewood fretboard. It was outfitted with the more enabling single-cutaway body and the highly touted Miracle Neck. Also, it was the only model in the 1953 brochure depicted with the fancy and functional Melita bridge, although the Electro II 6192 had also adopted this technology by then.

The Melita bridge was an innovation developed, manufactured, and provided to Gretsch by entrepreneur Johnny Melita. It allowed the guitarist to easily adjust each string's intonation through the manipulation of a sliding saddle system and thumb screw-locking mechanism. This was prior to the introduction of Gibson's Tune-O-Matic bridge, which claimed the same advantage. In his book, *50 Years of Gretsch Electrics*, Tony Bacon writes that Gretsch advocated the benefits of the Melita bridge in advertising as early as June 1952.

In its infancy, the model 6190-1 was introduced with a single DeArmond pickup (not yet called Dynasonic) in the neck position, a humble trapeze-style tailpiece with "Gretsch" engraved in its base, a celluloid tortoiseshell pickguard, and unbound f-holes. Individual white plastic button Waverly-style, open-back tuners resided behind the black pyralin Electromatic headstock overlay with white etched lettering and zigzag motif. The same clear control knobs, universal to the entire Gretsch line, were positioned on the lower rear, treble bout. The body depth of this Electromatic model was 3.25", slightly slimmer than the 3.375" depth of its 6182 contemporary and its forerunner, the 6185.

This 1953 model year 6190-1 example from the debut batch reflects the early features of the model. It is missing its celluloid pickguard, but does feature the zigzag headstock motif and clear plastic control knobs characteristic to each of the Electromatic models. *Photo Courtesy of Steve Wilson.*

The single-cutaway feature is an evolutionary highlight that relegated the non-cutaway body style to Gretsch's budget line models from this point on. *Photo Courtesy of Lee Howard.*

This late 1953 model year example is from the third and final batch of 6190-1 guitars produced (#124xx). Some of its features are already beginning to evolve, including the appearance of plain-topped chrome control knobs and chrome Waverly-style tuning machines. The bridge is not original. *Courtesy of Guitar Emporium.*

It is important to note that the 1953 model year 6190-1 represented the first 16" wide electric archtop that Gretsch produced with a cutaway body. The appearance of the cutaway body style of this period is directly related to the emergence of the electric archtop environment. Prior to amplification there was no practical reason to provide access to the upper reaches of the fretboard. The tone generated from those registers just did not have the volume to be useful in an orchestra situation. But with amplification these new tones could be heard, appreciated, and used to add unique sonic opportunities and texture to a guitarists' repertoire. Amplification and access to the fretboard changed a musicians' approach to the instrument. Ultimately, this advance impacted how music sounded and the single-cutaway body became dominant within the industry. Just in time for rock and roll.

When the 6190-1 was introduced, The Gretsch Company's approach to both manufacturing and marketing their guitar product line was being impacted by external influences. This 6190-1 model, and the company as a whole, were on the cusp of some exciting new changes. Both evolutions were affected by similar changes in a parallel consumer product industry that contributed an equally rich legacy to the 1950s.

Just three serial numbers later, in the same final batch, we see the transformation in full swing. This guitar features the new adjustable truss rod and "G" cutout tailpiece. It also displays the single model designation of 6190 on its label. However, the binding around the f-holes, change in top wood, and slimming of the body depth had not occurred yet. The bridge is not original. *Photo Courtesy of Rick Burda.*

1950s Automotive Industry Parallels

A pervasive trait in the popular culture of the 1950s was America's growing obsession with the automobile. Post war economic growth translated to more people being able to afford cars than ever before. Over a 30-year period, the American automobile changed dramatically due to technological advancements, changes in consumer tastes, and contemporary design aesthetics. In fact, this transformation process in the automobile industry actually influenced the evolution of the Gretsch product line on several levels.

Taking a page from General Motors' (GM) batch production manufacturing process, which included differing degrees of hand and/or skilled labor, Gretsch embraced this approach throughout their Golden Era. Gretsch serial numbers, from the period beginning around #5000 (1950), indicate that popular models were typically produced in batches of 50 or 100. It was not long before this practice extended to all their guitar models. Eventually, Gretsch coordinated production so that similarly constructed and dimensioned models, which used common jigs and tooling, were manufactured consecutively, thus more efficiently. Common and interchangeable parts (tailpieces, control knobs, tuners, etc.) were also used across many models in an effort to streamline the construction process.

Jimm[ie] Webster copied all the auto colors for the guitars. Caddy Green for example. JW always had Auto Brochures on his desk, working on different color schemes.

-Dan Duffy, manager, Quality Control,
The Gretsch Company (1957-1970)

In the mid-1950s, Gretsch followed the lead of the American automotive industry and boldly incorporated a dynamic pallet of unconventional paint finishes to their electric archtop guitars. Gretsch reportedly used the same DuPont paints that GM used. Metallic colors like Copper Mist and Metallic Gray had previously only been seen on Gibson's Les Paul (gold top) and ES-295 models. But Gretsch went further and employed interesting flat color finishes, including Cadillac Green, Oriental Red, Lotus Ivory, and, of course, Western Orange. Gretsch even combined some of these hues to create unique two-tone affects and several models displayed a lighter flat tone on the top of the guitar with a darker, sometimes metallic, color applied to the back and sides. The most extreme example of this new visual aesthetic was the introduction of the silver, sparkle-topped, solidbody Jet model (6129), which benefited from Gretsch's existing competency with drum materials.

Designed obsolescence is another GM manufacturing principal that Gretsch seemed to have assimilated into their corporate culture. The essence of this concept was the strategic introduction of structural and aesthetic changes to create consumer demand for new and improved products. Over the next three decades, The Gretsch Company produced regular design changes to most of their guitar models. Significant feature changes, such as pickup technology, fretboard ornamentation, and body dimensions

(among others) have been diligently documented. As a result, these features can help determine a particular guitar model year with a great deal of accuracy, even in situations where a serial number is unavailable.

Gretsch was more rigid and fastidious about the application of features and appointments to its guitars than virtually any other manufacturer, so much so that most Gretsch guitars can usually be dated by features and appointments alone.

-Jay Scott, *The Guitars of the Fred Gretsch Company*

In both the auto and guitar industries, the generation of a product line is often defined by the model year features it possesses. In other words, car buffs can easily distinguish a 1956 Chevy Bel Air from a 1957, based on some key feature differences. Likewise, the vintage guitar community is apt to discuss the benefits of certain 1959 models over the proceeding examples produced in 1958.

But within the Gretsch product line, changes were sometimes made more frequently than an annual design refresh. In fact, some models experienced changes, some subtle, others more significant, every few batches, in what seems to have been a constant state of modification. This contributes to a degree of sarcasm within the vintage guitar community and the charge that "every Gretsch guitar is a transitional example." In fact, this situation can be helpful in identifying and attributing a particular Gretsch specimen to its batch by simply cross-referencing its feature combinations. Another similarity between automobiles and guitars is the fact that model year may not always relate to calendar year, as both guitar and automobile manufacturers would customarily begin production of the next model year towards the end of the previous calendar year.

Examples of 1950s automotive brochures.

A—Gretsch "Convertible" Electric No. PX6199 in two   E—Gretsch "Rancher" Jumbo Flat Top Guitar No. X6022
     tone Copper Mist and Lotus Ivory (See Page 1)   in Western finish (See Page 13)

B—Gretsch "Corsair" Arched Body Guitar No. X6016 in   F—Gretsch "Clipper" Electric Guitar No. X6187 in
     Bordeaux Burgundy (See Page 11)   Jaguar Tan Finish (See Page 4)

C—Gretsch "Fleetwood" Custom-Built Guitar No. X6038   G—Gretsch "White Falcon" Electric Guitar No. PX6136
     in shaded brown and amber (See Page 8)   in white and gold (See Page 2)

D—Gretsch "Country Club" Electric Guitar No. PX6196   H—Gretsch "Streamliner" Electric Guitar PX6189 two-
     in Cadillac Green (See Page 3)   tone Copper Mist and Bamboo Yellow (Page 5)

GUITARS FOR MODERNS BY **Gretsch**

The 1955 *Guitars for Moderns* catalog. *Courtesy of Nick Anderson.*

A final parallel between the automobile and guitar industries is marketing. The radical increase in consumerism, and in turn competition, taught Detroit how to be more proactive in advertising. Car dealerships made their product line available to prospective buyers with full-color, glossy brochures and booklets.

Typically, early 1950s guitar dealers received a single hardbound comprehensive catalog of a company's entire instrument product line, including guitars, drums, and brass instruments. These were not intended for distribution to consumers. Dealers would also receive simple pricelist changes and they could write the company for certain model or product line specific brochures, which were typically black and white and could be circulated to interested customers.

Gretsch, however, embraced a more aggressive marketing tactic and in 1955, coinciding with their updated electric archtop arsenal, scooped the guitar world with the release of the *Guitars for Moderns* catalog, which featured a full-color cover. This catalog represented a landmark in the company's marketing and was the first to leverage full-color printing to reinforce the impact of its colorful product line. This catalog not only went to the usual dealer base, it was also reprinted and included in the November 1955 issue of *DownBeat* Magazine and then again in the October 1956 issue of *Country and Western Jamboree* magazine (although with some changes). This tactic brought the dynamic new Gretsch product line to the general public.

Gretsch Streamliner models 6189, 6190, and 6191 (1954)

The debut of the 1954 model year represented a coming out party of sorts for all the Gretsch electric archtop siblings. The 6190 models received a new name and its hardware was upgraded with plain-topped chrome control knobs, chrome tuning machine buttons, and the distinctive "G" cutout tailpiece. White binding now surrounded the interior of the f-holes, the guitar's top was made of maple, and an adjustable truss rod feature was added with the bullet-style truss rod cover above the nut on the headstock. In addition, a third model designation, model 6189, was launched to reflect a dynamic new color variation that went beyond what the other Gretsch models of the day were allowed to offer.

Another significant modification was thinning the 6190 body depth by half an inch, making its new 2.75" body the thinnest of the Gretsch electric archtop family. The 1956 catalog boasted that the model's "extra thin [body] feels so nice under your arm!" This last alteration was further recognition that with an electrically amplified instrument the mass of the body cavity had become less critical and the instrument's ergonomics were more of a consideration. This adaptation was appropriately characterized in the new name—the 6190 was now dubbed the Streamliner.

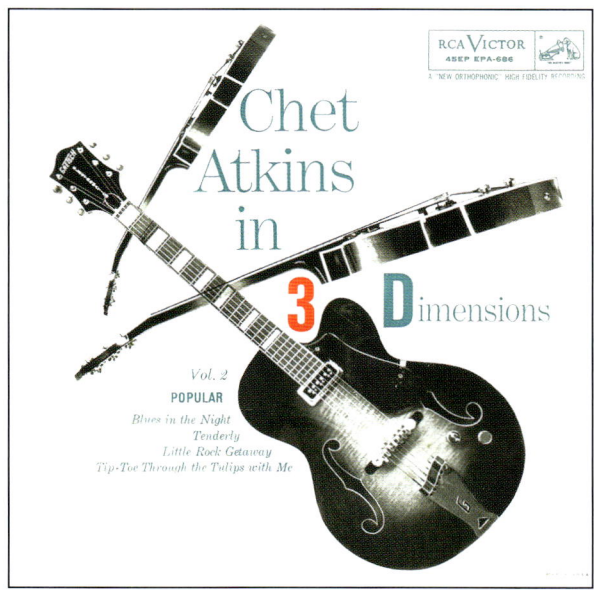

A very early 1954 model year 6190 was an interesting selection for the cover of the *Chet Atkins in 3-Demensions* EP (1955, RCA Victor).

Gibson's patent on the adjustable truss rod and headstock-located adjuster/cover, which was granted to Tim McHugh in 1921, ran out after World War II. Like other manufacturers, Gretsch adapted this style to all of their electric models beginning in 1953 with the inaugural batch of Duo Jets (model 6128). The addition of this adjustable truss rod to the Streamliner 6190 is clearly announced by the small bullet-style truss rod cover, which fails to conceal the zigzag design still underneath it. Another more subtle change that coincides with this advancement is the addition of a block inlay at the first fret, which was absent on the introductory 6190-1. *Photo Courtesy of Rick Burda.*

The March 1954 pricelist communicated the new Streamliner name to the Gretsch dealer base. The fact that the retail prices for the newly upgraded Streamliner models, 6190 ($225) and 6191 ($240), remained the same as the introductory pricing for the model, listed in the second *Your Album of Gretsch Guitars* brochure (1953), confirms two things. First, it suggests that the brochure was produced in reasonably close chronological proximity to this pricelist. Second, it reinforces 1953 as the timeframe for the introduction of the 6190-1.

The newly added model 6189, which retailed for $235, joined the existing two Streamliner models in the March 1954 pricelist. Curiously, the 6189 model was listed as possessing the Jaguar Tan finish, but it seems that this was a short-lived finish option for the Streamliner. It has only been documented on specimens from the first few batches produced. After the #154xx batch (mid-1954), it was apparently eliminated on this model and reassigned to the 6184 Corvette. From that point forward, the 6189 Streamliner displayed one of Gretsch's newest innovations, a two-tone combination paint finish inspired by the automotive designs of the day. This effect employed a television-friendly Bamboo Yellow top and a darker metallic hue known as Copper Mist on the back and sides. This event was celebrated in the 1955 Gretsch catalog, *Guitars for Moderns*, which displayed the two-tone Streamliner 6189 boldly on the full color front cover (labeled "H" on the image on page 50).

Interestingly, this 1955 catalog indicated that the Jaguar Tan finish option (now $240) was still available on the Streamliner through special order. In fact, the catalog displayed an illustration of a model 6189 guitar in that finish. However, no examples have been uncovered to suggest this happened with any frequency after the two-tone models came out. Nevertheless, this does provide an example where Gretsch used a single model designation (6189) to reference multiple finish options.

The first incarnation of the Gretsch 6189 model possessed a slightly metallic finish called Jaguar Tan. Jag Tan, as it is commonly referred to today, typically ages toward a dark champagne hue. *Photo Courtesy of Steve Wilson.*

A second version of the *Guitar for Moderns* catalog was released in October 1956. It was very similar to the 1955 edition, but predictably included increased retail pricing across the board for its guitar product line. Here the 6189 model is listed at $260, the 6190 at $250, and the 6191 at $260. By this time it had been over a year since a Jag Tan Streamliner or block fretboard marker neck had been produced. Yet, in their frugality, Gretsch elected to keep the same illustration from the 1955 catalog in this late 1956 publication. The final mention of the Streamliner model in Gretsch marketing material was the pricelist dated September 10, 1957. It lists the 6190 model at $265 and the 6191 and 6189 models each for $275.

Although the 1954 introduction of the Streamliner was highlighted by the debut of some wild (for the time) color finish variations, there are examples where the more traditional finishes (6190 sunburst and 6191 natural) display more select, highly figured wood, like maple, which were not used previously. *Photos Courtesy of Teddy Rasch.*

Streamliner Model Year Comparisons

A detailed review of the feature evolutions from each Streamliner model year follows below. It is intended to assist in the accurate dating of model 6190-1 and Streamliner guitars. It also illustrates The Gretsch Company's practice of incorporating regular and frequent product upgrades, which would be a prelude to the approach also taken with the company's next great 16" category electric archtop incarnation.

1953 Model Year

The 6190-1 models were introduced at batch #099xx. There is evidence to suggest this debut batch was manufactured at the end of 1952. These were the first Gretsch 16" category electric hollowbody models to have a single-cutaway body. The body was actually 15.5" wide and 3.25" deep, with a spruce top, and unbound f-holes. They were outfitted with a trapeze tailpiece, clear plastic control knobs, a celluloid tortoiseshell pickguard, and an Electromatic-style headstock with a slightly angled Gretsch T-roof logo and white etched zigzag motif. The bound fretboard had inlaid block markers with the exception of the first fret, where there was none. These guitars lacked an adjustable truss rod. Both the sunburst and natural finish options displayed the same 6190-1 model stamps on the label. Some examples have been found that lack a Melita bridge, although the brochure that first displayed this model shows one. Keep in mind, however, that these floating bridges are an easy component to remove or change and they are also quite valuable on the secondary market.

The last batch of the 6190-1-labeled Electromatics was #124xx. It already showed signs of change—the knobs were upgraded from the ubiquitous clear plastic to plain-topped chrome. Examples from very late in that batch also displayed an inlaid block marker on the first fret and a truss rod cover at the base of the headstock overlay, signifying the introduction of the adjustable truss rod. These may also have begun to receive the "G" cutout tailpiece, which was becoming standard in the Gretsch line for the 1954 model year.

The adolescent 6190-1 (batch #109xx), or pre-Streamliner, pioneered the single-cutaway feature on a Gretsch 16" category electric archtop. The trapeze tailpiece and bridge are not original. *Photo Courtesy of Guitars Beuzon, France.*

1954 Model Year

The next documented batch (#133xx) represented the fully transformed 6190 Streamliner models. The interior labels were stamped as 6190, 6191, or 6189 model designations. The transitional plain-topped chrome control knobs remained, as did the adjustable truss rod. This first version truss rod cover is the one referred to as the bullet-style and was often not large enough to conceal the remnants of the zigzag motif found on old stock Electromatic headstock overlays. Another structural modification was the thinning of the body to 2.75", a switch to maple tops, and the tasteful cosmetic upgrade of binding the f-holes. This batch was issued with the floating Melita bridge and Lucite pickguards replaced the previously standard tortoiseshell celluloid material. This group of guitars also contained the first examples of the new color finish for 6189 models. Evidence exists midway through this first 100 unit batch of the 1954 model year Streamliners that shows the transition to the arrow (only) control knobs.

A 1954 model year Streamliner with serial number #13753 played a vital role with Chet Atkins and became an important guitar to the future of The Gretsch Company. It was not part of a traditional batch, although more than one may have been produced. Its legacy will be comprehensively documented later in this book.

Headstocks from batch #154xx began to show a shortening of the vertical Electromatic designation to better fit above the truss rod cover and the zigzag remnants underneath started to disappear. This batch contained the last examples with the Jaguar Tan finish and the first with the two-tone, Bamboo Yellow and Copper Mist finish. This is also the last full batch produced with block markers on the fretboard.

This first batch 1954 model year Streamliner 6189 (#133xx) appears to be a very convincing old refinish to a Burgundy Bordeaux color. Period correct gold-plated hardware, atypical for this model, adds to the intrigue. The control knobs are still plain-topped, pre-dating the addition of the arrow motif. Several Gretsch models have been reported to have examples produced in custom colors, presumably on a special order basis from the factory. Although more common in the 1960s, examples from the previous decade have proven to be rare.
Photo Courtesy of Steve Wilson.

1955 Model Year

The Streamliners for the 1955 model year started at batch #167xx, which was the first of this model to display the new hump block, or Alamo, fretboard markers. Guitars from this group can also be identified by the fact that the Gretsch T-roof logo was re-positioned from the previously angled orientation to a placement that is perpendicular to the neck. Some 1955 model year examples of 6190 and 6191 possess highly figured wood tops. Several like this have been found in the #177xx batch, which was also the last to use the bullet-style truss rod cover. Much like their 6120 model sibling, only a couple of Streamliner batches were produced for the 1955 model year. From 1955 through 1958, the Streamliner model would employ the identical archtop body specification as the lauded, top-of-the-line Gretsch 6120 model. In essence, minus some ornamentation, the Streamliner represented a single pickup variation of that more celebrated guitar.

In 1955 the Streamliner model 6189 suddenly acquired a dual-personality with the introduction of a two-tone finish. This late batch #167xx example displays the Bamboo Yellow top and Copper Mist back and sides. *Photos Courtesy of Steve Wilson.*

1956 Model Year

In batch #186xx an elongated truss rod cover suddenly materialized and became standard equipment. Seemingly too subtle to constitute a new model year all on its own, in fact, it represented the defining feature for this and other Gretsch archtops from the 1956 model year. There is strong evidence that this Streamliner batch was manufactured at the very end of the 1955 calendar year.

As it turned out, 1956 was an unusually consistent year for the Streamliner. Batch #192xx shared the same feature package not only as the previous batch, but the next two batches as well (#203xx and #207xx). This is ironic when you consider what was happening to the 6120 model during the same period.

Even Chet Atkins paid homage to the Streamliner model by featuring this 1956 model year 6189 example as one of two beautiful blondes on his *Chet Atkins in Hollywood* album cover (RCA, 1961).

1957 Model Year

With five documented batches, the 1957 model year was the Streamliner's most prolific. Feature changes to batch #215xx included the removal of the vertical Electromatic designation from the face of the headstock. A simple, etched Gretsch T-roof logo remained on the black pyralin overlay. Gretsch also replaced the arrow control knob motif with a "G" indent knob featuring a large debossed "G" with an arrow piercing through it diagonally. The next few batches of this production year (#222xx, #228xx, #236xx, and #256xx) reflect a continuity of 1957 model year features, with the exception of the last 25 to 30 specimens from the #256xx group.

Most of the guitars from the #256xx batch should be considered 1957 model year examples. These were the first Streamliner models to feature the newer, more stylized orange/grey labels that replaced the former labels, which had a blue filigreed border. The last few guitars of this batch possess transitional 1958 model year attributes, including early trestle bracing inside the body, which predates by a batch or two the appearance of this same feature in the 6120 model. In fact, it would appear that these few Streamliners were the very first Gretsch guitars to be produced with trestle bracing. Although this new bracing system was created to support the pending change in pickup technology, many of these trestle-braced hybrid Streamliners continued to possess a Dynasonic pickup. There have been a few however, found at the very end of the batch that do reflect the updated pickup technology. These guitars also saw their Melita bridge transition to the new space control bridge that was common to several other Gretsch models introduced for the 1958 model year (i.e. Anniversary models).

A 1957 model year Streamliner 6189 with updated headstock. *Photo Courtesy of Teddy Rasch.*

1958 Model Year

The 1958 model year Streamliner illustrates the same overhaul experienced by many of the existing Gretsch archtop models. Foreshadowed in the last few specimens from the 1957 model year, batch #256xx, the 1958 model year attributes emerged.

Streamliner batch #266xx officially ushered in the significant aesthetic and functional changes that would define the 1958 model year for these guitars. First and foremost, the DeArmond Dynasonic pickup was replaced by the new Filter'Tron technology. The other obvious evolution was the application of a new brown headstock design displaying an inlaid Gretsch T-roof logo where the white, etched version used to be. Further adaptations include the tone control changing from a knob to a three-position switch, known as a mud switch. The tone control switch was repositioned to the upper bass side bout. Interestingly enough, although this #266xx batch exhibits the new Filter'Tron pickups, not all the guitars from this group have the trestle bracing, which was intended to be introduced in conjunction with the new pickup technology. The next batch would remedy this situation, incorporating trestle bracing throughout. Other modifications made at the end of the #266xx batch included relocating the volume control knob to the cutaway bout.

A rare last version Streamliner 6190 displaying its plain cover Filter'Tron pickup, smooth pickup surround, and neoclassic fretboard markers. *Photo Courtesy of Deke Martin.*

An early batch 1958 model year Streamliner 6189 with hump block fretboard markers, a Filter'Tron pickup, ebony fretboard, space control bridge, tone switch, inlaid headstock logo, and relocated volume knob. The tuners are not original. *Guitar Courtesy of Warren Harvey Bennett. Photo by Peter Journeaux.*

Near the end of the following batch (#271xx), some Streamliner examples featured the distinctive Gretsch neoclassic, or thumbnail fretboard markers instead of the hump block markers. These are the rarest Streamliners, with an estimated 150 examples represented in batches #271xx and #231xx. Not many have surfaced on the modern day vintage market.

The 1958 Anniversary (model 6117) benefited from the same Filter'Tron pickups as the higher-end models in the Gretsch archtop line. *Photo Courtesy of Teddy Rasch.*

Without official Gretsch documentation, or even credible anecdotal information, we can only speculate why the Streamliner model was discontinued in 1958. Not coincidentally, this was the year that Gretsch introduced the mid-range, single-pickup Chet Atkins 6119 model. But more importantly, it was also the year Gretsch released the celebratory Anniversary series, which included models 6117, 6118, 6124, and 6125. Today, the general consensus is that recognizing the company's 75 years in the business was an effort to make a short-term marketing splash. These guitars were available in single or dual-pickup formats and in sunburst or two-tone (green) finish options. They were very similar in specification to the 1958 model year Streamliner; in fact, they only lacked the elegance of bound f-holes and fretboards.

From a sales perspective, the Anniversary models apparently caught on immediately and no doubt challenged the Gretsch marketing department to reconsider the limited edition strategy that was presumably the original plan for these guitars. The company must have also realized the sudden redundancy that existed in their mid-range line and made the predictable decision to commit to the newer models.

The 6119 model received the Chet Atkins moniker, so it was bound to be around for awhile. Based on recently documented production history, no fewer than four batches of 6119s were produced in the 1958 and 1959 model years (between batches #282xx-321xx). During that same period the Anniversary production exploded—at least 17 batches were produced (between batches #277xx-320xx)—making it the darling of the mid-range line. It seems plausible that the Streamliner, which had a 1957 MSRP of $265 for sunburst 6190, simply fell victim to the sudden success of these newer single pickup 16" category electric archtop competitors and their promotional price of $198 for either the sunburst or two-tone models. Although it may never have been the plan, The Gretsch Company apparently decided to stick with a good thing. In the process the Streamliner became the odd model out.

This two-tone Anniversary model 6118 displays HiLo'Tron pickups, which the model inherited in 1960, clearly associating these guitars with the mid-range line. This model lost the trestle bracing feature at the same time. *Photo Courtesy of Soundstown.*

The Streamliner Model Legacy

The Streamliner was a particularly colorful model. For Gretsch, its legacy includes a notable run as an early electric archtop pioneer (6190-1) and a trend-setting member of the product line. It was Gretsch's first 16" category guitar with cutaway and unique color options. The 1954 Streamliner model, in particular, made some important evolutionary headway for the company, pioneering both fashion and function. As we will soon learn, the Streamliner directly influenced the birth of the next generation of the species, the model 6120 guitar, which would go on to become Gretsch's flagship model and a cultural icon.

Research suggests that there were fewer than twenty batches of Streamliners produced between its introduction as the 6190-1 Electromatic Cutaway in 1953 and its quiet discontinuation in early 1958. Throughout this period Gretsch typically produced batches of 50 or 100 guitars for a certain model at a time. Therefore, it would not be unreasonable to hypothesize that no more than 2000 of these guitars were ever manufactured. As a point of reference, in 1953 alone, Gibson sold in excess of 2000 Les Paul model guitars. From an industry perspective, this contrasting figure makes the Gretsch Streamliner a relatively low production example. It is also the primary reason why this model is an uncommon guitar 50 years later.

Admittedly not as sought after as the Chet Atkins signature line, vintage examples of this pivotal model are coveted by contemporary musicians, such as The Walkmen, who rely on vintage Streamliners to tap into "That Great Gretsch Sound!" *Photo Courtesy of Heather Schoeppach.*

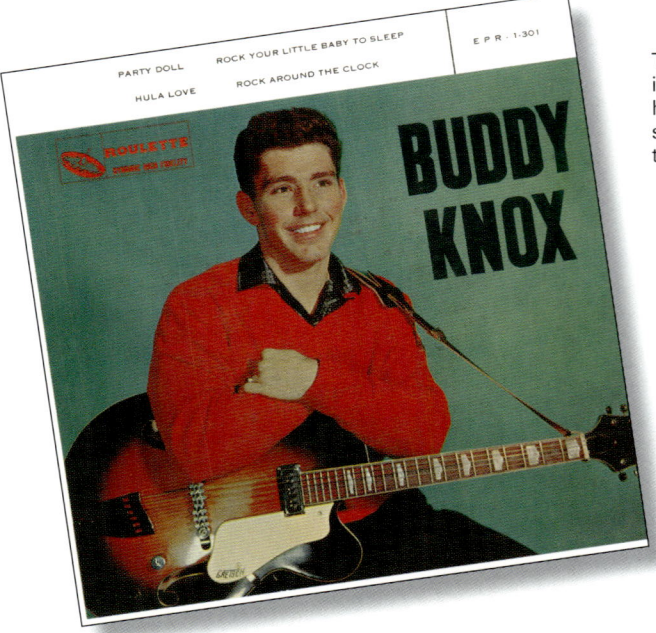

PARTY DOLL   ROCK YOUR LITTLE BABY TO SLEEP   E P R · 1·301

HULA LOVE   ROCK AROUND THE CLOCK

BUDDY KNOX

There was one artist from the period that was known for playing the Gretsch Streamliner model. Seen here on the cover of his self-titled record (Roulette Records, 1957), Buddy Knox had several songs on the charts in the 1950s. His biggest hit was the 1957 song "Party Doll."

The Gretsch Streamliner model did not become the guitar of tomorrow for one final reason—its single pickup configuration. For it to provide the musician with the maximum sonic flexibility, the guitar of the future would have to deliver the array of sounds that a multiple pickup configuration provided. This would be relatively easy to accomplish by simply adding a second pickup to the existing Streamliner model, which, one fateful day in early 1954, Gretsch actually did. The next chore would be to find somebody with the celebrity to endorse this new optimized Streamliner. Gretsch wonder-boy, Jimmie Webster, had something in mind, and once again Gretsch would look to Gibson to show them the way.

In addition to its low production totals, a more significant reason why the Streamliner model is not as coveted as other vintage models is its lack of association with a particular artist of note. Many of today's vintage guitar enthusiasts enjoy pursuing the guitars made popular in their youth. Some collectors, however, want to own the same instrument that an accomplished artist is known for using. Affiliations with celebrity artists like Jimmy Page and Eric Clapton have long been a driving force in the popularity, and value, of the late 1950s Les Paul and Stratocaster, respectively. The Streamliner had no such luck—a fate shared by most of Gretsch's 16" category electric archtops from the 1950s. A certain well-known picker from Georgia eventually changed all that.

It has been rumored that Gretsch made special order Streamliners equipped with dual-pickups. Solid evidence of this remains elusive. However, many examples exist with aftermarket modifications and added pickups. *Photo Courtesy of Dan Formosa.*

Les Paul and his Endorsement of Gibson Guitars

The Gibson Company had long dominated the guitar industry. Along the way they influenced many seminal developments, from the trend setting L-5 acoustic archtop format to electric amplification for guitars and the development of solid-bodied instruments. In each of these cases, The Gretsch Company followed the path that Gibson pioneered. One innovation that Gibson successfully exploited, however, had little to do with the technology of the instrument, but instead with how they marketed their new solidbody electric guitar model, introduced in 1952. Gibson collaborated very closely with one of the more notable players of the day in developing this model and decided to put his name right on it. This tactic might not have worked so well, had the name they associated with the model been that of somebody other than the great Les Paul.

In addition to collaborating on the concept and design of the guitar, Paul also provided his high profile endorsement of the model, playing it regularly in performances and lending his image for use in Gibson catalogs and advertising. Although it was not a new idea for artists to endorse brands and models of guitars, this was one of the first examples of a signature model, an innovative marketing approach that changed the industry from that point on. Interestingly, this was a concept Gibson had pioneered many years prior with the original signature model—the Nick Lucas acoustic flat top model. Today, signature guitar models are offered by just about every major guitar manufacturer.

Guitar Courtesy of Dave Rogers. Photo by Tim Mullally.

Influential Personality: Les Paul

Les Paul, born Lester William Polfus (1915-2009), was one of the most influential guitarists of the modern era. At the tender age of 17, Paul dropped out of high school and started his career in country music, using the stage name Rhubarb Red. He soon moved into jazz guitar, influenced by Django Reinhardt and Eddie Lang. In 1934, while doing radio work as Rhubarb Red, he began performing more jazz-oriented material under his own name, forming the Les Paul Trio in 1936. Coincidentally, Chet Atkins' half-brother Jim played in the original Les Paul Trio.

Paul's work with Fred Waring on network radio introduced the electric guitar to a nationwide audience, preceding Charlie Christian's rise in notoriety with the Benny Goodman Band by a year or two. In the mid 1940s, Bing Crosby not only featured the Les Paul Trio on his radio show, he also sponsored much of Paul's early experimentation with recording. In return, Paul performed with Crosby on his 1945 number one hit "It's Been a Long Time."

Hits of Les and Mary (Capitol Records, 1960).

Over the next few years Paul collaborated with a young vocalist named Mary Ford, who was an accomplished guitarist in her own right. Paul and Ford later married and continued to work together on music. In the late 1940s Paul and Ford pioneered what Capitol Records advertised as the "New Sound." which employed an early use of over dubbing. In his Les Paul biography on *MisterGuitar.com*, Richard Ginell writes that "in 1947, after experimenting in his garage studio and discarding some 500 test discs, Paul came up with a kooky version of 'Lover' for eight electric guitars, all played by himself with dizzying multi-speed effects." This unique and innovative work was released by Capitol Records and became a 1948 hit. As the 1950s began Paul and Ford were at the height of their popularity and influence. They applied the New Sound to jazz standards and produced many radio hits, including "Tennessee Waltz" (1950) and "Tiger Rag" (1952).

Les Paul has been referred to as "the Source." His immeasurable contributions to both the guitar industry and modern day recording were featured in the cover story of the December 1977 issue of *Guitar Player* magazine.

Always a tinkerer, Paul had experimented with electric guitar technology in the early 1940s. His development of the Log, a solid plank of pine outfitted with electrified pickups bolted onto a guitar neck and adorned with fake hollow wings to make it appear more traditional (Paul made these after-hours at the Epiphone factory), motivated him to advocate for a solid-bodied electric guitar. Paul made several attempts to convince Gibson of the potential such a deviation from their existing electric archtop line held. Then, in 1951, Gibson finally approached Paul about collaborating on a solidbody electric guitar. In what was a clear reaction to the success of the Fender Broadcaster model, Gibson produced the 1952 Les

Paul electric guitar. Now commonly referred to as the Gold Top model because of its unique metallic finish, it also incorporated dual-pickups into a more compact and comfortable single-cutaway solid mahogany body.

The original 1952 Les Paul solidbody. Its many offspring have become Gibson's most successful models and are still in production today. *Guitar Courtesy of Dave Rogers. Photo by Tim Mullally.*

Les Paul collaborated with Chet Atkins on two albums— the Grammy winning *Chester & Lester* (RCA, 1978) (pictured) and the Grammy-nominated *Guitar Monsters* (RCA, 1978).

The timing of such a relationship and product release, could not have been more opportune as musical tastes were shifting in new directions. However, the emergence of rock and roll in the 1950s, fully enabled by the solidbody electric guitar, made Paul and Ford's characteristic sound seem outdated by mid-decade. Paul was not able to crossover and appeal to the new generation of music consumers and he went into semi-retirement. During this period, he continued his experimentation with technology, including the development of on-board, over-dubbing capability via the Les Pulverizer unit. He made two albums in the 1970s with his good friend Chet Atkins and began playing regular shows in New York, which he continued into his 90s. Paul was inducted into the Rock and Roll Hall of Fame in 1988 and the National Inventors Hall of Fame in 2005.

The Gretsch Company could not help but take notice of the success Gibson's partnership with Les Paul had on this signature guitar model, which was verified in the marketplace. Between 1952 and 1953 almost 4000 Les Paul guitars were sold. The concept of leveraging the endorsement of a notable guitarist to sell instruments was an undeniable success. As would become their practice, Gretsch followed suit, attempting to duplicate Gibson's achievement. In doing so they understood that they would need to attract a name of equal status and clout within the industry. It was a foresighted Gretsch representative named Jimmie Webster who brought Chet Atkins into the fold and solidified a deal that would ultimately produce The Gretsch Company's greatest legacy.

Al Caiola

Mary Osborne

Sal Salvador

WHATEVER YOUR STYLE, IT'S GRETSCH BY A MILE!

Professionals, like these top Jazz artists, appreciate the full, rich sustaining tones they get in every register of their Gretsch guitars. Rave about Gretsch's new streamlined styling . . . the wonderful 'new feel' of Gretsch extra-thin modeling.

Why not try a Gretsch guitar? Whatever your playing style—there's a model for you. Write for FREE, new Gretsch Guitar Catalog . . . pictures over 30 different models, plus special Gretsch Electromatic Amplifiers and accessories.

GRETSCH The FRED. GRETSCH Mfg. Co., Dept. DB107, 60 Broadway, Brooklyn 11, N. Y.

In the early 1950s, Gretsch attempted to showcase its guitars by running regular ads featuring notable musicians in music and trade publications. The artists that were featured tended to be less universally recognized and presumably failed to influence the kind of consumer behavior that the Gibson signature model approach achieved.

Section III:

Jimmie Webster: The Man Behind the Scenes

Most of the design changes came from Jimm[ie] Webster. He would get the feedback from the stores. They would tell him what was selling for Gibson, Fender, and the rest of the guitar makers.

-Dan Duffy

In the early 1940s, Jimmie Webster's role within the Gretsch organization was that of a periodic demonstrator. Never officially a full-time employee, Webster would bill his time much as a consultant would. In January 1951 he served as a "special representative," demonstrating the newly released electric archtop line (Electro II models) in New York at a special promotional event. Soon he would be instrumental in providing creative input on guitar design and marketing alike.

Influential Personality: Jimmie Webster

Jimmie Webster (1908-1978) made his reputation as a jazz musician, playing with the likes of Woody Herman and Count Basie. As a musician he relied on his solid rhythm chops and periodic solo work to make a name for himself in the late 1940s and early 1950s. A hallmark of Webster's career was developing a fretboard tapping style he eventually called the Touch System.

PRESENTING

THE GRETSCH - DE ARMOND METHOD
FOR ELECTRIC SPANISH GUITAR

By JIMMIE WEBSTER

The Guitar Technique of Tomorrow
Explained for the Artist of Today!

This 1940 brochure provided the reader with the basics of equipment set-up. It also did not miss the opportunity to pitch Gretsch guitars and DeArmond products. The publication included a brief primer on the technique itself, claiming "by a little concentration and study on your part, you should be able to really go to town by yourself in a week." *Courtesy of Rod McDonald.*

Webster acknowledged that his inspiration for this method was the result of a demonstration he attended where hammer-on techniques were used to illustrate the highly sensitive nature of DeArmond pickups. Harry DeArmond was proud of his product line and he often demonstrated their abilities by depressing strings on a fretboard to produce tone. Seeing this, Webster, who was already working as an agent of The Gretsch Company, was motivated to develop an entire playing style based on this tapping action. Early efforts to promote the technique referred to it as "The Gretsch-DeArmond Method (for electric Spanish guitar)." Gretsch produced a 1940 brochure that provided instruction on the basics. Sometime later, however, it became less commercialized and was renamed the more consumer-friendly Touch System.

Webster had a piano background and using both hands on the fretboard probably came more naturally for him as a result. He documented his unique approach to the guitar in his 1952 method book, *The Touch System for Electric and Amplified Spanish Guitar*. In this publication he revealed that the chording used with an aggressive hammer-on technique eliminated the need for right-hand plucking or strumming. He would then use that free hand to tap melodies on higher frets and open strings. This system created more of an ensemble sound—the left hand chording provided the rhythm sections and the right hand tapped out the solo. Webster was an avid supporter of new technology and he provided a glimpse of his enthusiasm about these new directions in the foreword of his book: "Electronics brought out the hidden voices and tonal effects which had been lying dormant in the guitar for centuries, it was like finding many buried treasures."

Webster was an influential force in the design and production of The Gretsch Company's White Falcon model, introduced in 1955. He was a proponent of the larger bodied electric archtops because he felt that the bigger format lent itself to his Touch System. In 1958,

in an attempt to optimize the instrument even further, he successfully developed the Project-o-Sonic stereo guitar. These instruments employed sound engineer, Ray Butts' modified split Filter'Tron pickups to direct the signal from the upper three strings to one amplifier and the lower three strings to a second amplifier. Several Gretsch models were offered with this option. Gretsch apparently provided Webster the latitude to pursue this avenue, in part because of his belief that the Touch System would become a mainstream trend. In the foreword of his book, Webster makes some optimistic predictions:

The most startling discovery in the electronic field is the Touch System. This new revolutionary school of playing is the most modern, far reaching system to reach the guitarist since the inception of the guitar itself. [Those who have heard it] have been so electrified, thrilled, and enthused, with the Touch System that its universal adoption by guitarists everywhere is simply a question of time.

It is probable that these bold assertions are not just the work of a publisher trying to sell books, but that it actually reflects Webster's perspective—and it is apparent that Gretsch bought into it as well. In 1959, Chet Atkins produced Webster's RCA LP release entitled *Webster's Un'a-Bridged*, which provided a wonderful demonstration of what the Touch System, once mastered, and enabled by a stereo guitar, can produce. Webster continued to regularly promote the technique at trade fairs and industry events in an effort to create interest. Even though Gretsch's commitment to this technique apparently motivated Gibson to produce a competitive system, it seems that this particular evolutionary influence was not destined to have a long-term impact on the Gretsch electric archtop product line or the industry.

In the 1950s, Gretsch ran many of these "Spot Light" advertisements in popular music publications.

In the past few decades there have been some isolated examples of artists who successfully employed variations of the Touch System. Eddie Van Halen is notable for integrating his own approach with hard rock music, but a more pure example of the modern mastery of the system would be the jazz musings of Stanley Jordan. In the early 1980s, there was even an innovative electric stringed instrument introduced to the marketplace called the Chapman Stick that relied on what is essentially an application of the Touch System. However it generated only moderate adoption within a niche of musicians.

The reality is that 50 years later the Touch System technique is not only largely unappreciated it is basically absent from contemporary music. The vintage Gretsch stereo models from the period are, therefore, under-valued compared to the same models with conventional electronics. Although examples periodically surface in the vintage market, the electronic accoutrements (special wires and dual-jack box) are even less common.

Web'ster's un'a-bridged album (RCA, 1959).

When considering the various catalysts that triggered change within the Gretsch electric archtop product line of the 1950s, it is impossible to underemphasize the impact Jimmie Webster made. He unapologetically subscribed to the philosophy of providing regular updates to the product line and championed many feature adaptations. Some of these absolutely improved the package, either benefiting the musician, or providing a business advantage to the company. Others were ill-fated decisions made on his assumptions about the future of guitar playing and music, and some were simply thinly veiled attempts at promoting gimmicks as weak imposters for technology. As with anything in a consumer driven economy, the principle of natural selection ends up sorting all this out over time. Fifty years later, it is now obvious which of Jimmie Webster's contributions had substance and which were discarded into obsolescence.

Highly successful Webster contributions include:

- White Falcon guitar model 6136: Developed in 1954, it became as recognizable a Gretsch icon as the Chet Atkins 6120, but with significantly lower production numbers.
- Filter'Tron pickups: Worked closely with Ray Butts on the application of the Filter'Tron pickup, which addressed the humming issues that plagued the single coil Dynasonic technology. They also enabled Gretsch to gain internal manufacturing control of this important component. (Ray Butts Patent #2,892,371)
- Space control bridge: An internally produced component, this created a greater degree of control for the company. (Patent #2,918,837)
- Neoclassic (thumbnail) markers: Likely the most distinctive fretboard markers ever produced and a Gretsch trademark.
- Unconventional and highly colorful finishes: Scooped the industry and is one of the great legacies of the Gretsch brand.

Less than successful Webster contributions include:

- Project-o-Sonic stereo enabled Gretsch guitar models: The technology never took off. (Patent #2,964,985)
- Padded guitar backs: A feature the rest of the industry felt no need to emulate. (Patent #D-196,609)
- Tone-twister (1962): An attempt to provide subtle vibrato from behind the bridge. Resulted in a lot of broken strings. (Patent #D-196,678)
- T-Zone Tempered Treble (slanted frets) patent (1962): Incorporated one degree of slant above the twelfth fret to improve tonality in treble range. (Patent #3,353,433)
- Floating Sound Unit patent (1965): An attempt to improve sustain that resulted in suspect execution.
- String dampening (mute) system: Chet Atkins was apparently not consulted on the addition of these to his signature models. (Patent #3,134,288)

Today, Jimmie Webster is fondly remembered for his many positive contributions to the success of The Gretsch Company during its Golden Era. It seems that history has absolved Webster for most of his ill-advised gadgetry, devotion to the Touch System, and the tangential affects it had on the Gretsch product line. These have in no way diminished what is arguably his greatest contribution to the company—his role in recruiting Chet Atkins as an endorser of Gretsch guitar products.

This was an accomplishment easier said than done, but

Webster, ever diligent, courted the young guitarist, ultimately convincing Atkins to agree to co-develop a Chet Atkins signature guitar in early 1954. There was no way that Webster (or Gretsch) could have known what this new relationship with Chet Akins would ultimately mean to the future success of the Gretsch brand. In retrospect, however, this collaboration represents a defining moment that ultimately put Gretsch on the map in the Golden Era, and which keeps the company there today.

Courtesy of Joe Ensalaco.

Chet Atkins and his Endorsement of Gretsch Guitars

In early 1954, the young Chet Atkins was becoming well-established as a performer and was already providing glimpses of his future success. Jimmie Webster made it his business to try and link the Gretsch brand to that potential. Working closely with the design staff, and with preliminary input from Atkins, Webster oversaw the creation of a prototype guitar, reflecting what he (and Gretsch) thought would be the perfect mix of country music aesthetic and the performance features that an elite instrumentalist like Chet Atkins would desire.

Photo Courtesy of Michael Ochs Archive/Getty Images.

Influential Personality: Chet Atkins

Chet Atkins (1924-2001) is remembered as being arguably the most influential musician that Nashville and country music has ever had—but he did not appreciate being pigeon-holed into just that genre. He considered himself simply a guitarist.

Growing up in Georgia, Atkins first picked up the ukulele and then the fiddle. Then, supposedly, at the age of nine he traded his brother Lowell a pistol and some chores for his first guitar. Atkins became obsessed with music, opting to play his guitar rather than pursue the usual interests of kids his age. He was completely self-taught and by high school was an accomplished guitarist. In 1939, Atkins was influenced by the picking work of Merle Travis, which led him to develop and master a unique, right-hand technique of picking with his first three fingers, using his thumb for bass. This discovery dramatically shaped his playing style. The resulting sound possessed the complexity and clarity characteristic of his future work.

Atkins dropped out of high school in 1942 to pursue a job at WNOX radio in Knoxville, Tennessee. He spent the next few years moving around to other radio stations, often getting fired because he did not sound country enough. Then, in 1946, Atkins made his Grand Ole Opry debut as a member of Red Foley's band. His complex picking style and soft-spoken persona continued to work against him until Merle Travis' radio hits began to make Atkins' sound more desirable.

Atkins was asked to make some recordings for RCA in 1947, which subsequently sold poorly. Undaunted, he persevered, existing on studio work and WNOX radio gigs. In 1949, Atkins was asked to join Mother Maybelle and the Carter Sisters (June, Helen, and Anita) and relocated to Nashville in the mid-1950s. Now Atkins was busy with recording sessions and performances and his reputation was growing. Atkins scored his first hit single with "Mr. Sandman" (1954) and his album sales improved.

Around that time, when Atkins was managing RCA's Nashville studio, The Gretsch Company approached him to collaborate on the design of a signature series guitar. Oddly enough, Atkins admits to consulting with Les Paul regarding the type of royalty agreement he should make with Gretsch. That determined, this began a relationship with Gretsch that would last until late 1978, when disenchanted by the Baldwin Company's stewardship of the Gretsch brand, Atkins defected to consult for the Gibson Company.

In 1957, as rock and roll began to erode the public interest in country music, Atkins made a conscious decision to steer the RCA Nashville division away from fiddles and steel guitar, focusing instead on the singers. The resulting body of work was referred to as the Nashville Sound, which successfully maintained country music's viability during that period. It was not uncommon for country hits to cross over and achieve popular music success as well.

Through the 1960s Atkins made records of both pop standards and Jazz in his state-of-the-art home studio. He had his biggest hit single in 1965 with "Yakety Axe" and his albums were revered by other musicians for their unique and experimental approaches. Hugh Gregory, author of *1000 Great Guitarists*, described Atkins' impact with the following: "His striking use of muted, syncopated bass parts, dazzling deployment of the guitar's natural dynamics, and an open willingness to experiment with new sounds and effects have combined in a style that has been supremely influential, not only among country players but with guitarists from all musical areas." Atkin's success and stature within the industry won him the moniker of Mr. Guitar.

In 1968, he began a successful stint as the vice president of RCA's country division, signing talent such as Jerry Reed, Waylon Jennings, Dolly Parton, Charley Pride, and Willie Nelson. In the 1970s, Atkins recorded fewer records, focusing on the challenge of his executive duties. RCA ultimately became less supportive of Atkins' desire to play more jazz and he left the label in 1982, signing with Columbia Records, where he proved that he was a master of the jazz genre as well. Before his death in 2001, Chet Atkins had received eleven Grammy Awards and nine Country Music Association, Instrumentalist of the Year Awards. Along the way he was inducted into the Country Music Hall of Fame (1973) and the Rock and Roll Hall of Fame (2002). He is idolized by many for making incalculable contributions to modern guitar music.

The guitar that was presented to Chet Atkins in mid-1954 as a proposed signature model was in fact a special order Streamliner model (#13753). This maple topped, 21-fret guitar did not have a standard Streamliner model number assigned to it and was marked "Streamliner*special" on the label. The guitar, which was outfitted with an additional DeArmond Dynasonic pickup, had gold-plated hardware, including a Melita bridge, arrow control knobs, and Waverly (oval button) tuning machines. The finish was the distinctive transparent amber red and it was further adorned with Western appointments, including an inlaid steer's head on an un-bound headstock, large "G" brand on the body, etched images of cows and cactus in the block inlays (except for the first and last frets which were left un-etched), and a fancy belt buckle-enhanced gold "G" cutout tailpiece. Early photographs reveal that the original pickguard, made of a dark cellulous tortoiseshell material, displayed a complementary (to the headstock) steer's head motif along with the words "Chet Atkins" in a subtle plain text.

Acknowledging its evolutionary legacy, this prototypical 6120 specimen (#13753) was identified as a Streamliner Special on its interior label. Subsequent modifications to this guitar include the gold Lucite Chet Atkins signature signpost pickguard, which was clearly added later, evidenced by its ill-fitting bridge pickup notch. *Photo Courtesy of Russ Cochran and Chet Atkins, copyright ©2001. Used with permission.*

This wonderful photo of Chet Atkins backstage at the Grand Ole Opry depicts him holding the Streamliner Special prototype, easily identified by the unbound headstock and plain, un-etched fretboard markers on the first and last frets. Interestingly, the guitar, which originated with a "G" cutout cowboy belt buckle tailpiece, instead displays a vibrato assembly. This does not appear to reflect any of the standard Bigsby designs (first introduced in 1939), but instead looks to be the same vibrato that Atkins was known to use on his highly modified 1950 D'Angelico Excel. This could plausibly explain how and why Atkins determined he desired a production vibrato on the 6120 model.

Even more interesting than this feature however, is the date of the photograph. The Grand Ole Opry archives verified that this photo was taken in August of 1954. Based on the historically accepted rule of thumb around the chronology of Gretsch production, this date would seem too early for a guitar with serial number #13753 to exist. New research, however, indicates that this guitar was actually made for Atkins sometime in early 1954.

Chet Atkins in August of 1954 with the Streamliner Special prototype. *Photo by Gordon Gillingham, ©2008 Grand Ole Opry.*

Atkins approved the design of the Streamliner Special prototype, but insisted on the installation of a Bigsby vibrato tailpiece and improved sustain, which was, in part, addressed by the addition of a brass nut. To further enhance the model's sustain, subsequent production incarnations of the guitar replaced the Melita bridge with a simple, compensated cast aluminum unit on a floating rosewood base. Atkins claims to have protested the large Gretsch-style f-holes as well, but those comments went unheard until a few years later when one of Atkins' other signature models was conceived with thinner, simulated f-holes (Country Gentleman model 6122).

"Hey Ferlin, what do you say about this new Gretsch guitar they made for me?!" Chet Atkins showing off his Gretsch 6120 prototype to Ferlin Husky at the Grand Ole Opry in 1954. *Photo by Gordon Gillingham ©2008 Grand Ole Opry.*

A second prototype guitar featuring these requested modifications was quickly created (#13770) and has become accepted as the very first model 6120 Chet Atkins hollowbody guitar produced. This new prototype exhibited a fixed-arm, enamel-faced, Bigsby B6 unit, aluminum Bigsby bridge, as well as a nicely flamed Maple top, brass nut, and gold Lucite pickguard. Atkins is also captured in archive footage from 1954 playing his breakthrough hit "Mr. Sandman" on this historic guitar. Close inspection reveals that the gold pickguard does not yet display the Chet Atkins signpost insignia or Gretsch logo.

The back cover of the February 1956 edition of *Country & Western Jamboree* depicts Atkins with what is clearly the second prototype 6120 guitar, indicated by its unbound headstock and etched first fret inlay.

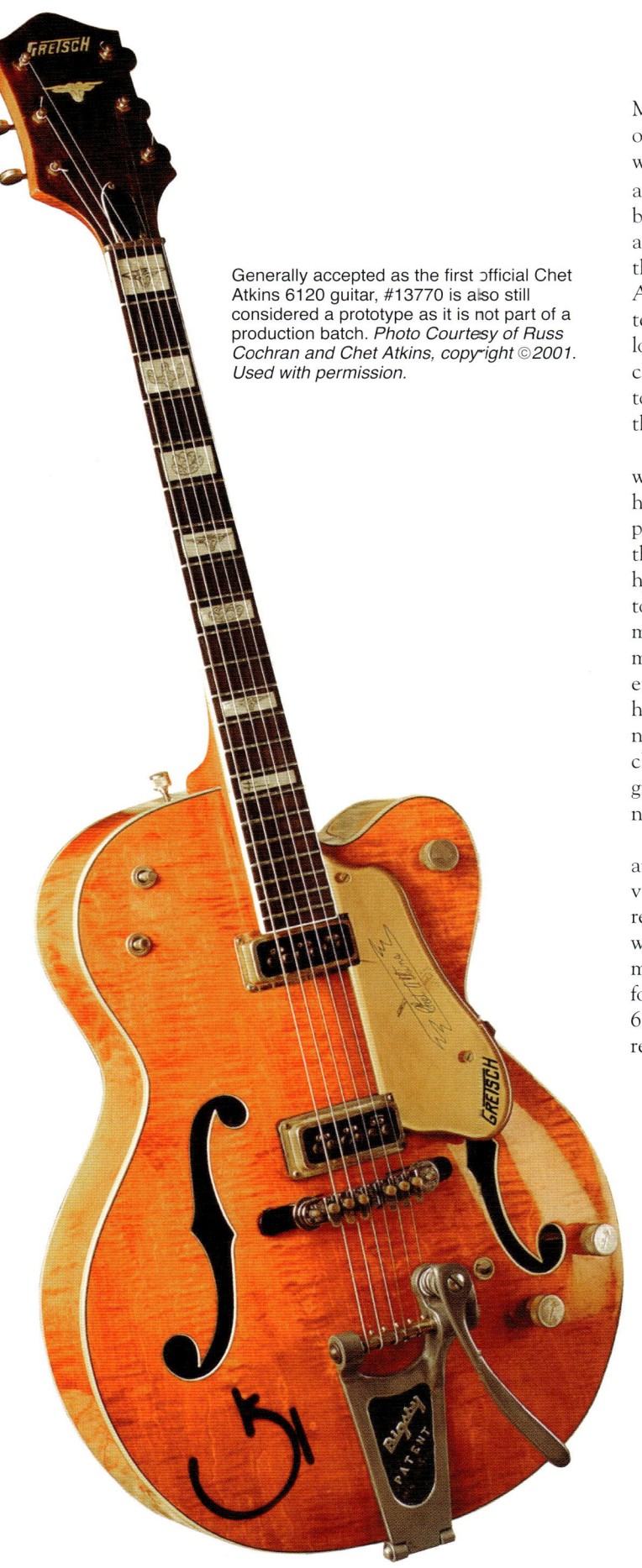

Generally accepted as the first official Chet Atkins 6120 guitar, #13770 is also still considered a prototype as it is not part of a production batch. *Photo Courtesy of Russ Cochran and Chet Atkins, copyright ©2001. Used with permission.*

Modern day photos show the guitar as having an old-style Melita bridge, much like its prototype predecessor, but this was not original to the guitar. Today, this guitar also possesses a modified wiring configuration with two control knobs at the lower bout and a switch where the third knob typically resides. The upper bass-side bout now has an added tone selector toggle switch accompanying the existing pickup selector switch, a schematic that in later model years (1958) became standard on the 6120. Additionally, these recent photos reveal that it has been outfitted with a later swivel-handle-style Bigsby vibrato unit. Atkins loved to tinker with his guitars, always experimenting and making changes he felt would improve their performance. It is not unusual to see photographs of them in various states of modification over the years.

It is reasonable to assume that this second prototypical guitar was yet another modified Streamliner. The components would have been readily available at the factory to make changes in the process of preparing this guitar for Atkins. In addition to the fact that it only has 21 frets, another telltale clue is the fact that its headstock was similarly unbound like the Streamliner Special prototype. By the time the first production batch of 6120 guitars was manufactured months later, the bound headstock was standard, making these two seminal examples unique in that way. Curiously enough, these two guitars are the only Gretsch examples that have surfaced (to date) from the #13700-13799 batch of serial numbers, creating a mysterious void in the factory production chronology. The fate of the other ninety-eight labels from that group is unknown. Both of these historically significant guitars now reside in the Country Music Hall of Fame in Nashville.

In a very literal sense, a metamorphosis had taken place and the Streamliner spawned a more flamboyant and functional version of itself . This time, however, the newer model did not replace the existing model, but would instead co-exist in harmony with it within the product line. As already noted, the Streamliner model continued to represent a successful mid-range instrument for the next four years, while the more flashy and charismatic 6120 model would go on to become the Gretsch brand's most recognizable icon.

Our ability to create a partnership with Chet Atkins and use his playing skills and his feel for the instrument and translate our skills into making what a player needs created that 6120 instrument.

-Fred W. Gretsch

Gretsch Chet Atkins Hollowbody Model 6120 (1955)

It seemed like a match made in heaven. Atkins received the recognition associated with having his own namesake guitar (presumably with Atkins endorsed design influences) and The Gretsch Company got a popular and loyal endorser of their new top-of-the-line guitar model. It was clear that Atkins intended to do his part to promote these guitars, making regular public appearances, appearing in high profile print ads, and providing frequent exposure for the instrument on his album covers. It was the beginning of a successful 25-year relationship and Atkins developed a great respect for Fred Gretsch Jr. He also got the opportunity to influence the design of several other subsequent signature models over the years. However, for many, he will be most remembered for his association with the big orange hollowbody.

Interestingly, Chet Atkins was widely quoted as saying that he really was not all that enamored with the Western appointments on that first prototype guitar. Because Atkins always considered himself as simply a guitarist, not necessarily committed to one genre, the cowboy trimmings rubbed him the wrong way. In his book, *Chet Atkins, Me and My Guitars*, he goes on to admit that the bright orange finish was not his idea either, calling it "hideous" and squarely placing the credit for that decision with Gretsch. He was also highly critical of the DeArmond Dynasonic pickups and accused them of dampening sustain as a result of their powerful magnets pulling on the strings.

It would seem, in retrospect that Atkins did not really like much about these guitars. These revelations just reinforce how eager he must have been to possess his own signature model guitar, as he initially acquiesced to most of those features. Ultimately, the Western motifs were eliminated in an effort to widen the 6120 model's appeal beyond the country and western category. It took another year after that, but Atkins was eventually able to resolve his displeasure with the pickups too.

Tony Bacon, author of *50 Years of Gretsch Electrics*, reported that in the December 1954 issue of *The Music Trades*, the 6120 hollowbody (and 6121 solidbody) were introduced as "Chet Atkins Country Style Electromatic guitars…" and that "both models would be available for delivery after January 1, 1955." There is no evidence that any guitars were shipped prior to this. The earliest documented batch of 6120 guitars begins at, or close to, serial #16450. It is important to point out that this first production batch was manufactured in 1954 (probably November or December), but represented the 1955 model year.

So, in early 1955, the world saw the first production batch of Chet Atkins 6120 model guitars roll out of the Brooklyn factory at a retail price of $385. It was an amalgamation of the previous 15 years of product maturation, a combination of successful features, and the adoption of advantageous traits from elsewhere in the industry. This was the model where Gretsch pulled it all together. The now famous amber-red finish, more commonly referred to as Western orange, first generation gold-anodized aluminum B6 Bigsby vibrato with fixed arm and spoon handle, along with all the cowboy trappings, aesthetically separated this beast from the rest of the Gretsch clan. The addition of a second pickup in the bridge position offered the guitarist more sonic options than its predecessor, the Streamliner model, and ultimately proved to be the dominant configuration in the industry. This combination of proven features made this guitar the first top-of-the-line 16" (actually 15.5") electric archtop that Gretsch had ever offered. The company was immediately rewarded with strong sales—the legend had begun.

Cover of the 1957 Winter issue of *Country and Western Jamboree* magazine. Atkins is holding the original Streamliner Special 6120 prototype.

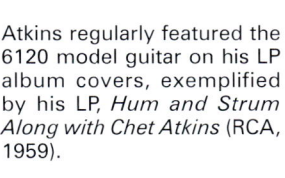

Atkins regularly featured the 6120 model guitar on his LP album covers, exemplified by his LP, *Hum and Strum Along with Chet Atkins* (RCA, 1959).

Atkins made periodic in-store appearances, here pictured with Ben Portman of Portman's Music in Savannah, Georgia. *Photo Courtesy of Jerry Portman and Portman's Music Superstore.*

It did not take long for the flashy looks and signature sound of the 1955 Gretsch 6120 model to catch the attention of a young guitarist named Paul Yandell, who was working with the Louvin Brothers band at the time. Later known for his long-time collaboration with Chet Atkins, Yandell recalls being impressed with the 6120, which he said was quickly becoming popular within the country and western music circles. Yandell decided to try one out, so he went to Kendall's Music store in Nashville, Tennessee, to trade in his three pickup Gibson archtop for a brand new Chet Atkins 6120.

Yandell has fond memories of that guitar, claiming that "it was as good as any Gibson I have played." When asked about the restrictive fixed arm of the first generation B6 Bigsby unit, Yandell recounted his experience of attempting to modify that feature, using a turn signal arm from an Oldsmobile in its place. He finished that story with a reminder that in those days there were no luthiers or guitar techs and musicians had to execute their own modifications. Yandell made many recordings with his trusty 6120 before finally trading it in for a Country Gentleman model after returning home from a stint in the military in 1961.

Courtesy of Paul Yandell.

By the mid-1950s, and the emergence of the 6120 Chet Atkins model within the Gretsch line, the concept of introducing regular feature changes to an instrument was firmly ingrained in the Gretsch corporate culture. This practice was employed to such a degree that the 6120 model seemed to be in a constant state of flux. Many in today's vintage community have voiced frustration at this fact, saying that no two 6120 model guitars seem to be alike and that

these transitional examples are difficult to accurately date. Since the Gretsch factory would periodically introduce these changes mid-stream, there is not always a clean-cut correlation of some features to a specific model year. There are also many examples of changes introduced mid-batch; so, even when two guitars are within just few serial numbers of each other, they may not share the exact same components.

Actually, these frequent feature evolutions can, for the informed Gretsch-pert, serve as a very accurate road map when trying to determine a particular examples' vintage. For the simple reason that certain feature combinations were so short-lived, many 6120 examples reveal their vintage and even batch origination if the observer carefully notes all of the clues. Hopefully the following review of each 6120 <u>model</u> year, and its associated features and changes, will better equip the reader for such detective work. Furthermore, if there is a question as to the originality of a particular specimen, this information provides insight to all the period-correct attributes one might expect to find within its batch. Please note however, that the cross-referencing of feature combinations becomes less scientific as a result of transient components like bridges, tailpieces, tuners, and pickguards, which have frequently been changed or modified over the course of 50 years. Unless you know that you have a completely original specimen, this fact could explain perceived anomalies.

As you proceed, please also keep some things in mind about serial numbers and model years. The lack of access to any official production records from The Gretsch Company has made the exact documentation of which batches fell into what production years problematic. Remember that an early 1958 model 6120 example, displaying all the appropriate model year features, may not necessarily have been manufactured in 1958. In the instances when feature changes were planned to fall at the beginning of a new calendar year, and were advertised in that year's catalog, those first batches of guitars with the new feature were typically manufactured in the prior year. The following narrative endeavors to define 6120 model year feature changes, with periodic, albeit less definitive, references to production and calendar year.

It is tempting to refer back to the company's official publications to confirm attributes of a particular model. But remember, Gretsch changed its guitars' features faster than they reprinted catalogs. We have already cited several examples where the catalog did not accurately represent the product line it promoted (see Streamliner and Corvette sections). Features were changed and new feature combinations created so rapidly on the 6120 model that the marketing material could not keep up.

The following grouping of 6120 batches into model year designations was determined by several factors, first, the generally accepted primary sources, including Gretsch Company publications and oral history. Factored into this is a comparative analysis of thousands of photographs of vintage 6120 specimens, as well as facts distilled from the rigorous examination of serial number data from the entire Gretsch guitar product line. It is not inconceivable that the future will reveal additional, currently undocumented batches or examples possessing feature attributes that might demand a recalibration of this grouping. Visit http://www.6120freak.com to keep abreast of any revelations that may revise the conclusions presented here.

1955 model year serial number batches:

#16450-16550: 100-unit batch*
#169xx: 100-unit batch*
#173xx: 100-unit batch*
*(6121 solidbodies included)

1955 Model Year 6120

It might seem counterintuitive that there were only three batches of Chet Atkins 6120 models produced for the 1955 model year. After all, leveraging Atkins' celebrity endorsement was the company's big new marketing device and they dedicated the entire inside front cover of the 1955 *Guitars for Moderns* catalog to these signature models. The reality is that the Brooklyn factory was only capable of manufacturing around 2000 guitars a year at that point. In the period between the first 1955 model year 6120 batch and the first 1956 model year batch, eight other Gretsch guitar models were also produced, with most yielding multiple batches. Throughout the Golden Era Gretsch typically produced batches of their guitars in groups of 50 or 100 units. The majority of 6120 batches were 100 unit groups, so this means just a few hundred 6120 specimens were ever manufactured with what are considered to be the classic 1955 model year features.

Chet Atkins 6120 examples from the 1955 model year can be easily identified by their bullet-style truss rod covers and gold anodized Bigsby B6 vibrato units with fixed-arm and spoon-handle design. The 6120 model, being a high-end representative within the Gretsch electric archtop line, was adorned with gold-plated hardware, including arrow control knobs, DeArmond Dynasonic pickup casings, pickup selector switch, and open-back Waverly tuning machines. All the Western features from Atkin's first 6120 guitar were present, including the "G" brand, engraved block inlays, steer's head headstock motif, and signpost graphic containing Atkins' autograph on the gold Lucite pickguard. The body measured 15.5" wide and 2.75" deep. The top was arched, pressed maple, the bound 12" radius fretboard was made of rosewood, the nut was brass, and the headstock had a thin white binding around its perimeter. On all but the very earliest of examples, a 22-fret Miracle neck joined the guitar's body at the 14th fret and the scale length was 24.5".

As noted, the lack of any earlier examples suggests that the guitars from batch #16450-16549 were the first production batch to be manufactured. This apparently occurred in late 1954 in preparation for the 1955 sales year. These debut 6120 hollowbody archtops were produced in the midst of a large run of several hundred Jet solidbody models. Interestingly, within this production run of 6120 hollowbodies, an estimated quantity of 25 or so Chet Atkins solidbody guitars (model 6121) were also produced, before the production line resumed the Jet solidbody manufacturing towards the latter half of the #165xx group.

A relatively short lived feature, but one that has nonetheless become synonymous with the Gretsch 6120 model is the famous "G"-branded body. Debate continues within the vintage community about the technique used to apply the symbol and it seems that examples of both actual branding (complete with over-singe) and routed versions exist. *Guitar Courtesy of Mitch Simpson. Photo by Lee Hiers.*

Apparently fewer than 70 of these 21-fret (seven Western block inlays) 6120 hollow-body examples were produced. They are the very first of the inaugural batch. *Guitar Courtesy of Vintage & Rare Guitars*.

Another interesting revelation about the initial 6120 hollow-body group is that the earlier examples within the batch exhibit 21 frets and seven Western block inlays, similar to Atkins' first two prototypical 6120's. However, a few hollowbody specimens from the end of that run—completed after the interruption of the 6121 solidbody guitars—have surfaced that have 22 frets and eight Western block inlays, which would remain the standard specification throughout the life of the model. With fewer than 70 guitars featuring the unique 21-fret attribute produced, this debut batch of Chet Atkins hollowbody guitars are highly desirable from a collectors perspective.

As one of the last guitars from the debut 6120 batch, this #165xx specimen is probably one of the very first examples produced with 22 frets. *Guitar Courtesy of Fred Stucky.*

Chet Atkins 6121 Solidbody Model

Since both the hollowbody and solidbody Chet Atkins signature models were launched simultaneously for 1955, it is plausible that the factory was hurried into making an initial quantity of each to equitably fill orders after the first of the year. The result was that the first Chet Atkins production batch (#16450 – 16549) was comprised of approximately 75 hollowbody 6120 examples and 25 solidbody 6121 model guitars.

When examining the batching approach of the Brooklyn factory in the late 1950s, it becomes clear from the serial number data that the 6120 model production was typically planned in sequence with other 16" archtops, particularly after the 1958 introduction of the 6119 and Anniversary models. From the start, however, the factory produced a few examples of the 6121 solidbody within many of the 6120 hollowbody batches. What is less clear is the motivation for the mixed 6120 and 6121 batches. This was possibly an effort to insure consistent color finishes between the two related models.

Other times this practice has occurred was when the White Penguin solidbody (model 6134) was periodically produced during batch runs of White Falcon archtops (model 6136). Presumably, like the Chet Atkins signature models, some dealers would market the two related models together, ordering examples of each. These occurrences might provide additional evidence to support the theory that the paint room controlled a lot of the production scheduling within the Gretsch factory. Once a certain pigment or stain was loaded, it seems that they went to great lengths to get all the guitars requiring that finish treatment through the system before having to wash up and go to another color.

Throughout the hollowbody format's single-cutaway era, the 6121 solidbody model reflected very similar features to its respective 6120 littermates. Although increasingly rare after the 1960 model year, there have been specimens found as late as the 1962 model year complete with the double-cutaway body styling of the period.

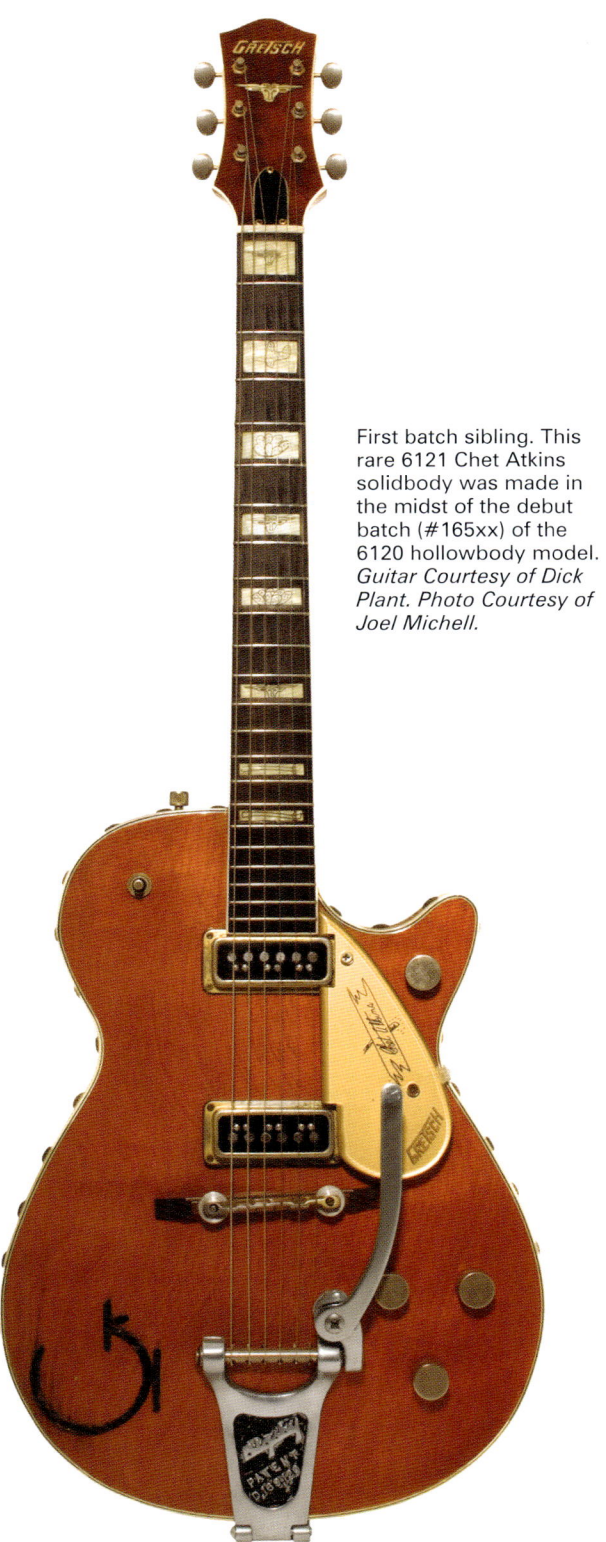

First batch sibling. This rare 6121 Chet Atkins solidbody was made in the midst of the debut batch (#165xx) of the 6120 hollowbody model. *Guitar Courtesy of Dick Plant. Photo Courtesy of Joel Michell.*

Specimens from the second batch of 6120 guitars (#169xx) are also highly desirable—it is from this group of 6120's that rock icon Eddie Cochran's famous guitar (#16942) originated. Typically this situation earns a premium for these guitars in the secondary vintage market. The premium price reflects the presumption that fans of the legendary rocker are willing to invest larger amounts to acquire an instrument so similar and/or related to his.

A harsh reality in the vintage guitar world is that when examples of vintage 1955 model year 6120s surface they are often not in their original condition. Many times the bridge has been changed from the factory original, compensated aluminum Bigsby bridge to something else. More times than not the something else is a thick bar-style, or rocking bar, bridge device. In other instances, but not to the same degree as the bridge, the perceived inconvenience of the fixed arm gold anodized Bigsby B6 vibrato unit has prompted it to be switched out for a swivel style—something Gretsch ended up doing themselves a few batches later. When the early factory original 1955 Bigsby units are modified it can result in the awkward looking chrome swivel arm, which is in contrast to the anodized gold base. More often than not, the entire unit is exchanged for a newer swivel arm equipped vibrato.

Only six serial numbers away from Eddie Cochran's legendary 6120, this guitar would be quite a catch for a true blue fan. *Guitar Courtesy of Fred Stucky.*

A 1955 model year 6120 from the #169xx batch. *Photo Courtesy of Crawford White.*

Consistent with the first two 1955 model year 6120 batches, it seems batch #173xx was also a run of 100 guitars, beginning at #17350. These would be the last of the classic 1955 model year 6120 specimens, as some subtle changes were already in the works for the next batch and, apparently, the new model year.

The rare 1955 model year 6120 specimens that are found with completely original features are usually guitars that were either played very infrequently or put into storage soon after they were bought. These classic 1955 6120 specimens remain highly desirable in the vintage market because of their distinctive Western ornamentation and reputation as the first of this legendary model.

The total output for 6120 guitars attributed to 1955 model year production is probably fewer than 250 instruments. This is based on adding the totals for the three documented batches above and subtracting a quantity of 6121 solidbodies from each batch. This is not very many guitars and explains why it is so rare to see a classic 1955 model year 6120 with an anodized gold Bigsby and bullet truss rod cover come onto today's secondary market.

Leave it to Randy Bachman, musician and Gretsch aficionado, to find such an outstanding 1955 model year specimen from the #173xx batch. *Courtesy of the Bachman Gretsch Collection.*

Every aspect of the original 1955 Chet Atkins 6120 package was Westernized. These leather straps depicting what is now referred to as the cows and cactus motif were no exception. *Photos Courtesy of Crawford White.*

Western Amplifiers

To complete the Gretsch outfit, true fans of the Western vibe might have also ordered a coordinating, model 6169 Electromatic Twin amplifier to complement their 1955 model year 6120 hollowbody guitar. At an MSRP of $175, these amps offered twin 11" by 6" speakers, six tubes, and 14 watts of output. This model accommodated three instrument inputs; two were full-range while the third was characterized as providing a "brilliant treble channel" for recording. Other features described in Gretsch marketing literature included a "built-in tremolo with foot pedal control, and speed regulator." A longhorn steer's head was displayed across the grill cloth and the outer covering was a buff, white leatherette trimmed in the same cows and cactus tooled leather as the cowboy-style guitar cases available for the 6120 model.

A larger Electromatic Deluxe version of this amplifier was also available with the same Western attributes (model 6163W) and retailed for $265. It possessed a 15" Jensen speaker, six tubes, and 25 watts of output. Humorously, the Gretsch literature points out that this amplifier was especially engineered to handle the needs of the electric accordion. Strangely enough, although listed, neither one of these Western-yle amplifier models was pictured in the 1955 *Gretsch Guitars for Moderns* catalog.

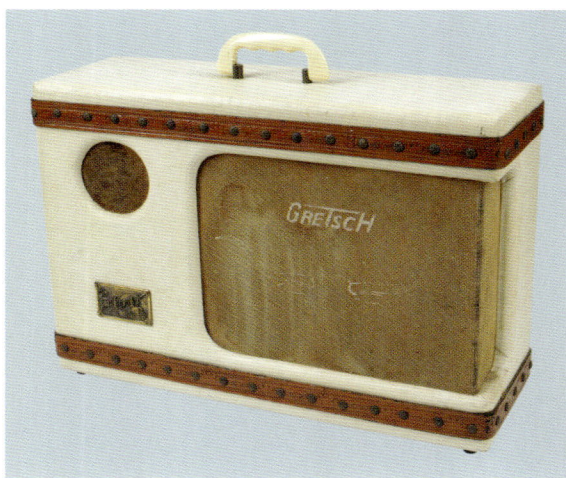

A 1950s Electromatic Twin amplifier, model 6169.
Courtesy of Fred Stucky.

1955 Red 6120 Sealed-Top Prototype

This famous and influential guitar was a special 6120 model prototype that Chet Atkins commissioned from the Gretsch factory. It featured many of the standard, classic 1955 model year appointments such as a "G" brand, gold anodized B6 vibrato with special extended fixed arm, bar bridge, Western block markers, a bullet truss rod cover, steer's head headstock, arrow control knobs, and a gold signpost guard. On the other hand, it had some very unique features as well. These included a finish that was redder in color and a closed f-hole solid top that was somewhere between 0.25" and 0.5" thick. Only light gray outlines of the f-holes are perceivable, presumably added for aesthetic value. The guitar was outfitted with prototypical pre-Filter'Tron Ray Butts-conceived stereo pickups. It also had two output jacks so, when split, the bass signal could be run through the Ray Butts-designed EchoSonic amp in echo mode while the treble strings would use the standard channel, which provided Atkins the tone he desired. A switch was installed between the two control knobs on the lower bout, allowing Atkins to switch between regular and stereo mode. Although the guitar was reputed to be uncomfortably heavy, this was a favorite recording instrument for Atkins. It is forever captured in history on the cover of his *Finger-Style Guitar* album (1956).

Chet Atkins with his cherished 1955 sealed-top 6120 at the Grand Ole Opry in July of 1956. Note that it still maintains the original 1955 model year neck with bullet truss-rod cover, Western block fretboard markers, and steer's head inlay on the headstock. *Photo by Gordon Gillingham, ©2003 Grand Ole Opry.*

Interestingly, when Atkins appeared with this guitar on the *Today Show* in April of 1957, the guitar had apparently experienced some modifications. In Chet Atkins' book, *Chet Atkins, Me and My Guitars*, he reveals that while in New York to do the *Today Show*, the guitar's neck was damaged in an accident. Fortunately, the Gretsch factory was close by and provided the required repairs in a timely manner. In photographs from that performance, it is clear that the guitar had in fact been completely re-necked, confirmed by the plain block markers on its fretboard and horseshoe-style inlaid headstock with an elongated truss rod cover.

In a 2007 interview, Paul Yandell surmised that this guitar was in fact the inspiration for the development of the solid top Country Gentleman (model 6122), another of Atkins signature models, released in 1957 for the 1958 model year. Yandell referred to the solid-top Country Gentleman as "basically the same guitar" as the solid-top 6120 prototype.

At some point Atkins gave this important guitar to his brother, who eventually returned it. Atkins then gave it to his nephew, Jimmy Atkins, who held it for a period of time. The guitar has since traded hands and currently resides in a private collection. More recently, this historically significant instrument was the inspiration for a limited edition reissue model that FMIC/Gretsch released in the Fall of 2008.

The famous, Chet Atkins 1955 sealed-top prototype. *Photo Courtesy of Russ Cochran and Chet Atkins, copyright © 2001. Used with permission.*

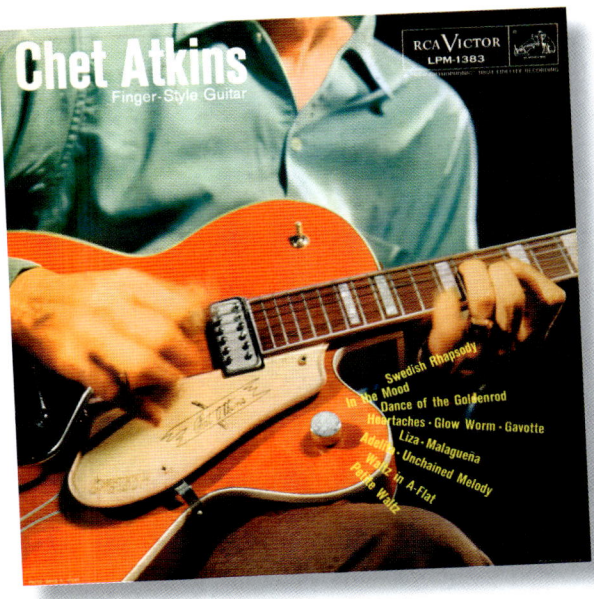

Chet Atkins' *Finger-Style Guitar* album (RCA, 1956).

Chapter

12

1956 model year serial number batches:

#182xx: 100-unit batch*
#185xx: 100-unit batch
#189xx: 100-unit batch
#200xx: 100-unit batch*
#208xx: 100-unit batch*
*(6121 solidbodies included)

1956 Model Year 6120

Consistent with the production of other Gretsch models, the 6120 experienced feature changes almost from the beginning. One characteristic, albeit a subtle modification, that was present in the #182xx batch, and that is recognized as an indicator of the beginning of the 1956 model year, is the disappearance of the bullet truss rod cover and introduction of a larger elongated cover in its place. In fact, the access cavity that this cover conceals did not change in size, so the motivation for the different cover shape is unknown. This truss rod cover modification, with a few exceptions, became evident across most Gretsch guitar models in the period just after the 6120 batch #173xx.

The changes reflected in the first model year batch for 1956 were just the beginning. This early #182xx specimen still retains a strong family resemblance to its relatives from the previous model year. *Guitar Courtesy of Andrew Morrison. Photo by Steve Hovery.*

The classic steer's head headstock with new-for-1956 elongated truss rod cover. Another subtle nuance not restricted to mid-1950s Gretsch 6120 examples is what is now referred to as a reverse "G" serif in the inlaid T-roof Gretsch logo on the headstock. This feature existed from the inception of the inlaid-style T-roof logo in 1953 and can be found in guitars as late as the 1957 model year. *Guitar Courtesy of Andrew Morrison. Photo by Steve Hovery.*

The other change appearing in this #182xx batch was that the Bigsby vibrato was modified from the gold anodized aluminum unit to a neutral, cast aluminum unit. These are sometimes referred to as the enamel-faced B6 Bigsby units, referring to the black enamel applied to the front of the aluminum base. This created more visual contrast for the raised letters of the Bigsby brand logo. Apparently, the introduction of a neutral metallic-colored vibrato onto a guitar that featured gold-plated hardware everywhere else did not offend the aesthetic tastes of the average musician, as this became a standard look for the 6120 model over its lifetime. The earliest of these new Bigsby units still retained the fixed-arm and spoon handle, which can be found throughout the following batch as well.

For most Gretsch purists, the #182xx batch is accepted as the beginning of the 6120's 1956 model year. Although these feature changes (i.e. simple truss rod cover and Bigsby color change) seem minor, they marked the beginning of more significant changes throughout 1956. In fact, there really is not a single classic 1956 model year feature combination. Consequently, as a result of its several mid-year alterations, it should instead be considered a "transitional" model year, in essence allowing the 6120 species to evolve from the original 1955 Western model to what most Gretsch fans consider to be the more vanilla 1957 model year feature package.

More concrete evidence supporting the fact that these first couple of (only slightly altered) 1956 model year batches are in fact from that model year, appears within the second batch of the model year (#185xx). Manufactured only 200 guitars after the previous 6120 batch, this group contains instruments with dated neck stamps marked December 1, 1955. These markings are only visible when the neck is detached from the body and are therefore elusive. However, another documented neck stamp from a Streamliner model found in the very next batch (#186xx) is marked January 1956, corroborating the attribution of the 6120 specimen. So, this seems to substantiate the fact that the #182xx and 185xx batches were manufactured at the end of the 1955 calendar year, in preparation for the 1956 model year, a practice the Gretsch factory would employ for the next decade.

A 1956 model year 6120 from the #185xx batch. *Guitar Courtesy of Dave Rogers. Photo by Tim Mullally.*

Guitar Courtesy of Jerry Duncan.
Photos by Stephen Davis.

Here is a rebellious member of the 6120 batch #185xx. Not only is it finished in a non-conforming, but factory original, brown sunburst, it also lacks the "G" brand on its body, which at this point in production history was standard on the 6120 model. Perpetuating the disguise further, the plain gold pickguard omits the characteristic Chet Atkins signpost etching.

Other than these differences, from a feature and specification perspective, this is a bona-fide model 6120 guitar. It maintains the steer's head motif on the headstock as well as the cows and cactus engravings on the fretboards' block inlays. Dual-DeArmond Dynasonic pickups, an enamel-faced Bigsby B6 with fixed arm and spoon handle, an aluminum Bigsby bridge, and brass nut are all requisite standards. The only other out of place feature is its "G" indent control knobs.

The actual identity of this unique guitar is revealed by its label, which is clearly stamped with the 6120 model indicator. This rare specimen is one of the earliest documented custom-finished examples of a Chet Atkins 6120 hollowbody to surface.

Courtesy of Deke Martin.

An early example from the #189xx batch that appears to be one of the last units equipped with the fixed-arm Bigsby B6 vibrato. *Guitar Courtesy of Mitch Simpson. Photo by Lee Hiers.*

Although the earliest specimens from the third 1956 model year batch (#189xx) have features consistent with guitars from the previous two batches, somewhere within this group some transformations began. For example, at some point in the #189xx batch what is now referred to as the breakaway handle B6 Bigsby unit first appeared. This design alteration was intended to be an improvement to allow the guitarist to fold the handle back out of the way when it was not required. Chet Atkins was accustomed to a more stationary vibrato control and preferred the fixed-arm-style Bigsby. The general consensus at Gretsch, however, was that this lack of flexibility might have a negative impact on prospective sales and the new breakaway design was quickly introduced. Perhaps it was too quickly introduced, as it soon became apparent that the new hinge design did not accommodate the control knob layout of the 6120 and only narrowly cleared the upper-most volume knob. A trip back to the drawing board produced a better solution, consequently making these breakaway Bigsby equipped guitars quite limited. The relatively few guitars that originally received the breakaway Bigsby units rarely retain them today. Much as the fixed-arm variety were similarly deemed unwieldy, both previous designs were often replaced by the newer swivel-style Bigsby arm once it was made available.

Other variations that made their debut among the last few specimens from the #189xx batch included the introduction of a new horseshoe motif inlaid onto the face of the headstock. This change coincided with another aesthetic evolution, the discontinuation of the engraved cows and cactus fretboard inlays. It appears that any guitar receiving the new headstock design also got the new plain block markers on the fretboard. This was the first obvious attempt at moderating the 6120's cowboy cliché and was presumably intended to provide an evolved aesthetic for the 1956 model line.

Courtesy of Deke Martin.

An exceptionally rare find. This is a 6120 example that not only sports the infrequently found breakaway Bigsby mechanism, but, as one of the last of the 189xx batch, also features the transitional plain block fretboard and short lived nail hole horseshoe inlay on its headstock. *Courtesy of Deke Martin.*

A rare, batch #200xx example of a 1956 model year 6120 with it's breakaway Bigsby B6 unit surviving intact. *Guitar Courtesy of Laurent Soriano. Photo by Jean-Louis Bessenay*

After the apparent failure of the hastily introduced breakaway handled Bigsby unit, Gretsch made an alteration. A more streamlined hinge mechanism for the, now slimmer, handle was incorporated into the #208xx batch, the last group of the 1956 model year. Often referred to as the Duane Eddy-style handle, it can be identified by the fact that the mechanism that prevents the handle from swiveling too far up into the string path resides on the handle itself. In comparison, more modern Bigsby technology incorporates this stop feature into the base bracket of the vibrato unit. It was this generation of new, improved swivel-handled Bigsby vibratos that became standard issue for the subsequent production batches of the 6120 model. From this point in the 1956 model year, until the end of the 1958 model year production, these Bigsby hinges typically employed a slotted-head bolt. Interestingly, the B6 units were manufactured with debossed patent numbers on the base, under the raised Bigsby logo, whereas the smaller (solidbody issue) B3 units were made with the patent number in raised characters.

The Duane Eddy-style Bigsby swivel handle. *Guitar Courtesy of Chris Guido. Photo by Rick Burda.*

The plain block fretboard markers existed throughout the next 6120 batch (#200xx). A specific feature characteristic to this #200xx batch is the occurrence of subtle nail hole details engraved into the inlaid horseshoe headstock motif. Only a few examples from very late in the previous batch seem to share this rare variation and beyond this group of 100 specimens, this particular nuance disappears. This batch may also have been the last to be equipped with the ill-advised breakaway Bigsby handle feature.

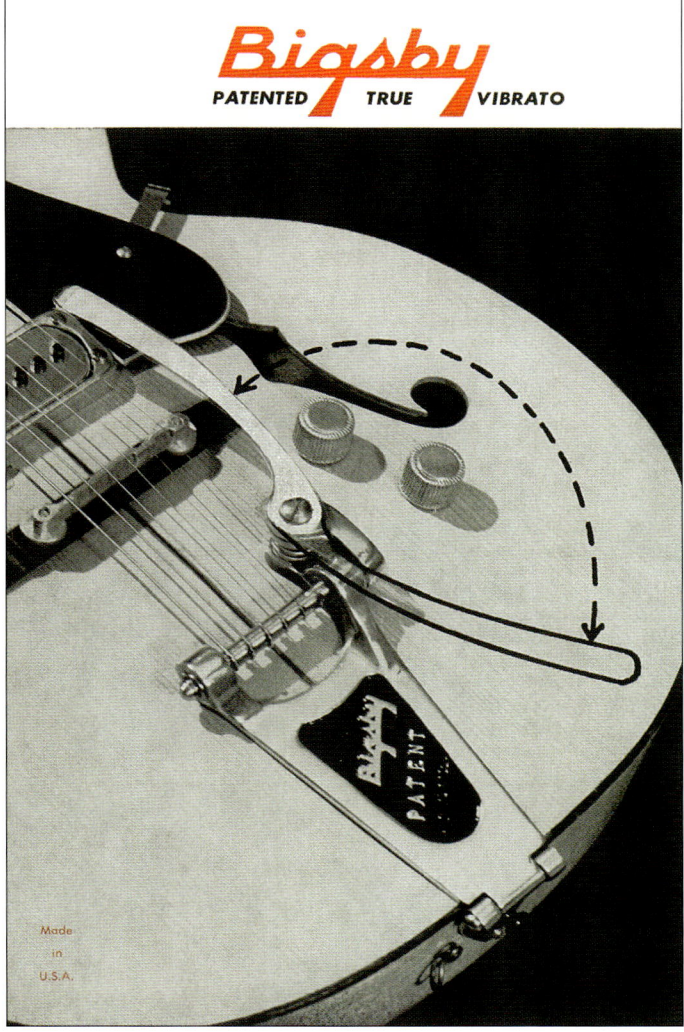

This brochure (c.1956) announced that "all Bigsby vibratos are now equipped with a stainless steel, swing away handle…" and references this new design as the Bigsby True Vibrato unit, available in three models.

An equally significant event occurred midway into the production of the #208xx batch, when the short lived plain block fretboard markers disappeared, and the hump block, or Alamo, markers were abruptly introduced. Since this batch also represented the swan song for the "G"-branded bodies, there may be fewer than 50, 6120 guitars in existence with both the "G"-branded body and hump block markers. A surviving, original bill of sale for one of these specimens indicates that it was sold on October 29, 1956 at the Simmons Music Co., in Denver, Colorado. This would again suggest that the 1957 model year features were first introduced sometime earlier in the fall of 1956.

This guitar displays a very rare confluence of features, possessing both the "G" brand and hump block inlays. Only a few other examples exist from production batch #208xx. *Guitar Courtesy of Chris Guido. Photo by Rick Burda.*

1956 Black 6120 Sealed-Top Prototype

After the success of the 1955 sealed-top 6120 prototype, Gretsch assembled another special 6120 model test guitar for Atkins. This guitar was 15.75" wide and 3" deep. It had a unique black finish, closed f-holes with gold sparkle inserts, and an enamel-faced B6 vibrato with the extended fixed arm that Atkins preferred. Typical 1956 model year features included the plain block markers, horseshoe headstock (with nail holes), elongated truss rod cover, arrow control knobs, and a gold (Gretsch logo only) pickguard.

Modern day photos of this guitar show it possessing dual-gold-cased DeArmond Dynasonic pickups. However, the September 1956 photo reveals that it was clearly outfitted with the white bobbin Ray Butts Filter'Tron prototype pickups. Some time after this 1956 photo was taken Ray Butts also installed pickup pole pieces in the fingerboard below the 15th fret to enable Atkins the opportunity to experiment with electronic octave effects. These

Chet Atkins back stage at the Opry in September 1956. This time he is wielding his black 1956 sealed-top prototype with early Ray Butts-conceived Filter'Tron test pickups. *Photo by Gordon Gillingham, ©2008 Grand Ole Opry.*

added pole pieces are clearly evident in more current photographs of the guitar, along with other subsequent modifications such as gold "G" indent control knobs, a swivel arm B6 vibrato, and a more standard Chet Atkins signpost pickguard. Atkins reportedly gave this guitar to RCA Engineer Bill Porter, who later sold it. For a period of time the guitar resided in the Scott Chinery collection, but has since changed hands. It was first featured in Tony Bacon and Paul Day's *The Gretsch Book* (1996, Balafon).

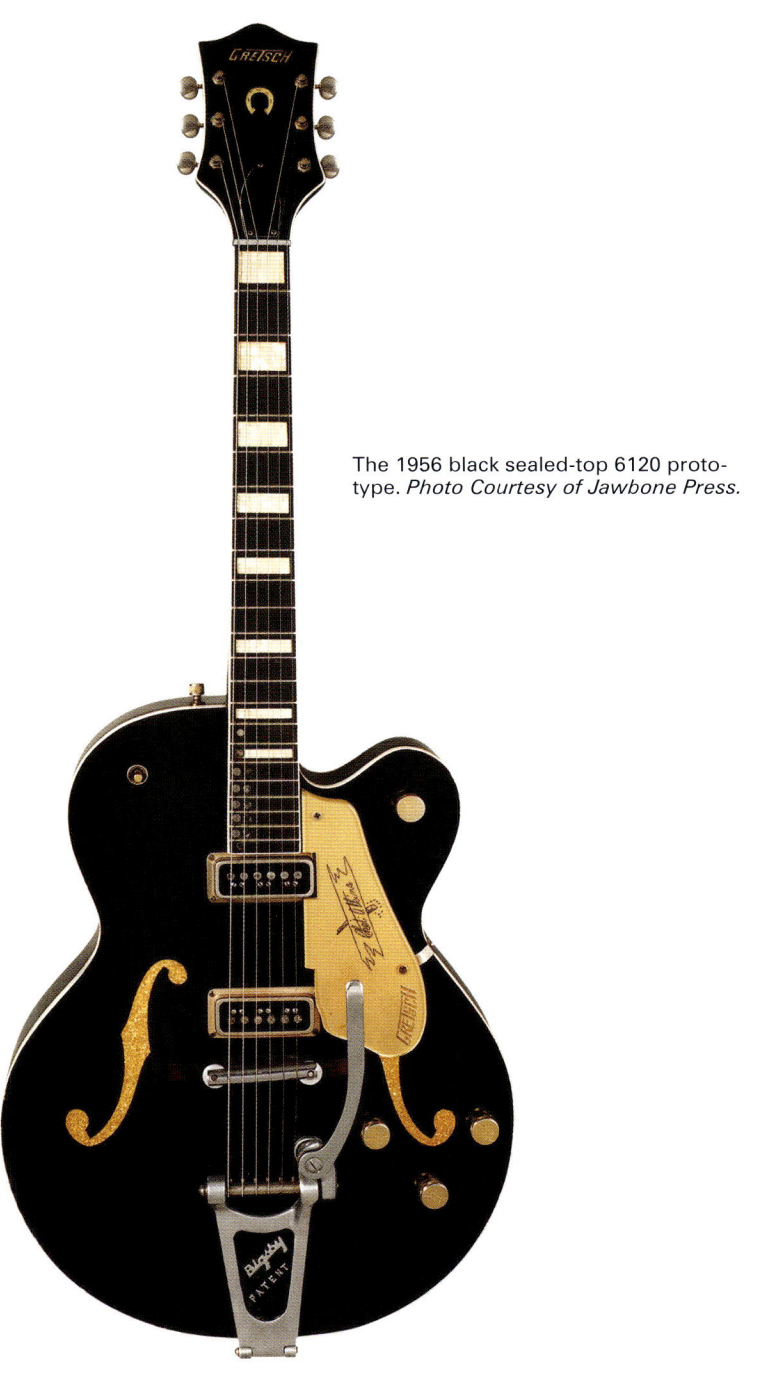

The 1956 black sealed-top 6120 proto-type. *Photo Courtesy of Jawbone Press.*

As a result of the Brooklyn factory increasing its total production to over 3000 units per year, five 100-unit batches of 1956 model year 6120 guitars were produced. Since most of those included a quantity of 6121 solidbody guitars they collectively yielded approximately 400 Chet Atkins 6120 hollowbody specimens.

The period that defines the 1956 model year is more ambiguous when compared to other 6120 model years that enjoy more obvious affiliations to a certain feature or a specific combination of features. Instead it might appear as if The Gretsch Company was taking this time to evolve the incumbent 1955 Western-style 6120 into something a bit more generic, yet still distinctive and tasteful. Once again there is strong evidence that by the end of the 1956 calendar year, the Gretsch factory had completed that process and was already producing the retooled version for 1957.

1957 model year serial number batches:

#216xx: 100-unit batch*
#220xx: 100-unit batch*
#224xx: TBD*
#232xx: 100-unit batch
#234xx: 50-unit batch*
#250xx: 100-unit batch
#253xx: 100-unit batch
#258xx: ~70 guitars from this 100-unit batch
*(6121 solidbodies included)

1957 Model Year 6120

Throughout the five previous eventful 1956 model year batches, the 6120 had experienced changes in fretboard markers, headstock inlay design, Bigsby technology, and body ornamentation ("G" brand). The Chet Atkins hollowbody had morphed into a different looking guitar. In contrast, the guitars from the 1957 model year remained remarkably consistent and all incorporate the same classic 1957 model year features as the initial batch (#216xx), which established the move away from the Western ornamentation.

Batch #216xx was the first batch produced without the "G" brand on the body. It was also the first full batch of 6120 guitars to display the hump block fretboard markers, which have become widely recognized as one of the signature features of the 1957 model year. In addition, examples from this #216xx batch were also the first to possess the "G"-indented control knobs, which replaced the previous arrow only motif. This is one of the few features that would endure, with only subtle changes in their knurled sides, over the next ten years.

Like its hollowbody brethren, the few 6121 solidbody guitars from the #216xx batch had also shed their "G" brands. Likewise, these solidbody models acquired the hump block fretboard markers late in the previous batch. *Photo Courtesy of Nick Anderson.*

A 1957 model year 6120 (batch #216xx) with missing pickguard, newer Bigsby handle, and (characteristic for 1957) ruddy-orange finish. *Guitar Courtesy of Warpdrive Music. Photo by John Sieger.*

Although the 6120 guitars of the following batch (#220xx) maintained all the same 1957 model year features, strangely enough, they were quite different from what was presented in the Gretsch Marketing material the company released around that same time. In October 1956 Gretsch distributed a copy of their 1957 guitar catalog in *Country & Western Jamboree* magazine. This catalog retained the same text and photo-illustration for the 6120 model as the original 1955 *Guitars for Moderns* publication. Gretsch did, of course, go the trouble of changing the prices and this latest edition of the Chet Atkins 6120 cost $15 more than it did in the previous catalog. This publication must have been a bit misleading, considering that guitars possessing the 1957 model year feature package were already being produced from the factory.

It is not clear how the company addressed the fact that dealers and consumers received 1957 model year guitars that looked considerably different from the first generation 6120 Western example depicted in the October 1956 catalog. It is interesting that Gretsch went to such lengths to de-emphasize the Western aesthetic in their product, but then elected not to promote those changes in the marketplace. Further evidence supporting the late 1956 introduction of the 1957 model year hump block fretboard markers is the discovery of another early #220xx example with an original bill of sale dated January 19, 1957. This would establish that neither this batch, nor any prior batch, could have been manufactured in the 1957 calendar year.

As has been previously established, the Gretsch factory's practice was to manufacture a quantity of 6121 Chet Atkins solidbody guitars in many, if not most, batches of 6120 hollowbodies. There is circumstantial evidence suggesting that a group of 6120 hollowbody guitars might exist in batch #224xxx. To date, several 6121 solidbody specimens have been documented from this batch. So, it either represents one of the very few (or only) batches exclusively comprised of 6121 examples, or there are some unusually elusive #224xx Chet Atkins hollowbody guitars floating around out there.

A 1957 model year 6120 example from the #220xx batch. *Guitar Courtesy of Chris Guido. Photo by Rick Burda.*

Where there is smoke there is usually fire. The existence of this 6121 solidbody from batch #224xx might just be an indicator that 6120 hollowbody examples exist from this batch as well. *Guitar Courtesy of Chris Guido. Photo by Rick Burda.*

This 1957 model year beauty from batch #232xx is another to have received a slightly browner amber-red stain. *Guitar Courtesy of Arnoud Holsboer. Photo by Daniel Nicolas.*

This 6120 example from the #234xx batch displays the classic 1957 model year features and is one of less than 30 hollowbody specimens from this (presumably) small 50-unit mixed-batch of 6120 and 6121 model guitars. *Courtesy of Frank Walboomers.*

The #232xx batch appears to have been a typical 100-unit run of consistently featured 1957 model year 6120s. However, batch #234xx may be one of the few smaller, 50-unit 6120 groups. This batch is also another case where a run of 6121 solidbody guitars was intermingled within the group, which means that there are even fewer 6120 hollowbodies in this particular group.

A first version Gretsch label. It has been reported that paper labels were introduced on higher-end Gretsch models around 1949, near serial number 4000. *Photo Courtesy of Herve Bessenay.*

The second style, a blue filigree-bordered label, was introduced in mid-1954, at serial number 15000. They are distinguished by the introduction of the famous Gretsch T-roof logo across the top. *Photo Courtesy of Herve Bessenay.*

The third style, an orange and gray label, was initiated at serial number 25,000. The first guitars to receive these were a batch of 1957 model 6120 Chet Atkins hollowbodies. *Photo Courtesy of Herve Bessenay.*

The #250xx batch of 6120 hollowbodies has the claim to fame of being the first of any Gretsch model to receive the newly redesigned interior labels, which were introduced sometime in the mid-1957 production year. These modern-looking labels were orange and gray and slightly larger than the previous blue filigree-bordered version. The new label still accommodated both the model number and the serial number. The model number designations were rubber-stamped onto the labels, which were pre-printed with the serial number.

Dan Duffy, recalling his days at the Gretsch factory, where he served as Quality Control Manager from 1957 throughout the Golden Era, has indicated that the labels were purchased in rolls. It is not unreasonable to surmise that the factory simply ran out of the first label design. The other possibility is that perhaps the existing labels were considered dated and in need of an upgrade. Regardless, the new orange and gray labels were installed in the #250xx batch of 6120 hollowbodies and they maintained the continuity of the sequential numbering system that Gretsch had employed throughout the previous decade.

Batch #253xx continued to consist of 6120 guitars displaying the classic 1957 model year features, although there are rumors of a random example possessing the "G" brand on the body. This is not incomprehensible, as it could be the result of a special factory order. Or perhaps a brave owner longing for the Western look made the "G" brand him/herself. What appears to be the last guitar produced in this batch was, however, the beneficiary of some special work done at the Brooklyn factory. The resulting guitar challenges much of what we all have come to recognize, and expect, in a Chet Atkins 6120 hollowbody archtop. (See feature on sunburst-finished 1957 model year 6120.)

Sunburst-Finished 1957 model year 6120

Frank Walboomers is the current owner of this rare 1957 sunburst-finished 6120 hollowbody (#25399). According to Walboomers, the original owner of the guitar was a jazz musician from New York who had a great admiration for Chet Atkins, but did not especially care for the flashy Western look of the 6120 model. He opted for a custom-ordered guitar in the more traditional brown sunburst finish. Likewise, considering the genre he worked in, there was apparently less desire for the effects that the Bigsby vibrato provided and more appreciation for the fine-tuning that the Melita bridge offered. Free of the Bigsby, this guitar had the added benefit of increased acoustic qualities.

Courtesy of Frank Walboomers.

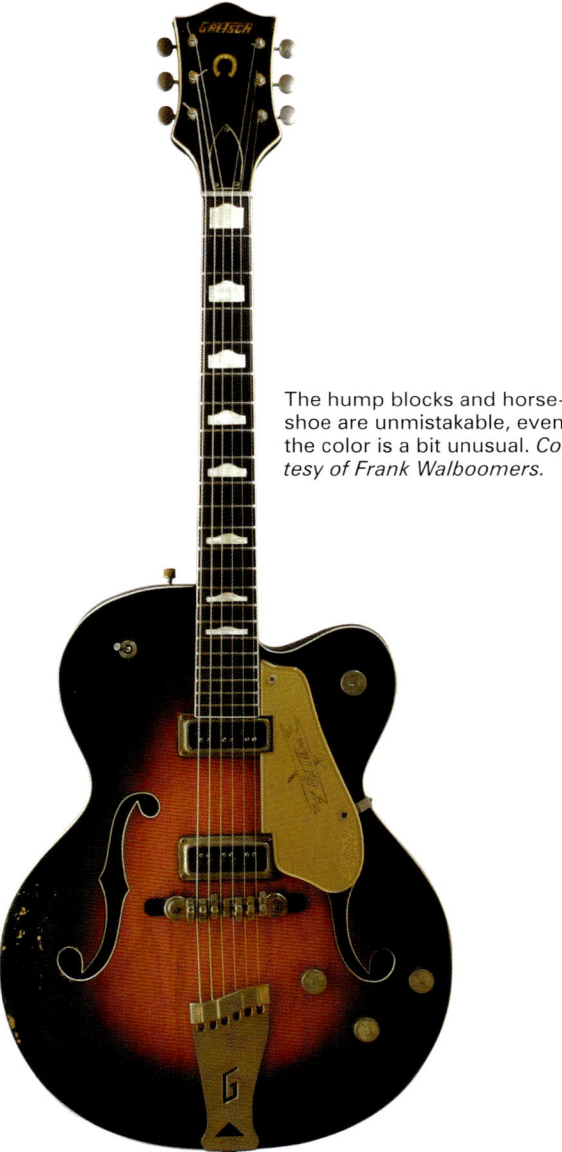

The hump blocks and horseshoe are unmistakable, even if the color is a bit unusual. *Courtesy of Frank Walboomers.*

The typical Chet Atkins 6120 hollowbody enjoys a distinctive visual impact—in no small part thanks to its signature orange-stained finish. To most, the idea of having a 6120 in anything but the standard orange finish seems counterintuitive. Customizing one in a sedate brown sunburst finish might even be considered heresy. This is why when a rare custom-finished 6120 shows up on the vintage secondary market, great pains are taken to verify that the finish is a factory original. Ordering a Gretsch guitar with a non-standard custom color was not necessarily unheard of in the 1950s, but it became more common in the mid-1960s.

For these reasons, this 1957 example has created quite a debate amongst the vintage Gretsch community. The fact that this brown sunburst-finished 6120 also possesses a "G" cutout tailpiece and Melita bridge suggests to some that it is no more than a Streamliner 6190 model with a second pickup installed. These detractors have had difficulty accepting the idea that anyone would go to the expense of buying a custom-finished 6120 for such inconsequential (in their opinion) differences.

The fact is, however, that the finish on this particular example has been certified as factory original by highly respected vintage guitar authorities. Another fact is that the label shows a faded, but authentic, 6120 model stamp and a serial number that falls at the end of a documented 100-unit batch of 6120 guitars.

Other clues indicating the true identity of this guitar include the lack of a white plastic tail pin, which came standard on the Streamliner model. The headstock overlay is clearly common to that of its 6120 siblings. Lastly, the appearance of gold-plated hardware suggests that this was not merely a modified Streamliner. Instead, this is a guitar made to order for a buyer who had specific ideas about what he wanted in a Gretsch electric archtop.

Finally, there is the #258xx batch of 6120 guitars, which is an interesting case, and one that creates a bit of a dilemma. This batch contains 6120 examples from both the 1957 and 1958 model years. One might wonder how that can be. It is true that all 100 guitars from this group were actually manufactured in the second half of 1957, but when considering model year, that is determined strictly by a guitar's features. So, the majority (approximately 70) of the #258xx batch is comprised of 6120 guitars displaying the standard 1957 model year features. One of these was the famous example (#25827) purchased by rockabilly pioneer Duane Eddy. Once again, the association of this batch with Duane Eddy will make other specimens from it more desirable to some collectors. Unfortunately, for those seeking other 6120 examples like Eddy's from this batch, the pool of possible instruments is smaller than they may think. This is because features from the next model year start to infringe on the last 30 or so specimens from the batch.

Some Gretsch enthusiasts feel the classic 1957 model year features tend to make this version of the 6120 species less desirable because the guitars lack the distinctive Western ornamentation of the 1955 model year examples and do not yet have the Filter'Tron pickups and trestle bracing of a 1958 model year guitar. On the other hand, there are other enthusiasts who feel this cleaner looking aesthetic and lighter overall weight actually make this vintage the more attractive package. It just goes to show how fickle the vintage guitar community can be.

Dan Duffy reports that each year of the Golden Era period the factory was under pressure to increase its production output. This fact is reflected in the increased number of 6120 instruments generated for the 1957 model year. Spanning up to eight batches, this resulted in between 550 and 700 hollowbody guitars produced. This calculation factors in an estimation of 6121 solidbody examples present in these batches. There are several reasons for the wide range of this projection—batch #224xx is unverified, the #234xx batch may be larger than 50 units, and the final batch (#258xx) had a reduced number (70) of 1957 model year guitars.

Never stagnant, Gretsch continued to refine and improve its flagship model. Long before the calendar had turned from 1957, the Gretsch designers were back at the drawing board preparing for the next evolutionary leap. The result was glaringly apparent in the 6120s of the 1958 model year.

This is a wonderful example that is less than 20 serial numbers away from the famous 6120 that Duane Eddy purchased brand new on September 20, 1957. The guitar provides insight into just how early in the year this last batch (#258xx) of 1957 model year 6120s may have been produced. *Photo Courtesy of Billy Straus.*

This batch #258xx specimen was one of the very last examples of a 6120 with classic 1957 model year features. Several serial numbers later, the hump block fretboard markers were replaced by the new neoclassic style (1958 model year). *Courtesy of Nino Fazio, Real Vintage Guitars, Italy.*

Chapter

14

1958 model year serial number batches:

#258xx: ~30 guitars from late in this 100-unit batch
#265xx: 100-unit batch
#269xx: 100-unit batch*
#276xx: 100-unit batch*
#284xx: 100-unit batch*
*(6121 solidbodies included)

1958 Model Year 6120

The Gretsch Company had big plans for the 1958 sales year. On the drawing board were changes in technology, bold aesthetic statements, and a modified lineup for the 16" category electric archtop models. After all, it was the Company's 75th Anniversary and they intended to make a big splash. The 1958 model year changes planned for the Chet Atkins 6120 were equally significant. They began to appear in the line somewhat abruptly, comprising approximately 30 guitars at the end of the #258xx batch.

Readily apparent modifications in the earliest 1958 model year examples included the emergence of the unique neoclassic (aka half-moon or thumbnail) fretboard markers. This aesthetic introduction created a distinctive visual effect that ultimately became synonymous with the Gretsch brand. Another change typically attributed to the 1958 model year, and associated with the advent of neoclassic markers, is an ebony fretboard. A subtler, and, as it turned out, relatively short-lived introduction in this eventful batch was the compensated bar bridge. These bridges are easily identified by their staggered post positions.

This late batch #258xx example is a rare specimen that still has DeArmond Dynasonic pickups, but also features the new neoclassic fretboard markers, as well as trestle bracing. *Photo Courtesy of Graham Hay.*

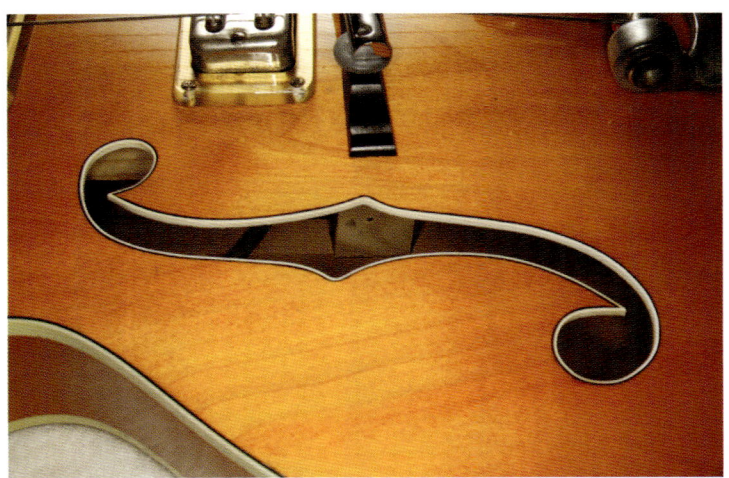

The wooden struts of heavy 1958 trestle bracing connect to bars running across both the top and back of the guitar's body. *Guitar Courtesy of Chris Guido. Photo by Rick Burda.*

Trestle bracing, we called it the internal bridge, was designed by Chet and Ray Butts to support the new Filter'Tron pickups. They called the bracing tone transfer bars. The bracing connected the top and back together, eliminating feedback. It was installed in most guitars that supported the Filter'Tron pickups.

-Dan Duffy

Trestle bracing was a big structural step in the 6120s' evolution that occurred unseen inside the guitar's body cavity. This was a system of wooden struts that connected a guitar's top to its back, providing rigidity to the body. It was an effective device that improved tonal sustain, but also reduced feedback inherent in hollowbody designs. It has been reported that this bracing was developed in anticipation of the new pickup technology that was planned for much of the 1958 Gretsch guitar product release. This early bracing has also been accused of making 6120 guitars from this era noticeably heavier than previous model year specimens. It seems that every guitar in the #258xx batch that received the new neoclassic fretboard markers was also produced with the trestle bracing. The next metamorphosis had clearly begun.

Inexplicably these updated guitars from the end of the #258xx batch did not include the new-for-1958 pickup technology and still retained the standard DeArmond Dynasonic units. However, the emergence of both the neoclassic fretboard markers and the trestle bracing are enough to anoint these as the first few official 1958 model year guitars. The 30 or fewer 6120 specimens that were released with this transitional mix of features are obviously rare and can be appealing to collectors, as they represent what would today be considered a limited edition run of a very unique hybrid feature combination.

Periodically, when tracking feature changes on Gretsch guitars, examples will surface with later serial numbers that still maintain the earlier feature. A plausible explanation for the seemingly intermittent occurrence of features within these transitional batches would be that the labels bearing the serial number were one of the last things to be applied to the guitars on the Gretsch assembly line. The few guitars with newer features were no doubt made later, or even at the end of the batch. Guitars are easily shuffled around during the various stages of assembly, so it was very possible that when the sequential serial numbers were applied the first few guitars with the newer feature received a lower (and earlier) serial number than some of the guitars with the older features.

Research confirms that the following batch (#265xx) was also manufactured late in the 1957 calendar year, in yet another example where Gretsch clearly intended to provide dealers with the new-for-1958 model year guitars as early as possible. Evidence for this production dating includes a factory invoice for a guitar from the debut batch of Country Gentleman (model #6122), published in Jay Scott's book *The Guitars of the Fred Gretsch Company*. This invoice confirms that this Country Gentleman, which was one of 50 made in the first half of the #264xx batch, was sold on December 23, 1957. In practical terms, that means that this, as well as other closely associated batches, were made sometime prior to the end of the 1957 calendar year.

This example is one of the last ten specimens of the #258xx batch. It represents yet another example where, within a batch, guitars get mixed up prior to serial numbering. As such, it shares the recently introduced compensated bar bridge with its sibling guitars in the batch. However, it lacks trestle bracing and still has the rosewood fretboard and hump block markers that the previous 25 (sequentially numbered) guitars had already abandoned for the new neoclassic/ebony combination. It would also be one of the very last 6120 guitars to leave the factory with DeArmond Dynasonic pickups. *Photo Courtesy of Nick Anderson.*

With the newly established ebony fretboard with neoclassic markers and trestle bracing already in place, this 1958 model year example unveils the Filter'Tron pickups and tone selector switch features. *Guitar Courtesy of Chris Guido. Photo by Rick Burda.*

Plain Filter'Tron pickup covers were in place for three batches of 1958 model year 6120 guitars. *Guitar Courtesy of Chris Guido. Photo by Rick Burda.*

The #265xx batch of 6120 guitars exemplified a change that would define the 1958 model year for many models within the Gretsch fleet. These were the first of the 16" category guitars to receive Gretsch's new, in-house manufactured, Filter'Tron dual-coil humbucker pickup design developed by EchoSonic amp inventor and Gretsch consultant, Ray Butts. From the beginning Chet Atkins did not like the DeArmond Dynasonic pickups, complaining in his 2001 book, *Chet Atkins, Me and My Guitars* that "they were too heavy on bass response, weak and inconsistent in the higher registers, and they hummed terribly." Ray Butts' ingenious approach with his Filter'Tron technology of wiring the two coils out of phase, to cancel out the hum, won Atkins over immediately.

I made a handshake agreement with Fred Gretsch and he held up his end until the day he died. You see, there wasn't anything in writing, so after he died, it took me a while to get a royalty check!

-Ray Butts, Gretsch consultant

Many historians have surmised that the primary motivator for the introduction of the Filter'Tron pickup was the success of the Gibson humbucking technology. Interestingly, it appears that Ray Butts' patent for the Filter'Tron might have been submitted earlier than Seth Lover's for the Gibson unit. Regardless, the fact that

Chet Atkins himself was a supporter of the new Filter'Tron was a huge catalyst for the change. Behind the scenes there were whispers about a falling out between Harry DeArmond and The Gretsch Company, as Gretsch wasn't getting the exclusivity it desired with the Dynasonic technology. These influences—in addition to the fact that Gretsch saw this as an opportunity to manufacture its own pickups for the first time—sealed the decision.

Examples from the #265xx batch typically display key 1958 model year features, including the dual-Filter'Tron pickups with plain covers, smooth plastic pickup surrounds, square notched pickguard, and a compensated bar bridge. *Photo Courtesy of Graham Hay.*

Early 6120 examples with Filter'Trons have unmarked or plain chrome pickup covers (aka pre-PAF). Several batches later Gretsch added the words "Pat Applied For" (aka PAF) onto the covers, in anticipation of their patent submission approval. This feature would change again during the 1960 model year, when the covers started featuring the actual patent number. These Filter'Tron-equipped guitars were also outfitted with gold plastic pickup bezels, or rings as they are commonly called. Authentic 1958 model year examples display smooth or un-sculpted versions of these plastic pickup surrounds, which are found spilling over into the first 1959 model year batch at #293xx. All batches after this display the sculpted version of the pickup rings identified by the grooves on their short dimension. Also, for a period of time, the gold Lucite signpost pickguards continued to have square notch cutouts, originally designed to accommodate the DeArmond Dynasonic pickup unit. Presumably, once these pre-fabricated guards were all used up, the notches were optimized for the more contoured Filter'Tron shape.

Guitar Courtesy of Dave Rogers. Photo by Tim Mullally.

A 1958 model year 6120 from the #265xx batch. *Guitar Courtesy of Dave Rogers. Photo by Tim Mullally.*

Another significant modification that was initiated for the 1958 model year was the replacement of the control knob affecting tone, historically located on the lower bout of the 6120 model. Beginning at batch #265xx, the tone control was regulated by a three-way switch, later affectionately coined the mud switch. It was positioned on the upper non-cutaway bout next to the pickup selector. In the up position this switch yielded full tonal colorization (aka mud). In the down position it added approximately half the effect of the up position. And when the switch was on the middle setting it provided no colorization at all—a clean channel.

In 1958, Gretsch augmented the Chet Atkins signature lineup with the introduction of the single pickup Tennessean, model 6119, another 16" category electric archtop. This 1958 model year example displays all the representative features, including its cherry red finish, bridge positioned PAF Filter'Tron pickup, and distinctive black sign-post pickguard. Often referred to as a single pickup version of the 6120 model, it lacks the fretboard and f-hole binding, as well as the headstock ornamentation of its big orange brother. With the exception of the very first few guitars from the debut group (batch #282xx), a feature the 6119 model possessed from the beginning was the zero fret, which the 6120 model would not acquire until the 1959 model year release.

Research indicates that less than 12 batches of the Chet Atkins 6119 model were manufactured with a single pickup and open f-holes. This would translate to approximately 1000 guitars produced (last batch #406xx) before the model's evolution to the Electrotone-style, dual-HiLo'Tron pickup version in 1961.

Chet Atkins' Workshop (RCA, 1961), featuring Atkins playing a 6119 Chet Atkins hollowbody model.

Yet another feature linked to this #265xx batch includes the appearance of the heel dowel on most 6120 examples. This may have been an effort to reinforce what history regards as a suspect dovetail neck joint design, employed by Gretsch on most of their archtop guitars. A few decades later the jury is in on this heel dowel modification—it is not well regarded. Today, after more than 50 years under the tension of their strings, vintage Gretsch archtops are notorious for requiring neck re-sets and the presence of this dowel and its underlying anchor screw only complicates that process.

Photo Courtesy of Larry Langell.

The 1958 model year for 6120 guitars was in full bloom by the inception of the #269xx batch. This group contained some 6121 examples, which also displayed the classic 1958 model year accoutrements, including Filter'Tron pickups, smooth pickup rings, tone switch, and compensated bar bridge. One of these solidbody specimens has an original bill of sale from Weaver and Sons Music Studio, Dearborn, Michigan, dated December 14, 1957. This would further reinforce the fact that this batch was also produced in the 1957 calendar year.

The 1958 model year 6120 guitars were the only vintage to feature the compensated bar bridge design that originally surfaced with the first few neoclassic, trestle-braced examples. These bridges were used throughout the 1958 model year production, but after only one batch into the next model year (#293xx) they were unceremoniously dropped in favor of a non-compensated design.

Batch #276xx was an uneventful batch of 6120 guitars that reflect common 1958 model year attributes with the previous two batches. Never complacent, however, Gretsch made additional factory refinements to some of the existing 1958 model year features.

A 1958 model year 6120 from the #269xx batch. *Guitar Courtesy of Chris Guido. Photo by Rick Burda.*

This is an interesting 6120 example that reflects most of the 1958 model year features. Its headstock retains the soon-to-be-modified wider winged construction. It does however diverge from the classic aesthetic of the day, by way of a horseshoe-less headstock overlay. These T-roof only headstocks are not unheard of, and examples have surfaced from several batches from this period, including #276xx and #284xx. *Guitar Courtesy of Jay Rosen Collection. Photo by Sibila Savage.*

Guitar Courtesy of Chris Guido. Photo by Rick Burda.

It seems the first of PAF Filter'Tron pickup covers appear in the #284xx batch, replacing the plain covers. This, the last batch of the 1958 model year guitars, may also be the first of the 6120 guitars to benefit from a new approach to fashioning the headstock from a single piece of wood. Prior examples possess what have come to be known as wings attached to either side of the main pegboard. These were simply glued on. Vintage instruments typically reveal their seams to varying degrees as years of string tension take their toll. This was often exacerbated by the unfortunate placement of some of the Waverly tuning machine screws, which at times were positioned right on the seam. This newer headstock is also a bit smaller than the previous winged design. The #284xx batch also possessed the first of the 6121 solidbody examples displaying neoclassic fretboard inlays, which lagged behind this features' introduction to the other solidbody Jet models by several batches. This last 6120 batch of the 1958 model year also spawned what is probably the most unique vintage Chet Atkins hollowbody specimen found to date (see Tenor 6120 feature).

The new-for-1959 model year wingless headstock. *Guitar Courtesy of Joe Nichols. Photo by Bill Baldock.*

The previous headstock design incorporated wings glued onto either side. *Photo Courtesy of Daniel Nicolas.*

Plain pickup covers gave way to the version inscribed with "Pat Applied For" (PAF) sometime during the #284xx batch. *Guitar Courtesy Gordon Dow.*

1958 Model 6120 Tenor

A very rare beast indeed, this Chet Atkins 6120 in a four-string tenor format was sold to musician Elvis Costello in 2005 by Gruhn Guitars in Nashville. Clearly a 1958 model year example (284xx batch), it reflects expected features such as Filter'Tron pickups (four-pole), smooth pickup rings, tone switch, and a heel dowel. It does not possess a zero fret, which was not introduced until the 1959 model year. Lacking the standard Bigsby B6 vibrato unit, it is instead equipped with a gold "G" cutout tailpiece and a space control bridge, which are consistent features on other non-tremolo equipped Gretsch electric archtops of the period. The simple dot inlays do however seem a little basic for this model, even on such a narrow fretboard. Quite rare, tenor specimens have been found for several of the Gretsch electric guitar models. Other than a couple of documented mini batches of Duo Jet tenors, the others appear to have been custom-ordered. This unique interpretation of the iconic 6120 might just be the only one of its kind.

Courtesy of Gruhn Guitars.

With the expansion of the Gretsch electric archtop product line for 1958, including the introduction of the Country Gentleman model (at batch #264xx), the Anniversary models (at batch #277xx), and the 6119 Chet Atkins single pickup hollowbody model (at batch #282xx), the number of batches of 6120 guitars were reduced to only four—plus the 30 guitars from the #258xx batch. Considering at least three of those groups included some 6121 solidbody units, the total factory output for 1958 model year 6120 hollowbodies is approximately 350-375 guitars. At almost half the production of the previous model year, this is a significant reduction and an explanation for why more 1957 model year specimens come up for sale on the secondary market than 1958 model year specimens.

David Lee (*left*) works hard on his 1958 model year 6120 in support of his band, The Legendary Shack Shakers. Poison Ivy (aka Kristy Wallace) of the notorious punk band The Cramps is known for playing a vintage 1958 model year 6120 she affectionately calls Big O, as well as producing some of the earliest psychobilly music in the 1970s. *Left: Courtesy of David Lee. Photo by Chelsea Hart. Right: Courtesy of Paul Redmond/WireImage/Getty Images.*

1959 Model Year 6120

1959 model year serial number batches:

#293xx: 50-unit batch*
#299xx: 100-unit batch
#307xx: 100-unit batch
#312xx: 100-unit batch
#316xx: 100-unit batch
#322xx: 50-unit batch
#325xx: 50-unit batch*
*(6121 solidbodies included)

I believe the zero fret (we called it fret nut in the factory) was in 1959 on the Chet Atkins 6120 guitars. It took the place of the metal nut. I was constantly rejecting guitars because the action wasn't low enough at the nut. The fret nut or zero fret was the perfect answer. This minor change saved many hours of production time.

-Dan Duffy

The 1959 model year was announced in batch #293xx with the introduction of the Gretsch Action Flow Fret Nut innovation. Today, most refer to this device as simply the zero fret. This was an additional fret, unconventionally placed adjacent to the nut—a direct result of Chet Atkins' playing style and his desire to have lower action at the nut. In conjunction with the introduction of the zero fret, the string nut was modified from a brass standard to a bone material. The zero fret feature is a defining attribute for the 1959 model year on the 6120 model.

A more subtle change, but one that purists always seek to verify, is the style of the bolt head in the swivel handle of the Bigsby B6 vibrato. Throughout most of the 1958 model year production, this bolt head was typically the slotted style. In batch #293xx, which appears to have been a small group of 50 units, however, it is replaced with a Phillips head version, a change that has no apparent functional benefit, but is associated with the classic 1959 model year feature package nonetheless.

This early 1959 model year example from the 293xx batch debuts the zero fret feature, as well as the Phillips head bolt in the Bigsby unit. This batch is also the last to display the leftover 1958 model year features of smooth pickup rings and compensated bar bridges. *Guitar Courtesy of Chris Guido. Photo by Rick Burda.*

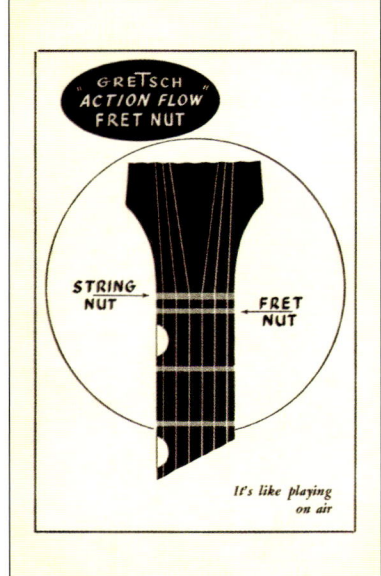

"It's like playing on air," claims this brochure for the Action Flow Fret Nut, often found in the case candy of 1959 model year 6120 specimens. *Courtesy Fred Stucky.*

It would appear that the majority of the 6120 guitars from the #293xx batch still possessed the smooth Filter'Tron pickup rings. There is evidence that this may have changed at the very end of that run and the introduction of the new-for-1959 rings are evident in just a couple late specimens from the batch. Some may argue that the existence of this trait makes this batch a 1958 model year group, but the reality is that the factory was probably just using up all the remaining stock of parts. The introduction of the zero fret feature is a substantial modification and one that would more plausibly indicate a new model year. The next batch (#299xx) clearly displays the new Filter'Tron pickup rings, characterized by its sculpted style and ridges in its short dimension, presumably for no other reason than aesthetic value.

The guitars produced in batches #293xx and #299xx (depicted here) display what have become recognized as quintessential 1959 model year features, including the zero fret, the Phillips head Bigsby bolt, PAF Filter'Tron covers, and sculpted pickup rings. However, they did not yet possess the much-heralded lighter trestle bracing and purportedly thinner tops. *Guitar Courtesy of Fred Stucky.*

Five-piece necks were found intermittently. *Photo Courtesy of Daniel Nicolas.*

At times there is debate within the vintage guitar community as to what production batches fall within what year designation. The lack of official production records from The Gretsch Company has admittedly made establishing these parameters less scientific than we would all desire. There are advocates on both sides of the model year versus production year philosophy. Actually, it would not really matter except in the case of the soaring popularity of the 1959 Chet Atkins hollowbody models, thanks to Brian Setzer. As a result, some (usually dealers) are compelled to try and nudge the 1959-attributed batches both back and forward a bit to reap the premium a 1959 vintage example can fetch in the marketplace. Again, the bottom line is that the desirable features are what should be important. Therefore, the 6120 guitars produced in batches #293xx and #299xx are attributed to being of 1959 vintage. Suffice it to say, just as the initial batches of 1958 model year guitars were produced in 1957, many of the 1959 model year guitars were actually manufactured in 1958, 1960 model year guitars in 1959, and so on.

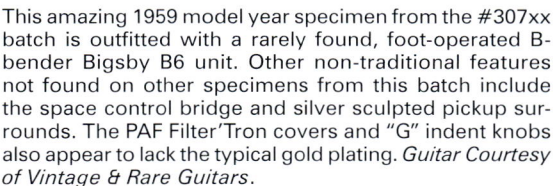

This amazing 1959 model year specimen from the #307xx batch is outfitted with a rarely found, foot-operated B-bender Bigsby B6 unit. Other non-traditional features not found on other specimens from this batch include the space control bridge and silver sculpted pickup surrounds. The PAF Filter'Tron covers and "G" indent knobs also appear to lack the typical gold plating. *Guitar Courtesy of Vintage & Rare Guitars*.

Apparently a patent had been applied for what was destined to be known as the True Tone Changer Bigsby unit. *Guitar Courtesy of Vintage & Rare Guitars*.

The #307xx batch of 6120 guitars continued to display a continuity of 1959 model year features, but this batch also contained many examples with a five-piece maple neck. This variation to Gretsch's standard three-piece neck design can be identified by the dual-stripe effect created from two separate ebony strips being sandwiched between the maple. The dual-ebony seam bisects the back of the headstock and neck, terminating at the heel cap. This feature seems to have been applied arbitrarily and exists sporadically in other models of this period as well.

Earlier 1958 model year Gretsch 6120 guitars are notorious for possessing what is now referred to as heavy trestle bracing, which was the first generation of this structural modification to the 6120 body design. In fact, the first few batches of 1959 model year 6120s also share this style of trestle bracing. However, guitars belonging to batch #312xx seem to have benefited from some production refinements in their trestle bracing, utilizing wooden feet to replace one of the rails. In addition, it is rumored that the thickness of the guitar's top was reduced. These examples have developed a reputation for being quite desirable as a result of the lighter feel and more sonically responsive top. Although less visible to the naked eye, these advancements are also considered classic 1959 model year attributes.

The 100-unit 6120 batch starting at #312xx exemplifies a trend in the Gretsch factory production process that illustrates its necessity to increase the factory's annual output with each new year. This batch is the third consecutive 6120 group that has been preceded, followed, or both by other similar 16" category archtop models. Since the inception of the 1958 model year Anniversary and 6119 models, the factory apparently recognized the production efficiency of manufacturing guitars with similar specifications in sequence. In essence, this turned individual 100-unit batches of these three respective models into super batches that allowed the factory to produce more total units with fewer time-consuming changeovers of jigs, templates, and equipment. For example, the #299xx batch of 6120 models was preceded by a batch of acoustic flat top models, but followed by several consecutive batches of Anniversaries and 6119 model guitars. This added up to a production run of 500 similarly specified guitars before they switched the line over to accommodate a batch of Jet solidbody guitars. The 6120 batch #307xx was also part of a super batch of 400 units that included Anniversaries and 6119 archtops, sandwiched between Jet solidbodies and a batch of 17" Country Clubs.

A typical 1959 model year 6120 from the end of the #312xx batch. *Guitar Courtesy of Chris Guido. Photo by Rick Burda.*

The last three documented batches of 6120 guitars with classic 1959 model year features are #316xx, 322xx, and 325xx. They are representative of the period of relative calm during the 6120s' evolution—their features consistent with the earlier #312xx batch.

The last 1959 model year batch (#325xx) appears to have been a smaller 50-unit run that also included a few 6121 solidbody examples. Hollowbody representatives from this batch are, therefore, rare. An interesting note about the 6121 solidbodies from this group is that they possess a zero fret. This would seem to be a late introduction compared to their hollowbody 6120 cousins, which had this feature throughout the six previous batches. Equally curious, the zero fret feature even made it on to three batches of Jet-style solidbodies before it debuted on the 6121 solidbodies.

Experiencing continued success with incrementally increasing its annual output, the Gretsch factory produced seven batches of the 6120 hollowbody for the 1959 model year, selling at an MSRP of $425. Several of these batches appear to have been smaller 50-unit groups and a few others included the requisite 6121 solidbody representatives. The total number of 1959 model year 6120 guitars produced might be in the range of 525.

With optimized features and a high profile celebrity partiality (Brian Setzer), many consider the guitars from the 1959 model year the pinnacle of the Chet Atkins 6120 model. Their escalating value on the vintage market confirms this. Ironically, most of the Brian Setzer-owned, vintage 6120s are actually 1960 model year examples—his famed Stray Cat guitar (#33024) is an example of this. Reasons for this misattribution include the guitar's 2.75" deep body, its enamel-faced B6 vibrato (which was not the guitar's original vibrato), and the simple fact that back in Setzer's mid-1980s heyday, the Gretsch production history was less understood than it is today. Realistically, this guitar and those from its batch are 1959 <u>production</u> examples, probably made sometime after mid-year. But as has been illustrated throughout the Gretsch Golden Era, the company's practice was to begin production of the next model year's instruments in the previous calendar year. So, the changes that are revealed in the batch containing the Setzer Stray Cat specimen, actually exemplify the emergence of the 1960 model year.

In all its glory. This dead mint 1959 model year 6120 from the #322xx batch is the Holy Grail for many 6120 collectors. *Guitar Courtesy of Fred Stucky. Photo by Sarah Stolfa.*

Chapter
16

1960 model year serial number batches:

#330xx: 100-unit batch
#337xx: 100-unit batch*
#341xx: 50-unit batch (TBD)
#345xx: 100-unit batch
#354xx: 100-unit batch
#359xx: 100-unit batch*
#367xx: 100-unit batch*
#376xx: 100-unit batch
#388xx: 100-unit batch
#394xx: 100-unit batch*
*(6121 solidbodies included)

1960 Model Year 6120

The use of the "V-cutout–Gretsch by Bigsby" tailpiece introduced this year differentiate the 1960 (6120 model) guitar from the '59 model.

-Jay Scott

There are two defining features that categorize a 1960 model year 6120 guitar. The first is the appearance of the cast aluminum V-style Bigsby vibrato, which replaced the previously standard black enamel-faced B6 Bigsby unit. This new look vibrato operated in the same manner as the previous design, but featured a triangular cutout in its base. It also acquired a debossed "Gretsch by Bigsby" designation on its face. The addition of this feature has historically defined these guitars as being from the 1960 model year. These new Bigsby vibratos first appeared on 6120 examples in the #330xx batch. Guitars from this group are quite unique as they represent the only batch of 6120 archtops with the combination of a V-style Bigsby and a 2.75" body depth. The very next batch of 6120 hollowbodies marked the beginning of the other 1960 model year attribute, a slightly shallower body.

This well-loved 6120 was one of the very first from the #330xx batch. It originally possessed a factory-installed V-style Bigsby vibrato. As a tribute to the impact Brian Setzer has had on American music, many fans have modified their vintage 6120 guitars to emulate that of the famous (similarly-modified) #33024 specimen that Setzer wielded through his early Stray Cats career. *Guitar Courtesy of Fred Stucky.*

Examples from this 1959-produced batch of 1960 model year 6120 guitars are highly coveted by Brian Setzer fans all over the world and they typically sell for a premium. Many of these #330xx Chet Atkins hollowbody guitars have ended up in the vaults of affluent overseas collectors.

This guitar from the #337xx batch was sent back to Brooklyn for a factory refinish by its original owner in the late 1960s. The result is a 1960 model year 6120 in walnut brown. *Guitar Courtesy of Fred Stucky.*

The space control bridge is not original to this gorgeous guitar from the #337xx batch, but everything else is. Its 2.5" body depth, figured grain, and V-style Bigsby make it the poster child for the 1960 model year. *Photo Courtesy of Larry Langell.*

Only seven serial numbers away from its flame-topped #337xx batch mate, this guitar displays a more sedate top. *Photo Courtesy of Frank Walboomers.*

In the second batch (#337xx) of the 1960 model year, which also originated several Brian Setzer-owned specimens, including the now famous "Steve Miller" guitar #33767, the 6120 model's body depth was reduced by a quarter of an inch to 2.5". This batch also contains 6121 solidbody examples that were similarly outfitted with the B3-sized, V-style Bigsby unit. The #337xx batch is also an instance where quite a few specimens have been found with highly flame-grained maple tops, which has contributed to the demand for guitars from this group.

So, instead of a single-feature evolution occurring in one batch of guitars, it seems the defining 1960 model year attributes were born out of a combination of batches #330xx and #337xx. It may be that the factory wanted to introduce the new V-style Bigsby vibrato but still had the older body style in the pipeline. Regardless of motives, this was not the first or the last time that Gretsch would introduce model year changes over several batches.

Specimens from the following batch (#341xx) are elusive, which suggests that this is another example of one of the few 50-unit batches. The features are unchanged from the prior group and, in fact, carry over some of the figured grain bodies, although the examples found from this batch typically have a more subtle grain pattern. This is also a batch where there are several specimens documented with five-piece necks.

Another beneficiary of the "Setzer affect" is the #345xx batch, which claims two representatives in Setzer's personal stable of vintage 6120s, and is a popular group with collectors.

This may be one of the examples in the #345xx batch without a five-piece neck. Inexplicably, this 6120 has a custom seven-position rotary tone knob installed to augment the standard mud switch, which is still operational on this guitar. *Guitar Courtesy of Chris Guido. Photo by Rick Burda.*

Photo Courtesy of Crawford White.

These littermates exemplify the gorgeous flamed-grain wood used on 6120 hollowbodies from the #359xx batch, as well as the difference in color fade guitars can experience over four decades.

Guitar Courtesy of Gordon Dow.

This 1960 model year 6120 from the #354xx batch illustrates the trend of subtle to moderate flame-grained examples. *Courtesy of Nino Fazio, Real Vintage Guitars, Italy.*

The cover of *Guitar Player* magazine's May 1982 issue is rumored by John Entwistle, bassist for The Who, to be the first time the magazine's cover featured a guitar (#35992) without an artist. Entwistle also owned a 6121 solidbody from this same batch.

Although this guitar belongs to the #367xx batch, it could be the twin brother of the famous Entwistle specimen. Not only is it another example of a highly grained 1960 model year guitar, but the striations in the grain actually match up quite closely between the two instruments. *Guitar Courtesy of Chris Guido. Photo by Rick Burda.*

Continuing its practice of producing a small quantity of model 6121 Chet Atkins solidbody examples within a larger batch of 6120 hollowbody guitars, this member of batch #367xx is one rare bird. *Guitar Courtesy of Chris Guido. Photo by Rick Burda.*

As this late example illustrates, the flames died down at the end of the #367xx batch. *Photo Courtesy of Daniel Nicolas.*

The next three 6120 batches all maintain the standard 1960 model year feature package. Batches #354xx, #359xx, and #367xx all continue to display figured maple ranging from the subtle to the wild in its intensity. Some of the most extremely flamed 6120 specimens originate from the #359xx batch, including several celebrity-owned examples. None is more beautiful than #35992, otherwise known as the Entwistle 6120, after John Entwistle. bassist for The Who. This guitar, in all its flamed-grain glory, graced the cover of the May 1982 edition of *Guitar Player* magazine. It was also prominently featured in the book *Bass Culture* (2004), in which John Entwistle posthumously shared his extensive collection of guitars and bass instruments. Although batch #367xx produced a few guitars with intensely figured grains, it seems the flames died down in later examples from this 100-unit batch.

Sometime in the period that corresponds to 6120 batch #376xx, a subtle feature change occurred. The actual patent number (2892371) began appearing on the previously blank right-hand tab of the Filter'Tron pickup covers. This newer style is referred to as the patent number cover within the vintage guitar community. Due to the transient nature of pickups and the emotional connection collectors/players have to the PAF moniker (mostly associated with Gibson humbuckers) it is not clear exactly in what batch the patent number first appeared. However, the last three batches of the 1960 model year seem to consistently have 6120 examples that possess them.

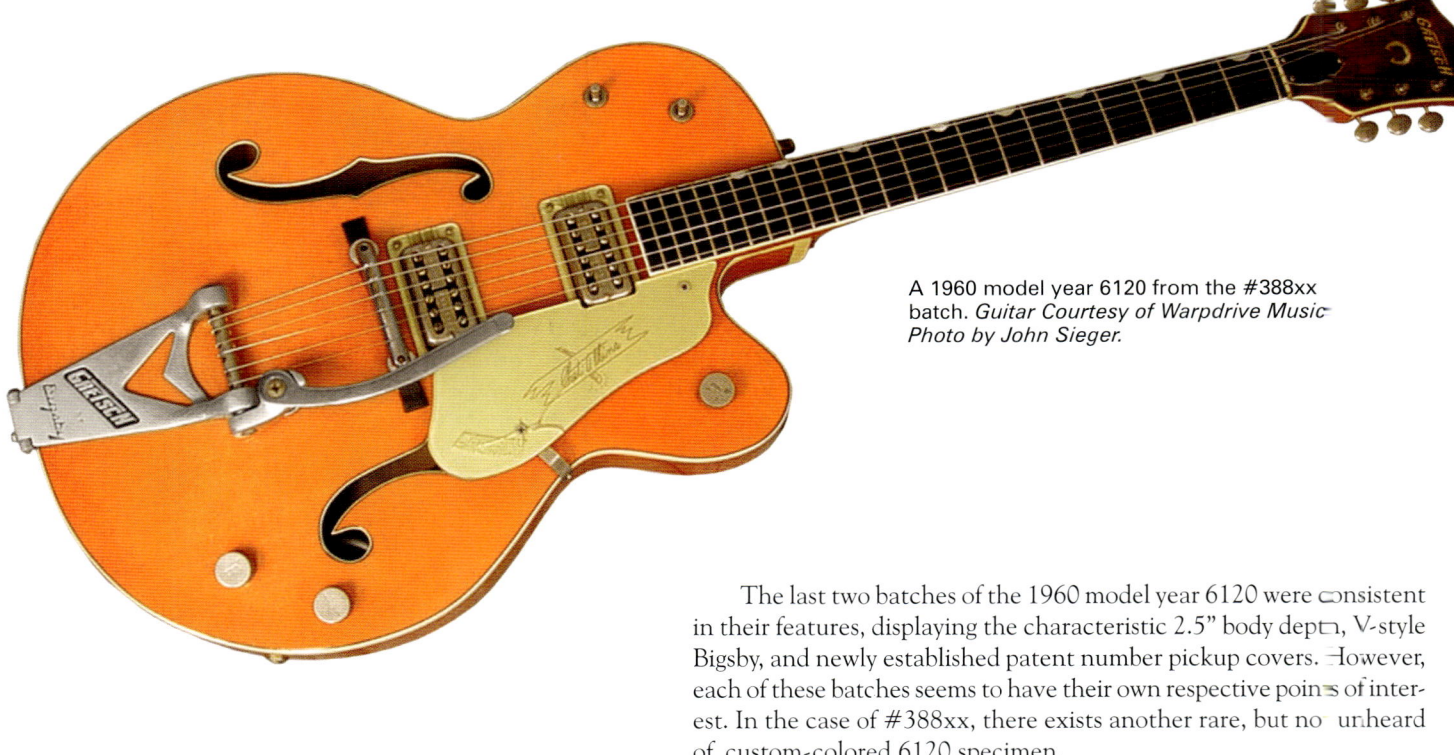

A 1960 model year 6120 from the #388xx batch. *Guitar Courtesy of Warpdrive Music Photo by John Sieger.*

The last two batches of the 1960 model year 6120 were consistent in their features, displaying the characteristic 2.5" body depth, V-style Bigsby, and newly established patent number pickup covers. However, each of these batches seems to have their own respective points of interest. In the case of #388xx, there exists another rare, but not unheard of, custom-colored 6120 specimen.

Once again, there is always the question of how and why someone would pursue a sunburst factory finish on a model 6120 guitar. This amazing 1960 model year specimen from the #388xx batch reveals some interesting details about its adoption on its surviving original bill of sale. This document confirms that on October 27, 1960 this Chet Atkins 6120 model guitar was purchased in Queens, New York. It was part of a package deal including the guitar, a case, a Supro amplifier (with cover), and footswitch, which all retailed for $592.25. The MSRP for the guitar was listed in the December 14, 1959 Gretsch pricelist as $475. As per this receipt, there is no longer a mystery as to the premium charged for the special sunburst finish, and it is cited on its own line item at $25. At less than a six percent up-charge, it would seem like there would be a lot more of these out there, but this assumes that viable dual-Filter'Tron-equipped, sunburst-finished alternatives were not available. They were, in the form of the Country Club 6192 model ($450) and the Anniversary 6117 model ($310). Purists will point out, however, that although more affordable, the Anniversary 6117 model had already switched to the HiLo'Tron pickup technology earlier in that same year at batch #355xx—it also lost the trestle bracing feature at that juncture. Likewise, during this time, the Country Club model was experiencing a period where its body depth was thinned to just under 2" deep. So, these alternatives may not have been as close to the 6120 specs as it may have appeared. It seems reasonable to consider that these custom-colored (sunburst) examples are as rare as they are because of a general unwillingness by most to compromise the 6120 model's most obvious signature feature, its Western orange finish.

Courtesy of the Vermont Collection of Fine Guitars.

Courtesy of the Vermont Collection of Fine Guitars.

The last batch of the 1960 model year (#394xx) produced something almost as rare as a custom finish in the form of a left-handed 6120 specimen. In fact, it is generally accepted within the vintage Gretsch community that Gretsch may have produced as few as 100 left-handed guitars for all models throughout the entire Golden Era. These were only manufactured on special order and as a result had some idiosyncrasies, including a mix of features from previous model years.

Finally, it has been determined that some late 6120 specimens from this #394xx batch are actually the first examples of the new-for-1961 model year body format. This handful of instruments is merely a prelude to the pending changes that officially debut in the very next batch.

Evidence shows that there were no fewer than ten batches of 1960 model year 6120 guitars produced, making it by far the most prolific year for the Chet Atkins hollowbody. At least four of these batches included a quantity of 6121 solidbody guitars and one batch may be a 50-unit group. With this in mind, the projected output of 1960 model year 6120 hollowbody guitars would be approximately 850 specimens.

Believe it or not, this ultra rare left-handed 6120 possesses a serial number that places it in the last 1960 model year batch (394xx). This is counterintuitive to many Gretsch detectives because features like hump block markers, enamel-faced Bigsby B6 vibratos, and the absence of zero fret should not normally exist on a guitar of this vintage. However, the body is a 1960-appropriate 2.5" deep, it has trestle bracing, and a period-correct patent number Filter'Tron covers. The plain gold Lucite guard is a common trait for the few Gretsch lefty guitars the factory produced. *Guitar Courtesy of Chris Guido. Photo by Rick Burda.*

I opened the case and it was bright orange and I thought, "Ugh! It's horrible, I hate it." I went home and went into my studio and plugged it in and it totally wrecked me out, It's the best guitar I've got now. It's the Chet Atkins model, with double pickups, f-holes and single-cutaway.

-Pete Townshend, The Who

Theater for Eric Clapton's comeback concert. Then on October 3, 1973, in a televised "Top of the Pops" performance, an ill-advised demonstration of showmanship (or temper as some observed) involved Townshend characteristically smashing his Gretsch onto the stage, severely damaging the instrument. This particular act of violence was captured and used as the footage for the very end of the Who documentary movie, *The Kids Are Alright* (1979). Townshend subsequently had the guitar repaired, miraculously bringing it back to playing condition.

Pete Townshend's 1960 model year 6120 made a rare live appearance at the Rainbow Theater in 1973. *Photo Courtesy of Debi Doss/Hulton Archive/Getty Images.*

This photo of Pete Townshend with his 1960 Chet Atkins 6120 is circa 1985 and testifies to the guitar's survival. It was an interesting selection for use on his *Pete Townshend Anthology* double CD release (2005, Eel Pie Recording Productions Limited). *Photo Courtesy of Malcolm Heywood.*

Brian Setzer was not the only celebrity artist to wield a 1960 model year 6120. Although he was not widely associated with this model, Pete Townshend used his Gretsch 6120 to record many of The Who's most popular hits. A gift from Joe Walsh in 1970, this guitar appears extensively on the albums *Who's Next* (1971) and *Quadrophenia* (1973). Townshend points to tracks like "Bargain" and "Won't Get Fooled Again" as examples that reveal the 6120 model's sound. On January 13, 1973 he played the Gretsch at London's Rainbow

Long before "The Devil Went Down to Georgia" took Charlie Daniels from country music star to crossover phenomenon, he was cranking out early rock and roll with his band The Jaguars and playing this custom 1960 model year Gretsch 6120. This was one of Daniels' very first electric guitars and it was purchased during late 1961. In addition to the wonderful white finish on this custom-ordered guitar, the binding is comprised of the same gold sparkle material used on White Falcon models. The fretboard is inlaid with Daniels' name and when the guitar was stolen in 1963 the name was amateurishly covered up to conceal the original owner's identity. Now fully restored, refinished, and back in Daniels' possession, this guitar is on permanent display at the Charlie Daniels Museum in Nashville.

Courtesy of Charlie Daniels Personal Collection.

Photo Courtesy of Brian Akers.

1961 Model Year 6120

The 1961 model year represented the last of the single-cutaway body format for the Chet Atkins 6120 model. The changes for 1961 were evident in batch #395xx, which was only separated from the previous batch of 6120 guitars by a small 50-unit batch of Chet Atkins 6119 models. Those 6119 model archtops, as well as this #395xx batch (also 50 units) both shared the defining feature for the new 1961 model year—an even slimmer body that measured a mere 2.25" deep. This transition to the shallower body coincided with a change to the neck heel shape as well. Unlike the previous design, this shallow heel stops significantly short of the binding on the edge of the guitar's back and is not as tapered down to the heel cap. Instead, it terminates more abruptly at the cap. Inside the neck joint another change was installed, and the previous (and problematic) dovetail design was modified to a mortise and tenon joint. Lastly, to accommodate this ultra-thin body style, the dowel and anchor screw device, used to reinforce the strength of the neck joint, was relocated from its previous heel position to the side of the pocket, visible in the cutaway.

1961 model year serial number batches:

#395xx: 50-unit batch*
#398xx: 100-unit batch
#407xx: 100-unit batch
#413xx: 100-unit batch
#423xx: 100-unit batch
#428xx: 100-unit batch
#431xx: 100-unit batch
#446xx: 50-unit batch
*(6121 solidbodies included)

Guitar Courtesy of Dave Rogers. Photo by Tim Mullally.

These kissing cousins are less than ten serial numbers apart within the #395xx batch. Both models display the new 1961 model year dowel position in their respective cutaways.

Guitar Courtesy of Chris Guido. Photo by Rick Burda.

Guitar Courtesy of Arnoud Holsboer. Photo by Daniel Nicolas.

The second two production batches for the 1961 model year 6120 hollowbody were consistent with the first, however, all around these batches signs of 1961 model year changes were obvious in other Gretsch models. The #398xx batch of 6120 hollowbodies, which was in all probability manufactured at the end of the 1960 calendar year, was directly followed by a 100-unit batch of Duo Jets, which appear to be the last of the single-cutaway format for this model. Likewise the #407xx batch of 6120 guitars was directly followed by the factory's debut of the dubiously innovative Gretsch Bikini (two-in-one) double neck guitar.

A 1961 model year 6120 from the #398xx batch. *Photo Courtesy of Crawford White*.

A 1961 model year 6120 from the #407xx batch. *Guitar Courtesy of Dave Rogers. Photo by Tim Mullally.*

Changes in pickguards are always difficult to track because they are so prone to being broken and/or replaced. It appears, however, that sometime late in the first half of batch #413xx the shape of the Chet Atkins signpost guard changed, acquiring a more scalloped radius around its back end. Today, this presents a challenge to model year identification in the field, as there are basically three 1961 model year batches with the older guard and three with this newer contoured signpost style. Unfortunately, to muddy the waters even further, these would not be the only pickguard variations ultimately found on 1961 model year 6120 examples.

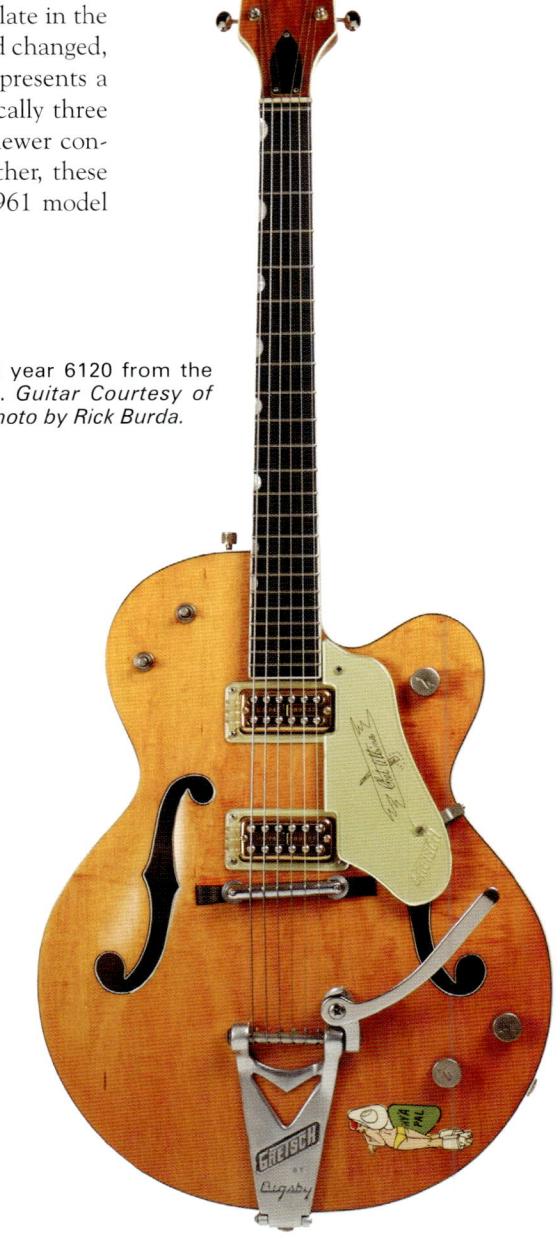

A 1961 model year 6120 from the #423xx batch. *Guitar Courtesy of Chris Guido. Photo by Rick Burda.*

A 1961 model year 6120 from the #413xx batch. *Guitar Courtesy of Fred Stucky.*

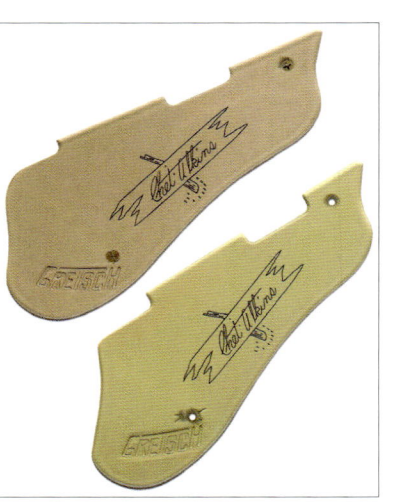

Photo Courtesy of Josh Bradshaw.

By the time the next batch (#423xx) of 6120s was produced, the Gretsch guitar product line had experienced some significant events. In the 1000 guitars produced between 6120 batches #413xx and #423xx, Gretsch introduced debut batches of the solidbody Corvette guitar (model 6132), the Electrotone Tennessean (model 6119), and the first of the double-cutaway Jet solidbodies. In the midst of all this change, the 6120 batches #423xx and #428xx remained consistent with each other.

In an example of variability within a batch, these two specimens produced in the first half of the #428xx batch are only 30 guitars away from each other, but note the varying position of the tone and pickup selector switches, as well as the volume knobs on the lower bout. Sharp eyes will detect yet another difference, as one of these guitars is probably the earliest example of a 6120 with a standby switch, a feature that doesn't officially appear until the next batch. *Guitar(s) Courtesy of Chris Guido. Photo(s) by Rick Burda.*

The slender 1961 model year 6120 pushed the limits of the conventional archtop body. *Guitar courtesy of Joe Nichols. Photo by Bill Baldock.*

The last two 6120 model batches attributed to the 1961 model year are #431xx and #446xx. In fact, they are the swan song for Chet Atkins 6120 model guitars produced with the single-cutaway body. Examples from these batches display a new Chet Atkins signature (only) pickguard, which replaced the previous signpost motif that was so identified with this model from its inception. These two batches also mark the introduction of a new standby switch feature, which endured through the pending Electrotone body transition and into the mid 1970s. The standby switch was an effort to provide the musician with a way to kill the signal to the amplifier when not playing music. Lastly, these guitars also debuted the plain bolt hinge on the Bigsby V-style vibrato.

The final batch (#446xx) of single-cutaway 6120 guitars was a small 50-unit group. These guitars represented a highly evolved form of what had been originally introduced just seven years earlier in the 1955 model year. Virtually every aspect of the 6120 guitar was modified over that period; some features were changed several times over. Through all those transformations the Chet Atkins hollowbody maintained its identity, remaining equally distinctive in both its visual and sonic impact.

There is strong evidence to suggest that this last batch of single-cutaway 6120 guitars was actually manufactured in the Spring of the 1962 calendar year. This would be unusual as the Gretsch factory typically began production of the next year's model line sometime in the previous calendar year. The fact that there were relatively few 1962 model year Electrotone 6120 batches might lend credence to this theory.

These last two batches of 6120 hollowbodies, which featured significant aesthetic (pickguard and Bigsby bolt) and functional (standby switch) modifications, could have been intended as 1962 model year single-cutaway guitars. Several other Gretsch models, including Jet solidbodies and Tennesseans found within a few hundred serial numbers of 6120 batch #431xx also display the newly inherited standby switch as the defining feature of their respective 1962 model year instruments. It would not seem unreasonable to apply that same rationale to the 6120 model of the same period. Of course, as thought provoking as this may be, the soon-to-be released Electrotone version of the 6120 will always be the accepted 1962 model year representative.

The last version of the 6120 single-cutaway format, complete with new Chet Atkins signature pickguard, plain bolt Bigsby, and the standby switch. *Guitar Courtesy of Chris Guido. Photo by Rick Burda.*

The 1961 model year is attributed as having no fewer than eight batches of the 6120 model, translating to approximately 650 single-cutaway hollowbody guitars produced at the Brooklyn factory.

When it was all said and done, the single-cutaway Chet Atkins 6120 hollowbody guitar had made its mark within the industry. In seven years of production the Gretsch factory had shipped approximately 3800 units of the 6120 model, a far cry from the more robust production totals of Fender and Gibson's electric solidbody stalwart models. It is this relative rarity, in conjunction with the classic sound and unique aesthetics that attract many of today's collectors and musicians to the 6120. It is also the many manifestations of feature combinations that make the pursuit of a specific vintage or batch specimen that much more challenging.

These aspects, in addition to the substantial price tag for a clean and original vintage 6120 have, at times, motivated some to take an alternative approach to acquiring one.

A rare last batch example (#446xx) illustrating all the expected features. The tuners are not original. There were only 50 guitars in this swan song group. *Courtesy of the Bachman Gretsch Collection.*

Chapter
18

6120 Conversions: Flattery or Fraud?

All vintage guitars have had to endure decades of use, changing hands, and travel and storage hazards to survive today. In the more than 50-year lifespan of these instruments, they have faced potential destruction and loss and the prospect of being cannibalized for parts. Some Gretsch models have encountered yet another obstacle to maintaining their original condition and identity.

Typically referred to as 6120 conversions, if done well, these lower-end Gretsch hollowbody restoration projects can appear nearly identical to vintage 1950s model 6120s. As previously noted, the Streamliner body dimensions and construction were the same as the celebrated 6120, minus the second pickup, a Bigsby vibrato, and some ornamentation. This fact allows luthiers to get a running start on making their own version of the 6120 model. Typically, the 6120 conversions that are attempted using other Gretsch models (Anniversary or Clipper) as donors, tend to be more innocently motivated by an effort to improve an instrument that is already in significant disrepair or in need of a refinish. Other times, however, craftsman attempt conversion projects out of curiosity to see if they can create a guitar that is similar to a vintage 6120 in appearance and/or sound. In fact, most conversion projects are harmless, but as prices for authentic and clean examples of vintage 6120s threatened to exceed the $15,000 mark, these conversions have, at times, been used to deceive prospective buyers of high-end 6120 guitars.

Although the other Gretsch models that share common dimensions and structural specifications with the 6120 model are sometimes used in conversion projects—to varying degrees of success—the Streamliner remains the most desirable donor. The common model years for Streamliner donors are 1957 and 1958. In each case both the 6120 and Streamliner share identical fretboard marker designs and pickup technology. In 1957 that combination was Dynasonic pickups and hump block markers and in 1958 it was Filter'Tron pickups and neoclassic markers. Another big advantage the Streamliner has over other prospective Gretsch donor models is that it already has the f-hole and fretboard binding, a labor-intensive modification. The 1958 model year examples also share the important trestle-bracing feature, although so does the Anniversary. For these reasons, Streamliner-based conversions can be so convincing that they are the most prone to being fraudulently passed off as authentic 6120 guitars.

Originally born as two Anniversary models, these guitars have been converted into Chet Atkins 6120 imposters.
Photo Courtesy of Ted Broman.

Experts can usually identify a converted Streamliner. It is no small task to make the required aesthetic changes look authentic and original. Achieving the specific color finish, age, and wear characteristics is a major hurdle. Not to mention the second pickup must be introduced with exacting precision to pass as a factory installation. In addition, Streamliner models have a white plastic tail pin protruding just below where the "G" cutout chrome tailpiece screws into the body. This is not a feature on a vintage 6120 model, which makes its presence, or evidence of its existence, a key indicator when considering possible Streamliner to 6120 conversions. Another, more subtle indicator is the fact that the aftermarket horseshoe headstock overlays that have been available over the years reflect more rounded characters within the Gretsch T-roof logo.

This Streamliner-based 6120 conversion has been executed very closely to 6120 specifications. *Photo Courtesy of Dave Aquirre.*

Of course a more definitive clue to the authenticity of a 6120 is the serial number. With Gretsch's practice of producing guitars in batches and applying sequential serial numbering to them (until 1966 when they changed to a date coding), newly compiled Gretsch serial number documentation makes it very clear as to which model a particular serial number was assigned, regardless of whether the model stamp is present or legible. Of course the serial number was only applied to these guitars on a paper label inside the body cavity, visible through the bass side f-hole. There are legitimate instances when, over decades, they have been lost, removed, or damaged beyond legibility. However, if a particular guitar is being represented as an authentic 6120 and there is any reason to believe it may in fact be a conversion—AND the serial number is not available—it becomes highly suspect.

In recent years 6120 counterfeits have been largely thwarted by the existence of serial number and batch statistics. However, modern day advancements in the process of relicing, distressing certain aspects of a guitar to simulate age, remains a threat. It is not out of the realm of possibility that armed with this same serial number information, fake labels could be forged in a very convincing manner. So, the bottom line should continue to be let the buyer beware, especially when you are considering a five-figure, highly collectible instrument like a vintage Chet Atkins 6120.

Cowboy Cases

One aspect that collectors always look for when evaluating a vintage Chet Atkins 6120 guitar is whether or not it comes with an original, leather-trimmed cowboy case. Originally marketed in the 1955 *Guitars for Moderns* catalog as simply the Gretsch Chet Atkins guitar case, these cases were available in both the hollow-body (model 6220) and solidbody (model 6221) formats at $58 and $54, respectively. These cases were sold separately, which means that not every 6120 has one. The outside covering on these overtly Western-styled cases was described as a rawhide effect with a brown, tooled leather trim. In fact, the earliest examples display what is an attempt to recreate a pinto horsehide on the outside. The illustration in the 1955 catalog shows this effect, however, most cases we see today have the plain off-white or buff leatherette covering.

A rare, first version cowboy case. *Courtesy of Gordon Dow.*

Another difference between the earliest cases from 1955 and the ones that followed in subsequent years is the color of the plush interior. For some reason the original emerald green interior, which featured a green Gretsch T-roof logo on a white satin banner, was quickly replaced by the more common burgundy/purple interior with a Gretsch logo banner in blue. The later style also displays a raised stylized "G" on the inside top of the case. It appears that the Ess & Ess Mfg. Company (Brooklyn, New York) made the cowboy cases for Gretsch, although manufacturers' markings are typically not visible on them. The company may have sourced the brass hardware from several suppliers over the years because some of these components can found marked "Excelsior" or "Lifton." The placement of the latches and feet on these cases occur in a couple of configurations as well, although no specific association to model year has been determined.

The more commonly encountered, second version cowboy case. *Courtesy of Fred Stucky.*

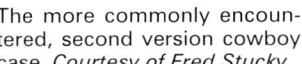

Over the life of the Gretsch cowboy case design there were several evolutions to the distinctive tooled-leather trim. Both the Western motifs depicted within the trim, as well as the color were modified over time. These samples appear in chronological order (top-to-bottom). *Courtesy of Fred Stucky and Gordon Dow.*

The cowboy-style cases continued to be offered, but they were not depicted in the 1960 *Gretsch Guitars Catalog No. 32*, and, surprisingly, they were listed for the same price they had been five years prior. The latest of the single-cutaway 6120 hollowbodies from the late 1960 and 1961 model years are often found to have cowboy cases with a black, tooled-leather trim. There are also examples of cowboy-style cases for the Electrotone double-cutaway 6120 format. The Chet Atkins guitar case, model 6220, was still being listed as a stock item in the 1965 *Gretsch Guitars and Amplifiers Catalog No. 32*.

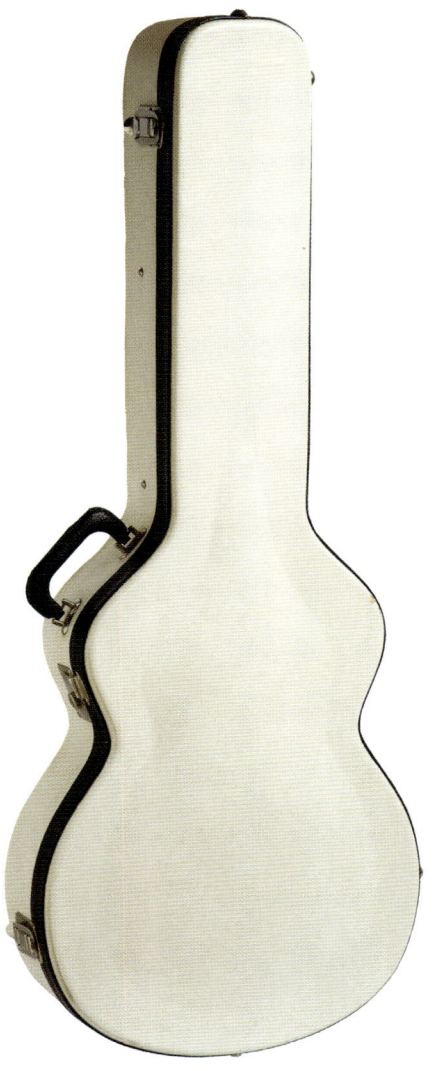

A third version cowboy case. *Photos Courtesy of Steve Wilson.*

Christopher Guido's Gretsch 6120 Collection

It has taken Christopher Guido 23 years to amass one of the most staggering single collections of vintage 6120 specimens known to exist. His thirty-two guitars span the evolution of the 6120 model from the 1955 Western-appointed fledgling to the highly refined last version of late 1961 and into the Electrotone era. These guitars tell the story of this iconic Gretsch model's glory years.

Guido's approach to the collection is meticulously comprehensive. Augmenting the thirty single-cutaway 6120 specimens are two extremely rare 6121 solidbody examples from the 1957 and 1960 model years. There is also a very early 1962 model year Electrotone double-cutaway representative and another slightly evolved version from 1964. Of course no collection of guitars like these would be complete without an ample stash of cowboy cases, authentic leather guitar straps, and a few Western-decorated Gretsch amplifiers. Clearly there is more to collecting Gretsch 6120 guitars than just acquiring orange guitars.

It was while he was still in high school that Guido was first attracted to the Gretsch 6120 model guitar through his growing interest in the rockabilly-styled music of Brian Setzer. In addition to the sonic lure of this instrument, he admits that the aesthetics of the guitar were equally appealing, both in its archtop format and color. It seemed appropriate that when Guido assembled his very first band for their very first practice session, their opening number was a run-through of the Eddie Cochran classic "Twenty Flight Rock."

Acquiring his first 6120, a 1957 model year, while still in college, Guido subsequently pursued an opportunity to pick up another after hearing the 1958 model year's exceptional Filter'Tron sound. The love affair was officially in full bloom and, unbeknownst to Guido, a collection had been born. Even with all the choices at his fingertips today, and his admission that the shallow body 1961 model year is his favorite 6120 format (he owns ten), that 1958 specimen along with his Fender brown Super amplifier remains his go-to rig for recording.

It would be an understatement to suggest that Guido exudes great passion for all model years of the Chet Atkins 6120 hollowbody. He explains that he never set out to acquire so many specimens and that he had no real objectives for the growing group. He simply allowed his gut and his budget to dictate its composition. Although he is content with the current lineup, Guido admits that there are a still a few voids—he is keeping his eye out for an opportunity to add that special 6120 that will better round out the collection.

Photo Courtesy of Rick Burda.

Gretsch 6120 Legends: Beyond Chet

The marketing magic of the Chet Atkins endorsement, combined with the harmonic convergence of feature combinations, resulted in a dynamic and unique sounding and distinctive looking instrument called the Chet Atkins 6120 hollowbody. It was the late 1950s and rock and roll had clearly established itself as the next big thing in music. Out of this genre there emerged a couple of notable artists who happily embraced this amazing instrument and in the process made the 6120 model guitar their own.

Eddie Ray Cochran (1938-1960) was an accomplished guitarist, whose influence within the rock and roll scene was diminished only by his tragic death in a car accident at the young age of 22. Growing up in California in the early 1950s, Cochran spent much of his time at the Bell Garden Music Center learning the basics of playing guitar. The owner, Bill Keither, was very supportive and would ultimately sell Cochran what would become his main guitar, the instrument with which he was most identified with, a 1955 Chet Atkins hollowbody model 6120 (#16942). This guitar was later famously modified with a Gibson black-covered, P-90 pickup in its neck position. Cochran was something of a prodigy, able to imitate and quickly master the work of his heroes, whether it was the triads of Johnny Smith, high-speed licks of Joe Maphis, or the bass melody picking style of Chet Atkins. These influences would help to shape his emerging versatility and style.

In January of 1955, at the age of 16, Cochran left high school to pursue his dream of becoming a professional musician. Partnering with Hank Cochran (no relation), The Cochran Brothers began to build a reputation on the West Coast country music circuit, which at the time provided more opportunity for newcomers than the Nashville scene did. During this time Cochran also became a regular and respected session player, further honing his abilities on the guitar. Then, inspired by the affect Elvis Presley was having on audiences, and intent on stardom, he decided to leave The Cochran Brothers act in 1956.

Cochran's growing popularity and good looks won him appearances in 1950s movies, including *The Girl Can't Help It* (1956) and *Untamed Youth* (1957). In 1957, soon after the release of his single "Twenty Flight Rock," Cochran toured with Buddy Holly. Later that same year his first and only album *Singin' to My Baby* was released. In early 1959, Cochran agreed to participate in the rock and roll movie *Go, Johnny, Go* along with many other acts of the day. Not only did this movie provide us with rare performance footage, this role reportedly prevented Cochran from accompanying Buddy Holly and Richie Valens on the fateful tour that ended in their tragic plane crash on February 3, 1959. Later that same month Cochran recorded "Three Stars" as a tribute to his lost friends.

Along with contemporary artists such as Gene Vincent, Cochran's career gravitated to Europe in the late 1950s, as the new teen idols began to dominate the airwaves in the United States. Legend has it, three young fans named John, Paul and George attended Cochran's March 14, 1960 show at the Liverpool Empire—just a month before his untimely death. In May of that year an album of his hits was posthumously released. A second album followed in January of 1962. Cochran's influence, particularly on British youth, was ultimately acknowledged when bands like The Who, the Rolling Stones, and The Sex Pistols all made successful cover versions of Cochran hits.

Although his career was cut short, Eddie Cochran's legacy as a musician remains strong. On January 21, 1987, Mick Jones was honored to induct Cochran into the Rock and Roll Hall of Fame. He will be remembered by most for his biggest singles "Summertime Blues" (1958) and "C'mon Everybody" (1959), as well as his devotion to his big orange Gretsch guitar.

Eddie Cochran. *Photo Courtesy of Michael Ochs Archive/Getty Images.*

Duane Eddy (b. 1938) is probably the single most successful instrumentalist of the rock and roll era. He first picked up a guitar at the age of five. At 16 he began performing around Phoenix, Arizona, where his family lived. It was during this period that he met Al Casey, whose collaboration provided Eddy the opportunity to develop a unique stylistic approach to the guitar. In September 1957, Duane purchased a Chet Atkins 6120 hollowbody guitar (#25827) at Ziggies Accordion and Guitar Studio in Phoenix. Subsequently, he and aspiring producer Lee Hazelwood produced a series of pop hits, including "Rebel Rouser" (1958) and "Peter Gunn" (1960), by employing a technique of selecting melodies with bass colored guitar parts and exploiting advanced recording devices like echo and tape delay. This combination allowed Eddy to achieve a raw, signature twangy sound when using the Bigsby vibrato, which was stock equipment on his cherished 1957 Gretsch 6120 model guitar. His 1959 debut album was appropriately named *Have 'Twangy' Guitar—Will Travel* and is considered a landmark achievement in rock and roll. With no fewer than five instrumental hits, the album was on the charts for 82 weeks, peaking at number five. This album was also unique because it was one of the first to be released in the newly developed stereo mode.

Eddy charted fifteen top 40 hits between 1958 and 1963. His lasting influence can be detected in much of the popular music of the following decade. Eddy continued to record through the 1960s and 1970s, but like many pop stars, he was over-shadowed by the British invasion and was apparently unable to bridge his sound to the next generation.

Then, 25 years later, in the mid 1980s, Eddy worked on a remake of his former hit "Peter Gunn" with the British band Art of Noise. The release achieved a top 10 hit in the UK and won a Grammy for best rock instrumental (1986). Eddy then embarked on a comeback album in 1987, recruiting some friends to record with, including Ry Cooder, John Fogerty, and George Harrison. Today, over 25 studio albums later, Duane Eddy remains popular with his fan base and continues to perform. His music has also been featured in a wide variety of films including *Forrest Gump*, *Natural Born Killers*, *Broken Arrow*, and *Scream 2*. Eddy was inducted into the Rock and Roll Hall of Fame in 1994 and the Musicians Hall of Fame in 2008.

The Power of Celebrity Endorsement

Did Cochran and Eddy play the Gretsch 6120 model because it was associated with the famous Chet Atkins? Or was it because this model's features and appearance were ideal for their music, image, and/or playing style? We may never really know. It does seem clear, however, that Gretsch was banking on increased sales as a result of Atkins' celebrity endorsement and association—and it still does today. It is interesting that they failed to duplicate the success they enjoyed with the Chet Atkins 6120 hollowbody and, in fact, did not really seem to try. There was an ill-fated attempt to market a Burl Ives, acoustic flat top guitar a year or two before Gretsch signed Atkins up. Beyond that, there were only two other examples of Gretsch creating a relationship with, and signature model guitar for, a notable artist of the day.

Duane Eddy. *Photo Courtesy of Central Press/Hulton Archive/Getty Images.*

Sal Salvador (1928-1999) was a young New Yorker, who honed his jazz chops with the likes of Johnny Smith, Mundell Lowe, and Tal Farow. His professional career got going in the 1940s and by the 1950s he had traded a life on the road for studio work. By mid-decade he was recording with his own quartet. Legendary for his versatility, Salvador was a master of comping and rhythm guitar, but he also built his reputation for single note solo work, which became a trademark of his long career.

In 1955, Gretsch added the Convertible (model 6199), a 17" electric archtop, to their line. This guitar was unique because its single DeArmond Dynasonic pickup and control knobs were mounted on the elongated pickguard, presumably to limit their influence on the resonance of the guitar's spruce top.

This was an elegant instrument aimed at the jazz crowd that featured bound f-holes and gold-plated hardware. Early examples had hump block fretboard markers, while later examples had the neoclassical markers (from the 1958 model year). The standard finish was a two-tone Lotus Ivory with Copper Mist back and sides, but Gretsch also produced a shaded (sunburst) finish as a special order. In 1959 the model name was officially changed to the Sal Salvador model, as he was notorious for having played his Convertible for several years prior. The last of these models was produced in 1967. It is unclear how many total Convertible/Salvador guitars were produced over its life span, but they are not very common in today's vintage market.

The work of the great Eddie Lang inspired **George Van Eps** (1913-1998) to pursue the guitar. Through the 1930s Eps worked with several band ensembles including a stint with Benny Goodman's orchestra. It was during this period that Van Eps developed an innovative chord-based lead style, which history seems to have marginalized in favor of the single string lead heroics of Django Reinhart and Charlie Christian.

In the late 1930s, Van Eps designed, and had Epiphone build for him, a seven-string guitar that possessed an additional bass string that enabled him to maintain bass lines while playing leads and chords. This technique has been likened to the finger picking style of Merle Travis and Chet Atkins. Better remembered for his session work, Van Eps made a few signature albums that showcased his unaccompanied mastery of the guitar.

Van Eps' performing career was already behind him when the Baldwin- managed Gretsch brand released the Van Eps seven-string models (model 6079 in sunburst and model 6080 in walnut brown) in 1968. This was a 17" hollowbody archtop with two dog-eared Filter'Tron humbucking pickups, three volume controls, a tone and pickup selector switch, and standby switch on the lower treble bout. Other standard Gretsch appointments were included, a "G" cutout tailpiece, a Lucite Gretsch pickguard, neoclassic markers, and a zero fret on an ebony fretboard. This guitar featured a distinctive asymmetrical headstock with a special engraved nameplate and a four and three tuner configuration to accommodate the seven strings. The Jimmie Webster-conceived tuning fork bridge was also standard. Six-string variations of the Van Eps model were also available (model 6081 in sunburst and model 6082 in walnut brown), and retailed for $100 less than their seven-string counterparts.

The Van Eps models were produced in relatively small numbers until 1972, and after that, only as a special order. This was apparently the Baldwin Company's sole attempt at exploiting a signature model guitar for someone other than Atkins. Consistent with many of Baldwin's ill-advised decisions, they had selected one of the least outwardly charismatic artists around to be the face of their product.

Both Salvador and Van Eps were elite guitarists, and loyal endorsers. Unfortunately, their respective success was too narrowly focused and did not relate to the masses. Popular music had moved away from jazz and orchestra swing to rock and roll. In what might be considered a missed opportunity, Gretsch seemed to overlook the influence that Bo Diddley might have provided as an endorser.

In the late 1950s, Diddley was conspicuously playing a red Gretsch Jet Firebird solidbody (model 6131), which appeared with him on the *Go Bo Diddley* album cover in 1959. There was also an obvious degree of collaboration, when in 1958, Gretsch made Diddley several custom solidbody prototypes including the Jupiter and the now famous rectangular bodied "Big B" guitar. But it was not until 40 years later, with the release of a lower-end version of the rectangular solidbody that Diddley made famous, that Gretsch capitalized on Diddley's status as a founding father of the rock and roll sound and music icon. Subsequently, in 2005, there was another collaboration between Gretsch, Diddley, and Billy Gibbons on the "Billy-Bo" Jupiter Thunderbird production model G6199.

Perhaps the late 1950s were just not an era when an African American artist could be considered for such an arrangement. The Gretsch marketing machine might have benefited from having an innovator of the rock and roll genre promote their solidbody products in an official capacity. Then again, Gretsch eventually went on to prove that they did not necessarily need to have an official endorsement deal to reap the benefit of a celebrity association.

It was just a few years later, in the mid-1960s, when a happy accident occurred that benefited Gretsch enormously. It was one of the more tangible examples of the power of pop music and its ability to impact the marketplace. With absolutely no effort on the company's part, Gretsch enjoyed an unofficial endorsement that resulted in sales of thousands of Gretsch guitars, even despite the musician's lack of any official ties with the company. It is for this reason that most accept the fact that next to Chet Atkins, The Beatles' George Harrison is responsible for more sales of Gretsch guitars than anyone else.

Harrison played a 1957 model year Duo Jet solidbody (#21179) in the early Beatles period and then a 1962 model year 6122 Country Gentleman, identified by its dual dial-up mute control knobs. This guitar was replaced by a 1963 model year Country Gentleman (with lever mute control), late in that same calendar year. Rounding out his Gretsch stable was a 1963 model year Tennessean, which was featured at the famous Shea Stadium concert in 1965. It has been rumored that Jimmie Webster was hoping to approach Harrison with a formal collaboration proposal, but apparently that opportunity never materialized. In 1962, however, Gretsch went as far as to make Harrison a prototype of a 12-string guitar, with the intention of it being a George Harrison signature model. This interesting one-off guitar is pictured in Andy Babiuk's book, *Beatles Gear*. It shows a 16" single-cutaway hollowbody archtop with bound f-holes. It is plausible that this was made with a 6120 body, as its serial number places its production right around the time of the first Electrotone 6120 batch. The guitar had a black finish with two SuperTron pickups, a "G" cutout tailpiece, and neoclassic markers on a wide fretboard with a zero fret. It also possessed a tone switch, a standby switch, and a large silver headstock plaque identifying it as "The George Harrison Model." Unfortunately, Harrison was not enamored with the guitar and gave it away it to fellow musician, John St. John, sometime around 1964.

Despite the lack of any contractual endorsement relationship, the Harrison influence created such a demand for Gretsch instruments that by the mid-1960s the Gretsch manufacturing plant was producing in excess of 12,000 guitar units annually. It was still not able to keep up with the demand—presumably, a good problem to have.

"Can't Buy Me Love." In this case Gretsch did not have to "buy" the love that their Chet Atkins electric archtop line was soon to receive as a result of George Harrison's high-profile use of them. Although forever associated with the Country Gentleman and Tennessean model guitars from the mid-1960s, in later years Harrison could be found playing his 1957 model year Chet Atkins 6120. *Photo Courtesy of Dave Hogan/ Hulton Archive/Getty Images.*

Section IV

Chapter
20

Music and Culture in the 1960s and '70s

The 1960s ushered in a new reality in the United States. The innocence of the 1950s gave way to feelings of disillusionment. The assassination of public officials, civil rights frustration, and war fostered a tension that began to polarize American youth. The mid-1960s was the Age of Aquarius and the Hippie movement was preaching peace and love. Many youth associated with this counterculture and were turning on, tuning in, and dropping out into a cloud of recreational drug use.

Instrumental music, driven by electric guitars, emerged as the teen-idol rock and roll of the 1950s died at the turn of the decade. No more apparent was this handoff than in 1960, when The Ventures released "Walk, Don't Run" as a fuller and more up-tempo sound than Duane Eddy's rockabilly-styled original. The Ventures were a harbinger of another trend because they promoted the Fender solidbody guitar and bass products almost exclusively. Other instrumental performers emerged from rockabilly influences, including surf rocker Dick Dale, who was also a disciple of Fender solidbody guitars. It was at this same time in history that the phenomenon of the garage band was born, motivating many amateur musicians to seek out electric instruments and make some noise.

On the East Coast the folk music revival was gaining momentum as a result of growing social unrest. Unfortunately for Gretsch the guitars that became the voice for the social and political causes of the day tended to be flat top acoustic models, a historically weak seller within the Gretsch product offering. Instead it was Martin guitars that Joan Baez and Bob Dylan were changing the world with. These influences, in conjunction with the relatively inexpensive cost of flat top acoustic models and their portability, motivated thousands of people to pursue the instrument. In his book, *Guitar, An American Life*, Tim Brookes describes the impact of the acoustic guitar on that time, asserting, "It was the guitar's finest hour."

By the mid-1960s guitar manufacturers were enjoying a new precedent of consumer popularity for their products. In his 1999 article in *20th Century Guitar*, Greg Gagliano reported that 700,000 guitars were sold in the United States in 1963. Then the boom began, coinciding with what was the beginning of the British Invasion. In 1964 the domestic annual sales of guitars jumped to 1.1 million then 1.5 million in 1965. By 1966 the trend began to level out and sales for that year were reported as being in the 1.4 million range. Gagliano also points out that almost half of those guitars were imports that year, signaling the beginning of another trend—overseas competition.

Sometime after the middle of the 1960s, rock and roll became less about creating music to dance to and more about creating music to listen to. Volumes were maximized and effects like vibrato, string bending, reverb, and sustain were distorted, generating walls of sonic energy. New sounds were being introduced to the guitar player's vernacular like "fuzz" and "wah." This new environment became the territory of the solidbody (Les Paul, Stratocaster, and Telecaster) and semi-hollowbody (Gibson ES-335 series) guitar formats. It is a bit ironic that in this age of feedback, the Gretsch hollowbody models of the 1950s, notorious for this attribute, were largely rejected by mainstream pop musicians. Instead they preferred guitars that had to be cajoled into producing this sonic disruption. By 1965, even Bob Dylan had gone electric.

As the decade of the 1960s wound down, the sound turned ominous. As music tends to reflect the times, it seems that frustration with the Kennedy and King assassinations and the war in Vietnam created an environment for music that was less about love and peace and more about primal energy.

The first of two new genres of music emerged from this chaotic time. Heavy metal introduced walls of dark sound, conjuring up mythical images and a vibe that made parents very nervous. Bands like Led Zeppelin and Black Sabbath surfaced out of England at the turn of the decade to popularize this new sound. They relied on blues based riffs, volume, and distortion from solid bodied guitars to drive their respective styles. Then, in the mid-1970s, punk rock, embodied by bands like the Sex Pistols in the UK and The Ramones in New York, channeled the voice of disenfranchised youth, expressing the irreverence and recklessness that a certain element found attractive at the time.

In the second half of the 1970s dance music was suddenly back *en vogue*, but it was not just on Lawrence Welk. Although RCA had invented the first musical synthesizer back in 1953, it did not become a threat to guitar-driven popular music until the late 1970s onslaught of disco.

Reinterpretation of the Chet Atkins Model 6120 (1962)

By the end of 1961, after seven years in production, the Gretsch 6120 was still a single-cutaway, dual-pickup, orange-stained hollowbody guitar. However, other than its basic shape and identifying color, not a single feature had evaded transformation since its inception in 1954. Over those seven years the 6120 model absorbed a constant barrage of modification. Amazingly, throughout this manipulation, it remained distinctive and one of the most identifiable guitars in the industry.

Stepping back and understanding all the various feature evolutions that the 6120 underwent in its first stage of life, it is not unreasonable to think the company had simply run its course with the old format. It was the early 1960s and the world was experiencing great change. Likewise, Gretsch was ready to overhaul the 6120 model and it apparently was not afraid to do it in a big way. It has been a commonly held assumption that the new 6120 aesthetic was motivated by Gretsch's habit of following Gibson innovations—in this case their highly successful ES-335 and Thinline series. There was, however, an equally compelling motivation for pursuing this new direction and that was the influence of Chet Atkins himself. Atkins felt that the sealed-top Country Gentleman model had a superior body design and he wanted his 6120 model name-sake to enjoy the same advantage. Regardless of motives, Gretsch endeavored to take the 6120 model in a completely different direction to maintain the guitar's relevance in the ever changing and competitive environment of the day. What followed was the most rigorous redesign that the 6120 model had experienced to date. It would be a complete reinterpretation of the physical structure of the Gretsch 6120 electric archtop guitar.

This decision to radically alter the 6120 model was fore-shadowed by the company's introduction of the Electrotone body design to the Tennessean (model 6119) in early 1961. Interestingly, there was no evidence of this departure in the 1961 catalog, which still depicted the 6119 as a true archtop with single (bridge) pickup and open f-holes. The reality, however, was that very early that year this model was being produced with the new-for-1961, sealed-top, single-cutaway body with two HiLo'Tron pickups, painted-on faux f-holes, and serial number stamped into the tip of the headstock. Incidentally, upgrading this Tennessean to a dual-pickup format left only the Anniversary (models 6124 and 6125) and the Clipper (model 6186) as single pickup options in the Gretsch electric archtop line, which relegated the single pickup configuration to budget-level guitars.

Note the 1962 model year dial-up-style mute control knob, featuring the same "G" indent knob as its neighboring volume controls. *Guitar Courtesy of Chris Guido. Photo by Rick Burda.*

A 1962 model year 6120 example from the #452xx batch. *Photo Courtesy of Teddy Rasch.*

So it was that this Electrotone concept was also destined for the 6120 model. It seems reasonable to surmise that the genesis of this feature, a sealed-top archtop, was originally inspired by the 1955 red single-cutaway prototype that Atkins relied on so often for recording. Like that early sealed-top prototype, the key sonic advantage this new design offered was that the lack of open sound holes decreased the amount of feedback that historically afflicted hollowbody instruments.

For some fans of the Gretsch 6120 model, this particular evolutionary tangent might be construed as too drastic an alteration, an affront on the spirit of the original 2.75" deep hollowbody from 1955. However, an objective analysis of the Chet Atkins 6120 model's seven year development suggests that the incremental thinning of the body, which first occurred in model year 1960 (2.5") and again in 1961 (2.25"), in addition to the ongoing modifications to the internal trestle bracing system first introduced in 1957(1958 model year), did not leave much more room to refine the traditional hollowbody format. So, sealing the top, removing the trestles, and taking the body down to a solidbody-like depth seemed like a logical progression.

This new Electrotone 6120 model, with its sealed-top and simulated f-holes, displayed several of the Jimmie Webster-inspired features not found on the previous single-cutaway format, including a string mute system and a snap-on back pad. The body width continued to be 15.5" across the lower bout, the depth was reduced to 2", and the scale length remained 24.5". Although this new semi-hollow, double-cutaway body created a very different visual effect from that of its forefather, the classic orange stained finish was one of the common threads from its past that allowed consumers to make the leap to recognizing it as a Chet Atkins 6120. Other characteristic features that were preserved included the neoclassic fret board markers, gold Filter'Tron pickups, gold Lucite Chet Atkins signature pickguard, "G" indent knobs, zero fret, horseshoe headstock motif, and an aluminum V-style Bigsby vibrato unit.

Under the hood the guitar also employed a new wiring harness, which used a plug and adapter mechanism to allow the Filter'Tron pickups to be removed without breaking any solder joints. Carryover functions like the mud switch and the standby switch remained in their traditional quadrants of the guitar's body. Likewise, the master volume knob remained a fixture on the treble cutaway bout.

There have always been dedicated fans of these second generation Electrotone 6120 guitars. These fans feel that the sonic capacity of these newly designed 6120s is no less accomplished than that of the single-cutaway hollowbody predecessor. However, it is a fact that many Gretsch aficionados, in retrospect, view this evolution as an ill-advised mutation and the beginning of the end for the Golden Era of Gretsch guitars.

Electrotone 6120: 1962-1966 Model Years

It is interesting to note that the 1961 *Gretsch Catalog No. 30* already depicted the double-cutaway Duo Jet and the solidbody Corvette guitar (model 6132), but still presented the 6120 model as a single-cutaway archtop. This catalog was prepared in 1961 and by then the company should have already known the double-cutaway fate of the 6120. Could this be more evidence that the Electrotone 6120 was introduced later in 1962? It is hard to tell, however, research supports the theory that no Electrotone 6120 guitars were manufactured in 1961, which would have been the traditional Gretsch approach. The redesigned 6120 made its first appearance in *Gretsch Catalog No. 31*, which is copyrighted in 1963. It describes the guitar as the "New slim 16" Electrotone Hollowbody with simulated f-holes, (and) new double-cutaway for ease of playing." The full color photo of the model on the opposite page of this catalog illustrates a 6120 with the newer mute lever control, which is period correct for the 1963 model year.

The 1960s Electrotone era Filter'Tron pickup with plug. *Photos Courtesy of Dennis Reed.*

Presumably a first batch (#452xx) specimen of the Electrotone 6120, this example is only about 600 serial numbers away from the last batch of single-cutaway 6120 guitars. It has potentiometer codes dated from the fifth week of 1962. *Guitar Courtesy of Jeff Dethlefsen. Photos by Tacuma Lampkin.* (above and opposite page)

Regardless, it would appear that sometime in the first half of 1962, a 50-unit group of 6120 guitars beginning at batch #452xx (retailing for $495), ushered in the Electrotone double-cutaway body for the Chet Atkins 6120 model. Evidence suggests that there are only four or five subsequent batches that relate to this introductory model year.

Courtesy of the Vermont Collection of Fine Guitars.

It appears that there was only one group of model 6121 solidbody guitars manufactured with the double-cutaway body format. It occurred as part of the #475xx batch of Electrotone 6120 guitars. These instruments are incredibly rare and may be the last 6121 models produced. It is likely that there were no more than 25 made. In spite of the significant evolution that their 6120 hollowbody cousins were experiencing, these solidbody examples were less influenced by the introduction of the Electrotone (double-cutaway) body and more aligned with the rest of the Jet-style solidbody models, which had converted to the double-cutaway body style by batch #420xx. Assuming that these are the sole examples of double-cutaway 6121 guitars, they too will be the only specimens of this model to posses the Chet Atkins signature-style pickguard and standby switch features. Standard attributes remained, including the zero fret, horseshoe headstock in-lay, neoclassic fretboard markers, and V-style B3 Bigsby (not depicted in this example).

The feature changes that the Electrotone double-cutaway 6120 model experienced from the debut 1962 model year to the 1966 model year are relatively subtle. Unlike the single-cutaway forerunner from the 1950s, which seemed to revel in its constantly changing appearance, these 6120 models of the 1960s maintained more visual continuity throughout the decade. In fact, after the first model year (1962) it becomes almost impossible to distinguish between 1963, 1964, and 1965 model year examples based solely on features. However, there were a couple of feature modifications along the way that are useful in dating the Electrotone 6120 guitars of this pre-Baldwin era.

String Mutes

String mutes were a dubious innovation intended to dampen the strings to varying degrees with foam pads (aka mufflers) placed near the bridge. It is unclear how popular this feature was in the 1960s, but that did not stop Gretsch from making it standard issue on thousands of Electrotone 6120 guitars.

This Electrotone 6120 (#657xx batch) was probably made in 1964, but based solely on features it is hard to say which model year it represents because the features on 1963, 1964, and 1965 model year examples were so consistent. *Guitar Courtesy of Chris Guido. Photo by Rick Burda.*

Muffler pads dampen the strings when they are engaged. *Guitar Courtesy of Jeff Dethlesfsen. Photo by Tacuma Lampkin.*

Black felt on the two-position mute lever identifies it as belonging to a post-1965 model year guitar. *Photo Courtesy of Daniel Nicolas.*

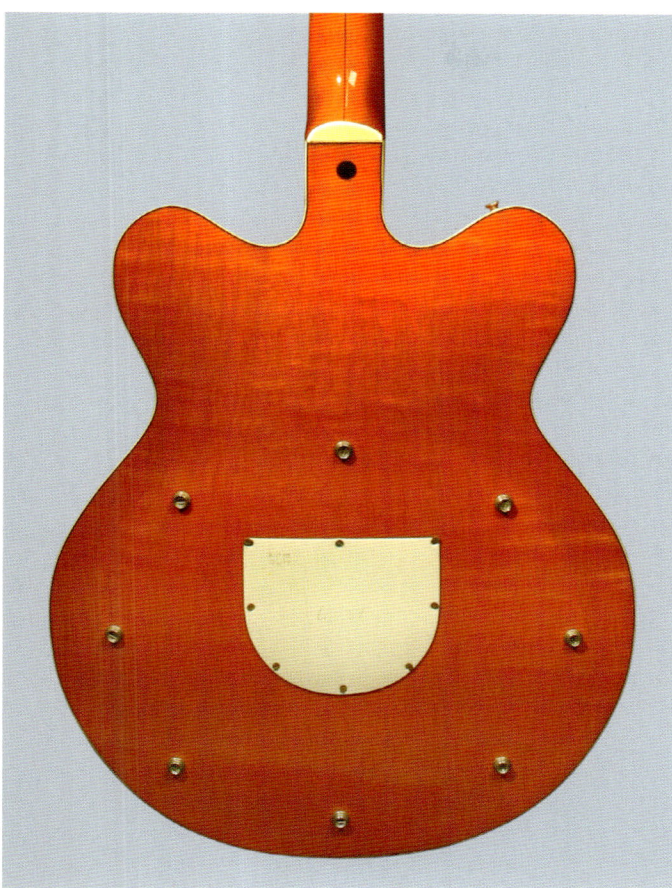

Photo Courtesy of Teddy Rasch.

red valve felts for their baritone horn model and they were the perfect solution for the guitar mute lever as well. These felts are also a key to dating Electrotone 6120 specimens. From the time the mute levers were first introduced (around batch #476xx) they were bright red in color. Then around batch #794xx (late 1965 or early 1966) the felt changed to black and stayed that way until the levers and mute systems were removed from the model in the early 1970s. Be aware that these mute lever felts are easily changed. A red felt merely provides a guideline for determining the vintage of a 6120 example as pre-1966, but is in no way definitive on its own.

Photo Courtesy of Steve Wilson.

"For added comfort and playing ease, a springy pad of foam rubber on the guitar back cushions pressure and eliminates fatigue." (1965 *Gretsch No. 32 Catalog*) The earliest back pads were made of a soft, nylon-like material with gold fluting around the edge. They tended to wear quickly and for the 1963 model year (and beyond) the factory transitioned to a tougher, simulated black leather material that was probably vinyl (Gretsch patent #D-196,609).

As a result, the new Electrotone 6120 had a secret. Behind the patented black snap-on back pad (supposedly there for comfort and to prevent belt buckle rash on the back of the instrument) there was a white plastic access door. Many assumed that this was a solution to one of the sealed-top's drawbacks, a lack of access to the guitar's electronics—traditionally enabled by open f-holes. In fact, this mysterious door was for the installation and maintenance of the mechanism that operated the string mute system. In 1971 the mute system was removed from the 6120 model, as was the access door, but the back pad remained for some time afterward.

The first generation of the double-cutaway 6120 guitars utilized a dial-up string mute control, which provided the musician a variable application of dampening. A standard "G" indent-style control knob, identical to the volume knobs, was used to engage the feature. This mute control was changed to a knurled two-position lever for the 1963 model year guitars. This makes the identification of an inaugural 1962 model year Electrotone 6120 fairly easy, as the dial-up mute control is exclusive to that period. There are at least four batches of Electrotone 6120 guitars that possessed the dial-up mute knob feature, which translated into only several hundred total guitars.

The new-for-1963 model year mute control lever had a felt disc at its base that was intended to protect the wood of the body surrounding it. Dan Duffy reports that these felt discs came from the Gretsch factory's brass instrument department. Gretsch used

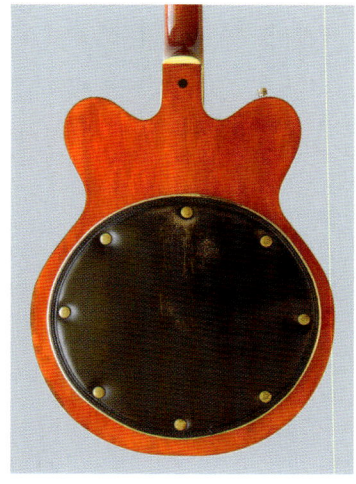

Photo Courtesy of Ian Morris.

The other change implemented in the 1963 model year 6120 Electrotone design was a more durable snap-on back pad made of a black synthetic material (probably vinyl) that simulated leather. This was an upgrade from the 1962 model year when the back pads were made of a soft (perhaps nylon) material that was prone to getting beat up from the constant friction created by contact with the musicians body.

Nashville Headstock Plaques

Early in 1966 the 6120's name was modified to the Chet Atkins Nashville, signified first by the appearance of a metal nameplate, or plaque affixed to the face of the headstock, and then soon after with the addition of the word "Nashville" to the Chet Atkins signature pickguard. The incorporation of this new name did not change the fact that these guitars were still considered to be 6120 models.

The Nashville headstock plaque is a post-1965 model year indicator. *Photo Courtesy of Daniel Nicolas.*

Photo Courtesy of Rob Hoffman, Montaine Antiques.

These headstock plaques appeared abruptly in the middle of a large 200-unit batch of 6120 guitars (sometime around #80870). This batch was the last group of 6120 guitars produced during the sequential serial numbering period, so these few examples are the only Nashville examples utilizing that system. The new plaques were also accompanied by a new finish treatment on the headstock overlay. The previously used brown was lightened, and in many cases transformed to a bright orange, which coordinated more closely with the hue of the body. For quite awhile, guitars with these headstock plaques continued to possess the traditional horseshoe inlay underneath the plaque and some owners have preferred to remove the plaque as a result, leaving four small holes around the horseshoe motif as evidence. It appears as though the Nashville pickguards were introduced a batch or two after the first headstock plaques, however, the transient nature of this feature makes it risky to emphasize it as a primary indicator of a guitar's vintage. Both the headstock plaque and Nashville pickguard endured on the 6120 model until early 1972, when the plaque was discontinued and the guard modified substantially.

Serial Numbering System

The most reliable method for dating a Gretsch guitar of this period remains the serial number. Over the years the successive feature modifications, the changes in serial numbering systems, and some periodic anomalies within the Gretsch factory have generated skepticism about the integrity of these numbers. Recent research, however, has validated the system as highly predictable and logical.

The pre-1966 sequential serial numbers were stamped into the tip of the headstock on Electrotone 6120 specimens. *Guitar Courtesy of Chris Guido. Photo by Rick Burda.*

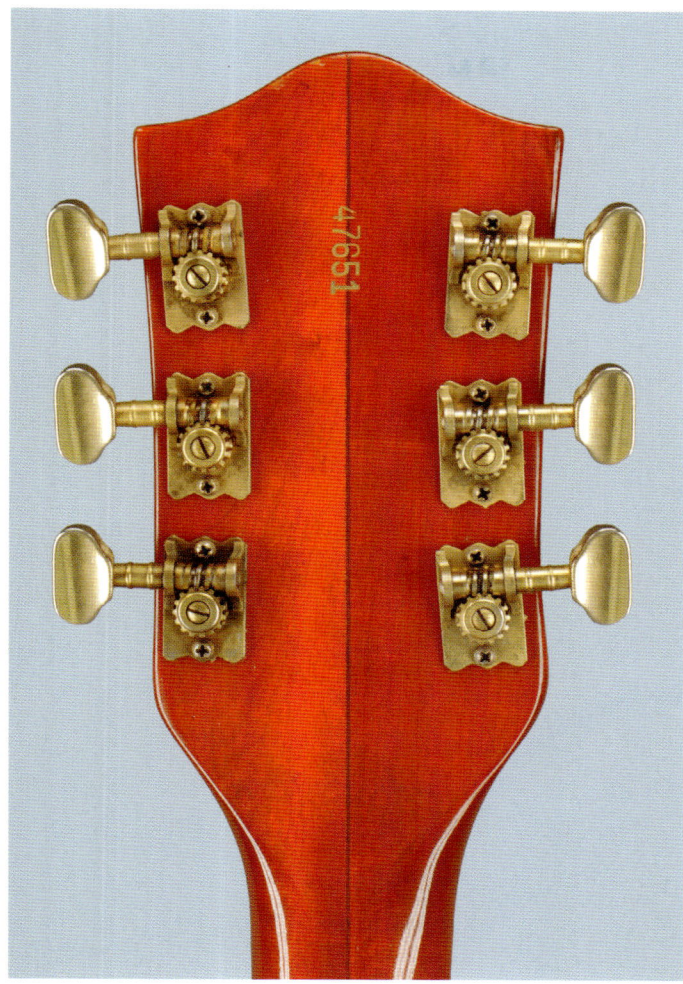

In August of 1966, the serial number system was changed to a date-coded approach and relocated to the back of the headstock. *Guitar Courtesy of Gryphon Stringed Instruments. Photo by Grant Groberg.*

Since the Electrotone's sealed body design did not conveniently accommodate labels inside the body cavity, the company began to stamp the serial numbers into the tip of the headstock on the 6120 model (1962). These stamped numbers are often difficult to read. In August of 1966, the serial numbering system changed from the sequential approach used for the better part of the previous two decades to one that was date-coded. This change coincided with the relocation of the serial number, which the factory began printing on the back of the headstock. In late June of 1967, the words "Made in the USA" were added to that same location.

In the date-coded system the first digits represent the month of production. This may be two digits if the guitar was produced in October, November, or December. The next digit would represent the last digit of the production year. This numbering was only placed on the back of the headstock from 1966 to 1973, which, fortunately, means that the year digit was never confusingly duplicated. The rest of the digits are reported to be an indicator of production volume—the number of total instruments manufactured that month. For example, serial number #871146 would correspond to the 1146th guitar made in August 1967.

Unfortunately, in some cases the date-coded serial numbers resemble the old sequential system. For instance, a 6120 example with the serial number #68152 might be perceived as being from 1964, but it could also be an example from June 1968. The key in this case is where the serial number is located on the headstock. If it is stamped into the tip of the headstock, it is a 1964 model year example. If it is found printed in gold on the back of the headstock, it is surely a specimen from 1968 and should also have the Nashville headstock plaque, Nashville pickguard, and black felt mute lever features mentioned previously.

Some Anomalies

This Nashville is a typical post-1965 specimen with the exception of its odd four-digit serial number (#1131). *Photos Courtesy of Ryan Costa.*

Every once in awhile in today's vintage market, a Nashville 6120 will surface with all the features of a post-1965 specimen (black mute lever felt, headstock plaque, and Nashville pickguard), but it will also have an odd, four-digit serial number stamped on the tip of its headstock. It appears that when the Gretsch factory changed from its sequential numbering system to the date-coded approach, there was a time gap between systems. It is theorized that these four-digit numbers were applied to several Nashville batches during this interim. These gap serial numbers can actually be found all they way into the early five-digit (10xxx) range and are also prevalent on Anniversary and Astro Jet models. For open f-holed archtops like the Anniversary, the serial numbers were still on paper labels. The labels themselves appear to be the same as the traditional orange and gray design, but the orange color on these mid-1960s versions tend to be a little more red and the slogan "That Great Gretsch Sound" has replaced the previously imprinted "Musical Instrument Makers Since 1883."

This seemingly anomalous serial number is neither sequential nor date-coded. These labels were used during the period between the two primary Gretsch serial numbering methodologies. Both this Anniversary model guitar's features and potentiometer date codes (February 1966) confirm that it was manufactured in early 1966. *Photo Courtesy of Woody White.*

The guitar is more than 40 years old, but its label is more than 50. *Photo Courtesy of Andy Anderson.*

This Nashville is a typical post-1965 specimen with the exception of its odd four-digit serial number (#1131). *Photos Courtesy of Ryan Costa.*

Then there is the mysterious lost roll of 1000 sequential serial numbers from 1957. Although it is true that the orange and gray labels were introduced at #25000, mysteriously, the last of the former blue, filigreed labels are found in the #239xx batch (Corsair model 6014), which leaves a gap of 1000 serial numbers before the 6120 batch introduced the new style at #250xx. As hard as it might be to fathom, it would appear that these 1000 labels (perhaps one roll), technically the last of the old design, were misplaced and not used for almost 10 years, leaving a void in the 1957 production sequence. Evidence of this is in the many Anniversary model examples that display mid-1960s features but carry the blue, filigreed circa 1957 labels and 24xxx serial numbers. As one of the few open f-holed

archtop hollowbodies left in the Gretsch line by the mid-1960s, the Anniversary was apparently chosen to use up the found labels. Not all the labels were physically used, but the numbers were. Other Gretsch models of the period, like the Country Gentleman, can also be found with late 24xxx serial numbers on their headstock plaques.

This phenomena has created no small amount of confusion for vintage Gretsch fans 40 years later. It is plausible that the decision to use the misplaced labels after so many years was driven by the characteristic waste-not want-not philosophy so engrained in the Gretsch factory culture. Research now suggests that the labels were reintroduced during the period when Gretsch was switching from its sequential serial numbering approach to the date-coded system. This period is admittedly convoluted, but the features (and potentiometer codes) of the guitars that carry these #24xxx serial numbers are consistent with both early 1966 production, as well as the earliest specimens with date-coded serial numbers.

Evidence to support the theory that Gretsch specimens found with either the four digit, the #10xxx, or the #24xxx serial numbers, are all in fact from the period between the time in early 1966 when the sequential system ended (sometime before #82500) and the first date-coded examples began (August of 1966), is based on the mid-1960s features found on the respective guitars. Another compelling fact is the consistently dated potentiometer codes (November 1965) that have been documented in guitars from each of these categories. This appears to substantiate the conclusion that these specimens are all of the same vintage, produced at the Gretsch factory during a relatively narrow window of time. This may also explain why so few Gretsch guitars attributed to the 1966 model year surface on the secondary market today.

Electrotone 6120 Feature Exceptions

Gretsch Chet Atkins Guitars

A great name. A great sound. Internationally famed RCA Victor recording star, Chet Atkins, and Gretsch guitar specialists created a spectacular series...

6122   6120   6119

COUNTRY GENTLEMAN
The most desired electric guitar in the world. Superb styling with its slim 17" double cutaway Electrotone Hollow Body with simulated "F" holes. Gold-plated Gretsch Bigsby Tremolo and Tailpiece. Filter 'Tron bridge pick-up and Super 'Tron 11 fingerboard pick-up. 24-karat gold-plated metal parts. Double muffler, standby switch and padded back. Rich mahogany-grained finish.
6122 Chet Atkins Country Gentleman Electric Guitar. $650.00

NASHVILLE
The guitar that set the standard of hollow body popularity. Beautifully finished in highly polished amber red, it's slim . . . 16" Electro-

tone Hollow Body, just 2" thick . . . . Easy to handle and play. Features Gretsch Filter 'Tron twin electronic heads. Built-in muffler and standby switch. Gretsch Bigsby Tremolo and Tailpiece. 24-karat gold-plated metal parts and padded back.
6120 Chet Atkins Nashville Electric Guitar. $500.00

TENNESSEAN
Distinctively styled and known for its famous Chet Atkins sound, the Tennessean has these all-time great features. New slim 16" Electrotone Hollow Body of 2" thickness with simulated inlaid "F" holes. Gretsch Bigsby Tremolo and Tailpiece. Double Hi-Lo 'Tron pick-ups and standby switch. Dark cherry red finish.
6119 Chet Atkins Tennessean Electric Guitar. $400.00

EXCLUSIVE GRETSCH FEATURES

- **BUILT-IN MUFFLER** . . . allows you to muffle your strings without using your hands.
- **STANDBY SWITCH** . . . holds your tone settings so you can turn power on and off without loss.
- **INLAID MOTHER-OF-PEARL NECK** . . . stunning Neo-Classic fingerboard with unobstructed smooth playing surface.
- **PADDED BACK** . . . adds comfort and playing ease with cushioned foam rubber back.
- **FILTER 'TRON HEADS** . . . give you pure sound by eliminating all electronic hum and distortion.
- **ELECTROTONE HOLLOW BODY** . . . advanced in design, slim and distinctive in looks, resonantly brilliant in sound.

The 1965 Gretsch guitar and amplifier catalog (No. 32) still listed the double-cutaway 6120 as the Chet Atkins hollowbody model, so this 1966 brochure would have been the first announcement of the new Nashville name.

A byproduct of the 1966 date-coded serial numbering system is the more definitive attribution of vintage for Nashville models going forward. Unlike the 1950s, for this era of guitars, fewer references are made to model year and the features that distinguish a guitar from one period to another. Instead, the date-coded serial number provides a more exact timeframe for when a particular instrument was manufactured. So, when a guitar is classified as a 1968 Nashville, it is because the serial number indicates it was made in 1968, not because it has certain features universally identified with the 1968 model year.

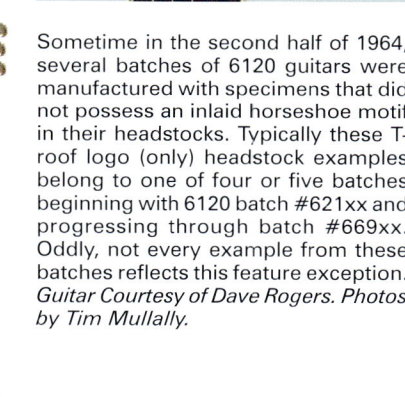

Sometime in the second half of 1964, several batches of 6120 guitars were manufactured with specimens that did not possess an inlaid horseshoe motif in their headstocks. Typically these T-roof logo (only) headstock examples belong to one of four or five batches beginning with 6120 batch #621xx and progressing through batch #669xx. Oddly, not every example from these batches reflects this feature exception. *Guitar Courtesy of Dave Rogers. Photos by Tim Mullally.*

There seems to be a number of Nashville 6120 guitars made in late 1966 that display a dark black headstock overlay. It appears that guitars produced in December 1966 possess this variation. Chet Atkins apparently acquired one of these late 1966 examples to pose with for a photograph that was used on the cover of his 1967 re-release of *A Session with Chet Atkins* (1967, RCA). This is another temporary feature adaptation—the headstock overlays of guitars from January 1967 reverted back to the bright orange stained finish. *Photos of Guitar Courtesy of Andrew W. Billek.*

There is no way to know definitively why Gretsch employed the periodic and infrequent feature exceptions we see in 1960s era 6120 specimens today. These are not considered evolutionary events that contributed to the ongoing refinement of the model, but are instead a blip on the aesthetic radar, occurring in just a few batches, then reverting back to the previous state. The motivations could be as simple as the factory needing a temporary alternative because they ran out of a certain part. To date, any attempts to distill real significance from these occasions have been dismissed as pure speculation.

This 1965 model year 6120, by way of its horseshoe headstock motif and red mute lever felt, exemplifies the short period when the Gretsch factory used HiLo'Tron-style, open-faced pickup casings on their Filter'Tron pickups. Many of these are found to be from a large 200-unit batch (#76650-76850), produced in the 1965 production/calendar year. Ironically, this would actually become a standard look for a future iteration of the model. *Guitar Courtesy of Warpdrive Music. Photo by John Sieger.*

Special Production 6120 Examples

Late in the 1962 model year, production batch #475xx had all of the standard 6120 Electrotone features, including the dial-up mute control and string dampening system. This guitar originates from that batch, however, presumably a custom order, it does not have the internal mute mechanism, the mute control, or the access door typically located behind the back pad. *Photos Courtesy of Steve Wilson.* (left and below)

As featured in the February 1989 issue of *Guitarist Magazine,* English rocker Marty Wilde owns a very unique 6120 example. Based on its serial number this guitar was produced at the very end of a documented batch (#525xx) of double-cutaway Electrotone 6120 guitars in late 1962. Inexplicably, this guitar not only maintains the previous style single-cutaway format, but has open f-holes as well. Other throwback features include large block fretboard markers and a mid-1950s control layout that omits the, by then, standard tone switch. Not a complete departure from the design of the time, this example does employ a zero fret under its custom monogrammed truss rod cover and a newer Chet Atkins signature pickguard. The gold-plated Bigsby B7 vibrato unit was not standard on 6120 guitars in any era, so it appears to be the perfect addition to this irreverent anomaly. Wilde bought this unique guitar in the early 1980s on Denmark St. in London. *Guitar Courtesy of Marty Wilde. Photo by Marc Platten.*

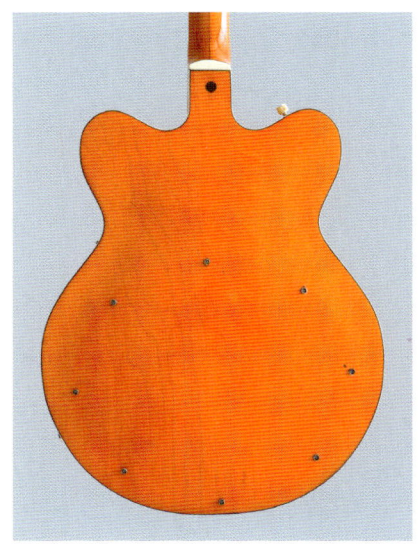

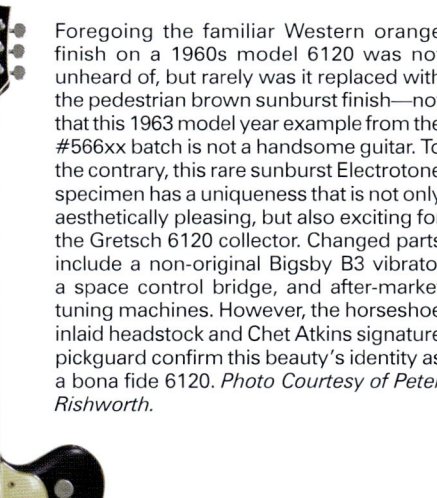

Foregoing the familiar Western orange finish on a 1960s model 6120 was not unheard of, but rarely was it replaced with the pedestrian brown sunburst finish—not that this 1963 model year example from the #566xx batch is not a handsome guitar. To the contrary, this rare sunburst Electrotone specimen has a uniqueness that is not only aesthetically pleasing, but also exciting for the Gretsch 6120 collector. Changed parts include a non-original Bigsby B3 vibrato, a space control bridge, and after-market tuning machines. However, the horseshoe inlaid headstock and Chet Atkins signature pickguard confirm this beauty's identity as a bona fide 6120. *Photo Courtesy of Peter Rishworth.*

Gretsch, like most American guitar manufacturers, made periodic customized examples of their more popular models. They would do almost anything, for a price. This was a way for musicians with special requests to get the features they desired or create a novel or unique visual effect by ordering a custom colored finish. Because the premium required was presumably not insignificant, these custom orders tended to be rare. This rarity can translate into value decades later in the vintage guitar marketplace, however, when an atypical example surfaces, it is important to verify its authenticity. In the case of simple hardware features, or custom finishes, it is easy enough for these modifications to be made after-market. These changes can be very difficult to verify as factory originals. Here are a few examples that have been scrutinized by many a Gretsch-pert.

Guitar Courtesy of Chris Guido.
Photo by Rick Burda.

Guitar Courtesy of Chris Guido. Photo by Rick Burda.

Resembling a 1964 model year Tennessean rather than the other 6120 guitars from its batch (#6C3xx), this custom-finished guitar breaks all the rules of the day. The deep walnut finish is only the beginning of these departures, as it has a 2.5" deep, proper hollowbody torso complete with bound, open f-holes. It lacks the mute apparatus, accompanying mufflers, and control lever of the standard Electrotone design of the period. It boasts a gold-plated V-style Bigsby vibrato and bar bridge, and a gray and orange label inside its trestle-less body cavity that confirms its identity with an authentic 6120 model stamp. Lastly, the figured maple headstock overlay with its horseshoe motif and Gretsch T-roof inlaid logo contrasts nicely with its jet-black translucent background.

Features that are consistent with the other, more typical, Electrotone 6120 examples from the batch include neoclassic markers on an ebony fretboard, dual-gold-plated Filter'Tron pickups with sculpted surrounds, a tone switch, a standby switch, zero fret, "G" indent control knobs, and a gold Chet Atkins signature pickguard.

The origins of this one-off guitar are unknown. Whoever instigated its creation was presumably not a fan of the direction that Gretsch had taken the 6120 model. Since a pre-1961 model year single-cutaway

6120 example would have been viewed as simply a used guitar back in 1964 (prior to the vintage guitar craze), the owner presumably opted for a brand new guitar, just built to a previous model year's specifications.

There are always skeptics when it comes to the authentication of a custom made guitar like this one. In this case they might suggest that the 2.5" depth simply makes this guitar a 1960 model year sent back to the factory for refinish and re-label. If that were the case, however, the body should have trestle bracing, which it does not. In addition, a 1960 model year would not have a standby switch, which was introduced in 1961, as was the signature pickguard.

This guitar's signature guard lacks the scalloped radius typical of the 1961 model year examples and is consistent with the pickguard shape on its contemporary Electrotone examples from the #603xx batch. It is plausible that these elements could have been added, along with the gold plating on the V-style Bigsby vibrato, as part of a factory refurbishment. But the fact that the guitar's label reflects a very early serial number from a documented batch of 1964 Electrotone 6120 guitars is a quandary, or at least a coincidence, as there would appear to be no reason for the factory to associate it with such a batch.

Sometimes light can play tricks on the eyes, but not in this case. This is a walnut brown 6120 example produced in 1965 (#703xx). This color option has been documented on several Electrotone 6120 examples and is accepted as a factory original custom color. *Courtesy of the Bachman Gretsch Collection.*

For many Gretsch enthusiasts it is hard to conceive of a 6120 model guitar that is not orange. However, there were some musicians who apparently preferred a more understated aesthetic for their guitar and were prepared to pay extra for it. Here we see a rare bird indeed. Produced in December 1966, this Gretsch Nashville displays all the standard features of that period with the exception of its gorgeous black finish. *Guitar Courtesy of Warpdrive Music. Photo by John Sieger.*

Yet another apparent anomaly found amongst a batch of factory standard Electrotone 6120 guitars, this unique example is purported to be from 1965. This mystery single-cutaway, open f-hole 6120 has been the focus of great debate within the vintage Gretsch community. Its standard Nashville 6120 features include dual-Filter'Tron pickups, sculpted pickup surrounds, V-style Bigsby, bar bridge, standby switch, tone switch, and zero fret. For some this guitar is openly accepted as being produced in 1965 based solely on its serial number (#80914) and the conventional wisdom of Gretsch chronology.

Its serial number not withstanding, this guitar's single-cutaway body makes it a throwback to an earlier generation of 6120 models. Furthermore, it possesses a shallow neck heel and dowel in the cutaway. This was unique to the 1961 model year for 6120 guitars, the last of the ultra-thin (2.25") single-cutaway bodies. Consistent with its deviation from the regular Nashville of the day, the neoclassic markers are on a bound rosewood fretboard instead of ebony. The Chet Atkins signature pickguard just is not quite right either, with its oddly styled T-roof logo. The signature may look a bit out of position as well, but other, more traditional 6120 examples from this batch show it in the same position. Perhaps this was in preparation for the pending "Nashville" designation that was included just under the signature on pickguards of subsequent batches.

The introduction of gold-plated headstock plaques in this batch was fortunate—this example's plaque is a key to verifying the guitar's identity as a Chet Atkins Nashville Model. Possessing what is clearly a red stain finish, rather than the traditional Gretsch orange, this specimen risks being misconstrued as anything but a Nashville 6120. Finally this example lacks the, by then mandatory, mute system synonymous with Electrotone 6120 guitars from the 1960s.

Clearly not associated with any model year, based on its unusual features, it would seem this unique Nashville 6120 example's vintage is more appropriately determined by its calendar year production. A revealing fact about this guitar is that its potentiometer date codes (137 65 47) translate to mid-November 1965. More standard Nashville 6120 double-cutaway Electrotone examples from this #809xx batch have yielded the same potentiometer date codes, as have 6120 specimens from several previous batches. This gives some plausibility to the idea that this entire batch—not just this red hollowbody example—was produced very late in 1965. It is probably even more reasonable to suggest that these, the last sequentially numbered 6120 guitars (batch #809xx), as well as all of the following Gretsch batches leading up to the transition to date-coded serial numbering, were manufactured in early 1966.

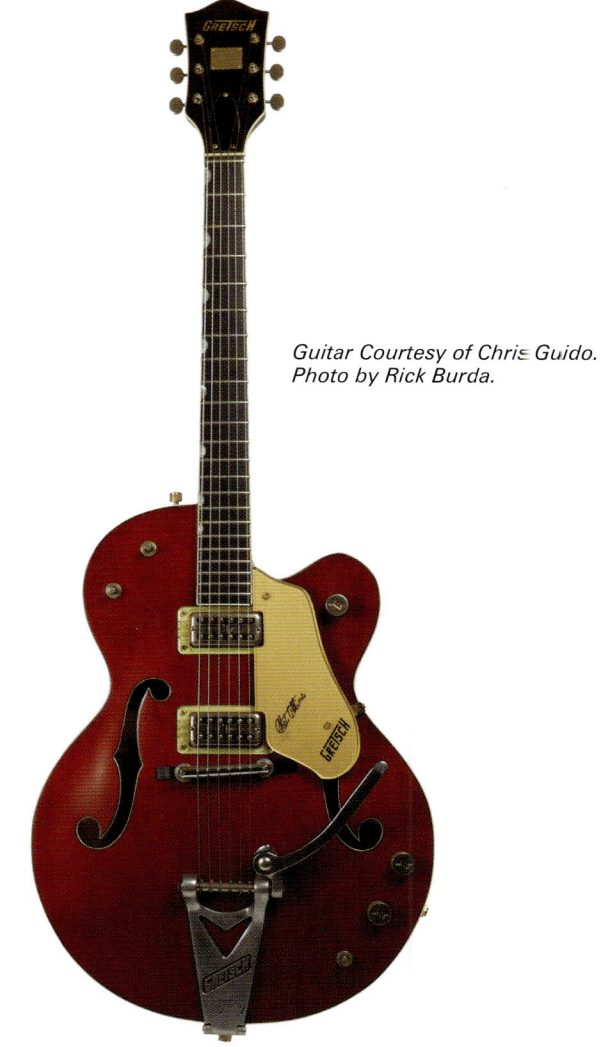

*Guitar Courtesy of Chris Guido.
Photo by Rick Burda.*

Once again, there are also those who strongly feel that this guitar is nothing more than a 1961 model year 6120 that went back to the Gretsch factory for a major refurbishment and repair in late 1965 or early 1966. This camp believes that with the extreme modifications this guitar may have received, including the red refinish, rewiring of electronics, and addition of Nashville nuances, the instrument also received a new label and serial number for future tracking purposes. The fact that this guitar does have the trestle bracing and does not have the mute system that was integral to all double-cutaway Electrotone bodied 6120 and Nashville guitars of the mid-1960s, convinces some that this is the most practical explanation.

Regardless of its genesis, it seems that Gretsch produced an eccentric custom ordered instrument for a discriminating customer, who just had to have something unique or specific and was willing to pay for it.

Nashville 6120: The Baldwin Years (1967-1980)

In 1967, Fred Gretsch Jr. made the fateful decision to sell the Gretsch guitar brand to the Baldwin Piano Company, which was looking to diversify its portfolio of musical instrument brands. Still reaping the market share benefits from the unofficial association with George Harrison, sales were good, so financially it was the right time to sell. This decision, however, alienated many of the long-time Gretsch employees, including Jimmie Webster, who distanced himself from the brand not long after the Baldwin buyout.

I was very disappointed. In Brooklyn my uncle told me he'd sold the business and I told him I wanted to buy it and he said, "Well, Baldwin had cash. So they bought it."

-Fred W. Gretsch

In late June 1967, the factory began to add the words "Made in USA" to the back of the Nashville headstock, adjacent to the serial number. Soon after, in early July, the previously ubiquitous chrome over brass "G" indent control knobs were changed to a brushed aluminum style with fluted sides and a black screen-printed "G" arrow motif on the top. Then, in August, the factory officially changed the tuning machines on Nashville 6120 guitars from the long employed open back oval-shaped Waverly design to the Van Ghent style, which had flat-edged buttons.

An August 1967 Nashville shows the tell-tale black felt on its mute lever, a Nashville signature pickguard, headstock plaque, and Van Ghent tuning machines. *Guitar Courtesy of Warren Harvey Bennett. Photo by Peter Journeaux.*

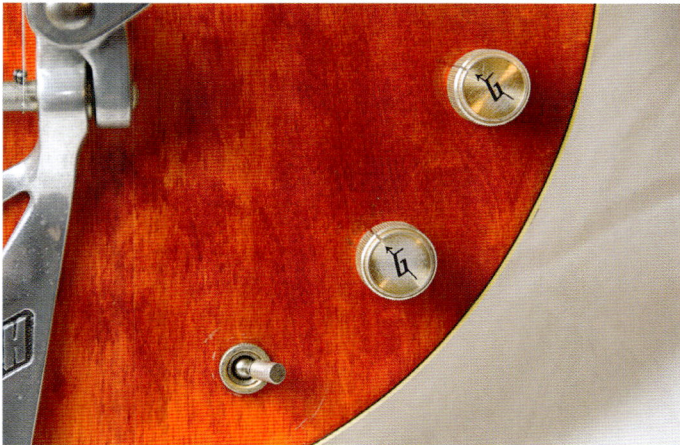

Second generation (aluminum) control knob design introduced in early July 1967. *Photo Courtesy of Ian Morris.*

Made in February 1967, this black beauty has had a few modifications since then, including a new tone selector switch, a gold Bigsby aluminum bridge, and what appears to be a rare double-sided fretboard with inlaid neoclassic markers on each side. These fretboards can also be found on left-handed Gretsch examples, as well as the mid-1960s Monkees model (6123). *Guitar Courtesy of Warpdrive Music. Photo by John Sieger.*

Evident on specimens produced as early as the spring of 1969, these enclosed-style tuners were utilized on all subsequent batches of the Nashville 6120 model. *Photo Courtesy of Ian Morris.*

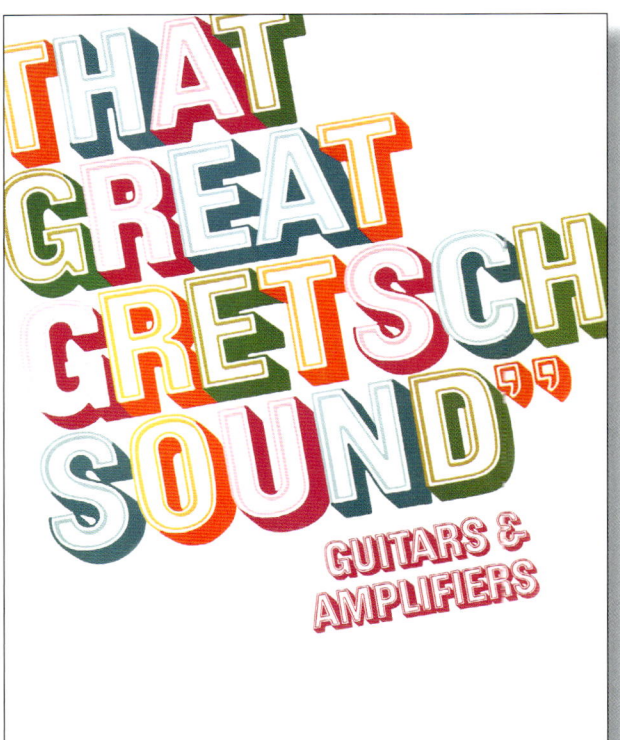

CATALOG NO. 33

That Great Gretsch Sound catalog (#33, 1968). An accompanying pricelist (April 1, 1968) announced the Nashville model's $500 MSRP.

That Great Gretsch Sound catalog (#33, 1968) presented the Nashville with the same basic specifications, still characterizing the signature color of the model as "amber red." Today, 6120 specimens can be found from throughout the Electrotone era that vary significantly in the color and transparency of their orange-stained finishes. Some variability is to be expected as guitars are subjected to differing degrees of exposure over 40 years time. These finishes can range from an almost golden tone through a wide palette of orange shades that can even border on a reddish appearance. Some examples are quite transparent and reveal the natural grain of the underlying wood, while others display a decidedly opaque finish that can sometimes resemble a bright pumpkin. As distinctive as the Western orange finish is to the 6120 model, there are examples of double-cutaway specimens where custom finishes have been applied, including black, walnut brown, standard brown sunburst, and even the rumored cherry red stain.

The March 1, 1969 Gretsch guitar pricelist shows the Nashville 6120 retailing for $550. At this point it is apparent that the model had become more of a mid-range instrument within the Gretsch line. Not only was it priced $100 less than the Country Gentleman (model 6122), it was also significantly less expensive than the $700 Viking (model 6187), and exactly half the price of the Stereo White Falcon from that period.

In 1970 Gretsch's guitar manufacturing facility relocated from the Brooklyn plant to Booneville, Arkansas, and in 1972, the New York offices moved to Chicago. By this time, most of the Gretsch models had been relegated to "also ran" status by many of America's youth, who favored the Fender Stratocasters and Gibson Les Paul models their guitar gods wielded in the late 1960s.

Gretsch Nashville 6120 model from December 1971. *Photo Courtesy of Ian Morris.*

A subtle, late 1971 adjustment that carried through to the 1972 Nashville production was the addition of the word "The" to the headstock plaque. *Photo Courtesy of Ian Morris.*

Falcon-lite? It may not have all the glitz and gadgets of its White Falcon cousin, but this unique Nashville 6120 example made in November 1971 looks awfully elegant in white, black, and gold. The presence of open f-holes supports the possibility that this was a custom ordered guitar from the ground up. It is an indisputably sexy instrument. *Guitar Courtesy of Warren Harvey Bennett. Photos by Peter Journeaux.*

The first sign that the Nashville 6120 was once again going to evolve into something new was in January of 1971, when two feature evolutions occurred. The first was merely an aesthetic change to the color of the headstock overlay. Previously the gold Nashville name plaque sat against an orange-stained headstock that coordinated with the rest of the guitar's finish. The 1971 models adopted a dark brown tone on the face of the headstock, which provided more contrast with the plaque. The second, and more dramatic modification was the discontinuation of the notorious string mute system, standard on all Electrotone era Nashville 6120 models throughout the previous decade. Coinciding with the mute system's departure was the disappearance of the access door behind the back pad. As fundamental as the string mute feature was to the double-cutaway Nashville 6120's identity, it was just the beginning of a greater metamorphosis to come.

A slight modification to the date-coded serial number was introduced in January 1972. A blank space was added between numbers—the digits to the left of the space represented the month of production and the first digit to the right of the space identified the year designation. The remaining digits continued to indicate production volume. For example, a guitar marked with serial number #1 2126 would be the 126th guitar made in January 1972.

This last version Nashville 6120 from January 1972 displays all the appropriate features of the model year, including the omission of the mute system, which also did away with the access door behind the back pad. *Photos Courtesy of Derek See.*

Sometime in early 1972, the last of the orange-finished, sealed-top Electrotone body Nashvilles were produced and the 6120 model designation was officially discontinued. This represented a bold departure by Baldwin, abandoning what had been such a mainstay icon of the Gretsch brand. By May 1972 the Chet Atkins Nashville, which maintained its identity in name only, had been re-invented into something very different, yet again.

It is difficult to estimate how many units of Electrotone 6120 and Nashville model guitars were produced in the decade after the demise of the single-cutaway 6120 hollowbody. The factory began producing smaller batches in the late 1960s. However, compared to the 6120 hollowbody these Electrotone 6120 models were produced over a longer period of time, when the Gretsch factory was increasing its annual output. This would suggest a significantly greater number of these 6120s were produced. The high volume of Electrotone 6120 guitars on today's vintage market reinforces this assumption. It might not be unreasonable to guess that there could have been as many as 10,000 Electrotone 6120s manufactured.

Nashville Model 7660 (1972)

In late spring 1972, a significantly evolved form of the Gretsch Chet Atkins Nashville guitar emerged, model 7660. Abandoned were features like the distinctive orange finish, string mute system, back pad, and the sealed top. This generation of 16" wide by 2.75" deep guitars was barely recognizable to its forerunner; displaying a burgundy red finish, open f-holes, and a headstock that lacked a name plaque, as well as the traditional truss rod adjustment and cover. The scale length of this new creation was still 24.5", but the neck now joined the body at the 18th fret instead of the 14th. Also at this time, the new Baldwin era squared-off pickguard was introduced, still bearing the Chet Atkins signature and Nashville model designation, but lacking the previously ubiquitous Gretsch T-roof logo. The aforementioned truss rod adjustment (Burns inspired gear box) now resided in the back of the guitar, concealed by a black triangular plate located just under the neck heel. Although still referred to as Filter'Trons, the 1972 Gretsch humbucker pickup more closely resembled HiLo'Trons, with their open case, black bobbin face, and metal surround ring. Initially, and for the first two years of production, the serial number was still stamped on the back of the headstock along with "Made in USA." The August 1972 Gretsch price sheet still listed the Nashville as amber red, retailing for $595.

In 1973 the Nashville model 7660s stamped serial numbers sometimes included a space between the month designation and the other numbers and sometimes it did not. It seems that as the year wore on and the serial numbers got longer they simply eliminated the space. Sometime in 1974, paper labels containing both the model number and serial number were reintroduced inside the body of the guitar. Most serial numbers from this period, which were hand-applied, have a hyphen between the month and year. Some examples, however, have surfaced with modified paper labels that have a machine-stamped serial number that lacks the space and the hyphen. These narrow labels have an orange border across the bottom and are actually Gretsch drum labels that had the top two-thirds trimmed off. These borrowed labels appear to have been anomalies and the black-bordered label with hand written numbers would survive until the demise of the model.

Familiar features that managed to make the jump to this newly anointed model 7660 Nashville included the V-style Bigsby (referred to as "Bixby" throughout the 1975 and 1978 Baldwin-published catalogs), tone switch, standby switch, neoclassic fretboard inlays, zero fret, and printed aluminum "G" arrow control knobs. The earliest examples (most of 1972 and 1973's production) came with gold-plated hardware and a coordinating gold pickguard. This changed to chrome-plated hardware and a matching silver pickguard combination in 1974, although there are examples found from subsequent years that possess the gold package, suggesting that this was an option, perhaps made available at a premium.

The Gretsch Chet Atkins Nashville, model 7660.
Photo Courtesy of Mass Street Music.

Production of the 7660 model Nashville continued through 1974 and 1975 without any perceivable changes. The June 1, 1974 pricelist reported its retail price at $695. By this time, the once distinctive Nashville model looked like it had devolved to, in essence, a double-cutaway variation of the Tennessean model. Midway through 1976 the guitar abruptly lost its standby switch feature, even though the illustration of the model in the 1978 catalog still shows it. There is evidence that this model was produced through December of 1978, but no evidence is available to determine exactly when the guitar was officially discontinued or how many total examples were produced. Although these late model 7660 Nashville's can be outstanding guitars in their own right, it is difficult for most vintage Gretsch enthusiasts to consider them in the same category as the big orange single-cutaway of the 1950s.

There are guitarists that will attest to the fact that many Baldwin-era Gretsch electric archtops are as fine an instrument as they have played, and there is no doubt that many excellent quality examples exist. However, many feel that the products Baldwin created during the 1970s can be of inconsistent quality, and many guitars are found with such chronic issues as to suggest the factory experienced periodic lapses in quality control. Another bad omen to the brand was the devastating affects of not one, but two separate fires at the Boonville plant in 1973.

A 1974 Tennessean, model 7665.
Photo Courtesy of Mass Street Music.

A 1974 Nashville, model 7660. *Photo Courtesy of Mass Street Music.*

Legend has it that it was during those catastrophes that the official Gretsch production history was lost, leaving us to speculate decades later about when and how the various feature evolutions occurred within the Gretsch guitar product line. The company made a valiant effort to recover from this dark period, and guitar production continued until around 1980, when the operation was finally abandoned. There was one last attempt to resurrect guitar manufacturing by establishing a Mexico production site, but it was short-lived

Chet Atkins had a couple of late Baldwin-era successes with the Super Chet electric archtop in 1971, and then the Atkins Axe and Super Axe solidbody models in the mid-1970s. Modest sellers, these were decent guitars that have always been underrated. Shortly after Fred Gretsch Jr. passed away in 1979, Atkins felt it was time to sever his relationship with the brand that had become something so very different from what he had known. He has been quoted as saying that the only reason he stayed on as long as he did was the great respect he had for Fred Gretsch Jr. By then it did not take much to convince Atkins that it was in his best interest to jump ship and partner with the Gibson Company on yet another signature model, the SST (solidbody acoustic-electric, 1981). This was followed by the Gibson incarnation of the Country Gentleman model in 1986.

This 1976 example illustrates the final iteration (no standby switch) of the Chet Atkins endorsed Nashville guitar, a name that had been integral to the Gretsch brand over the previous 10 years. *Photo Courtesy of Mass Street Music.*

The Gibson Company created a signature model for Chet Atkins and called it the Country Gentleman. This guitar incorporated several not-so-subtle inspirations from the classic Gretsch 6120 hollowbody, including a bright orange finish, neoclassic markers on an ebony fretboard, and a Bigsby B6 vibrato unit. Although lacking the traditional Atkins-favored sealed-top, this open f-hole archtop guitar employed a solid center block inside its ultra-thin 1.75" body. *Photo Courtesy of Matt Morris.*

Section V

Chapter

22

Music and Culture in the 1980s and '90s

It might be just as well that the Gretsch guitar brand was on sabbatical in the 1980s—the musical landscape was not very friendly to what their product line had to offer. Although disco was dying, the synthesizer-heavy sounds of new wave did not leave very much room for guitar heroes. With only a few exceptions, including Ted Nugent, George Thorogood, and Steve Howe of YES, hard rock bands didn't really feature hollowbody archtops. Pop bands and country acts were likewise employing solidbody guitars. Jazz was about the only bastion left for the archtop during this period. Many of those artists, such as George Benson, who collaborated with Chet Atkins on two tracks for Atkins' 1985 jazz-oriented album *Stay Tuned*, were playing instruments from Asian-based manufacturers like Ibanez, Cort, and Sammick. These brands were successfully infiltrating the United States' electric archtop market niche.

The thing that the old Gretsch archtops still had going for them was their visual impact. At a time when hair bands were thrashing away on pointy, imported solidbody guitars, the rare occasions when a musician played full hollowbody guitar generated some attention. This is how MTV impacted the future of the Gretsch brand. As the pop acts of the day endeavored to look cool, what better way to achieve this than to trot out a big old Gretsch hollowbody in your music video? For many nascent Gretsch fans, seeing the White Falcon in Adam Ant's early 1980s videos was their baptism into the Gretsch universe. But that was just the tip of the iceberg for Gretsch's revival, pending the arrival of a rockabilly star with an affinity for Gretsch guitars.

The skinny tie and spandex-wearing bands of the 1980s soon gave way to the grunge movement seemingly over night in the 1990s. The synthesizers disappeared and were replaced with, in many cases, vintage (or at least used) guitars. Alas, the walls of sonic energy that emanated from the Seattle sound were no less friendly to the hollowbody archtop guitar format. Newsweek Magazine characterized the period as such: "Grunge is what happens when children of divorce get their hands on guitars." There were a few notable artists, however, that valued Gretsch guitars. Dave Grohl, formerly of Nirvana, wielded a Gretsch White Falcon in one of his late 1990s Foo Fighters videos, proving once again the power of the Gretsch aesthetic within that medium. Likewise, guitarist Keith Scott was seen playing Gretsch hollowbody guitars in the early 1990s music videos of Bryan Adams. And when the Eagles got back together for the infamous Hell Freezes Over tour in 1994, they employed several Gretsch guitars in their arsenal.

Late in the decade, in the midst of all the angst of the time, there was a surprising reemergence of a sound from a previous generation. With a little help from a 1998 TV ad for The Gap, swing was re-popularized, and for the first time in a long time it was cool to dance again.

Rebirth of the Gretsch Guitar Brand and Reintroduction of the 6120 Model (1989)

In October of 1984, after years of frustration, Fred W. Gretsch, great grandson of founder Fredrick Gretsch, was finally given the opportunity to buy back the company that bore his family name, which he announced in January 1985. Soon after reacquiring the brand, he set up a headquarters in Savannah, Georgia. In an in-house newsletter called *The Gretsch House Telegram* (Winter 94/95), Fred W. Gretsch disclosed that it took several years after the reacquisition to be in a position to build guitars again. One of the dilemmas was the lack of any design specifications or schematics for the vintage Gretsch models. Fred W. Gretsch commented: "With the lack of these plans and blueprints, we went to Gretsch collectors and literally borrowed their best instruments." He described how they embarked in a process of "copying their own guitars."

Working closely with longtime Gretsch mogul Duke Kramer, and Gretsch aficionado and collector Randy Bachman, the company produced the first prototypes that would ultimately re-launch the brand. Gretsch then established a manufacturing source at the Terada factory in Japan.

In 1989 the first models of the new Gretsch guitar product line were announced in what has become known as the *Truly* catalog. It featured 18 instruments—eight electric archtop guitar models and four electric solidbodies— all of which captured the essence and style of the Gretsch Golden Era. The flagship of the group was, of course, the 6120 model, once again named the Nashville, as Chet Atkins continued to be under contractual obligation to the Gibson Company. It was offered in two variations, the Nashville Western (6120-W) with the full Western appointments and the more vanilla Nashville 6120. Other than the "G" brand, which was actually a decal, on the body, cows and cactus fretboard makers, and signpost motif on the pickguard, these two models were identical, however the 6120-W also had the option of a cowboy case covered in cream leatherette vinyl with dark brown trim. It had been almost 30 years since the big orange single-cutaway hollowbody had been available, and there were lots of people wanting to recapture that look, as well as "That Great Gretsch Sound."

The timing of this launch was excellent, as the baby boomer disciples of Duane Eddy and Eddie Cochran, teenagers in the late 1950s, were now reaching the age when they had the discretionary income to invest in such symbols of their youth. With vintage 6120 examples selling on the secondary market for two to three times what these new reissues sold for, the latter immediately became an attractive option.

The 6120-1960 may not have been as exact a reproduction as intended. *Photo Courtesy of Mass Street Music.*

Photo Courtesy of Jesse Whiteside, Folkway Music.

The *Truly* catalog reported the following specifications, common to each of the two 1989, 6120 models. The guitars had a standard 24.5" scale length and a laminated maple body that measured 16" wide by 2.75" deep. They displayed block inlays on a rosewood (ebony stained) fretboard (12" radius) and gold Lucite pickguards displaying only the Gretsch T-roof logo. Other features included over-sized bound f-holes and a curly maple headstock overlay with inlaid horseshoe design. The models' 24k gold-plated hardware consisted of "G" indent control knobs for volume and tone, dual-Filter'Tron pickups, pickup selector switch, tuning machines, roller bridge, and a V-style Bigsby vibrato.

Taking a few years to get reestablished, and acknowledging that the 1989 Nashville offering was more of a hybrid design, Gretsch made a concerted effort to pay homage to, and provide a more exacting reproduction of, one of the popular 6120 iterations of the past. They released the G6120-1960 Nashville in 1992. This guitar maintained the 24.5" scale and single-cutaway laminated maple body measuring 16" wide with a fretboard radius of 12". It also had dual-Filter'Tron pickups, a horseshoe headstock motif, signpost pickguard, and the same famous Gretsch-orange stain as the first reissue from 1989. It did, however, receive the 1960-appropriate, 2.5" body depth. Further adherence to 1960 specifications resulted in its acquisition of a tone switch, zero fret, and neoclassic fretboard markers. The hardware was 24k gold-plated with the exception of the period-incorrect, enamel-faced Bigsby B6 vibrato. The addition of a space control bridge was an equally curious decision.

Quick to recognize how successful the retro-styled reissues were, Gretsch decided to try and recapture the marketing magic they had leveraged all those decades prior with their association to a premier guitar hero of the day. Chet Atkins was unavailable, and frankly a lot less popular by then, so Gretsch endeavored to find another high profile, highly respected, influential guitarist to promote their brand.

The list of candidates was pretty short. Not many had made their Gretsch guitar a staple of modern music in the two decades leading up to the rebirth of the Gretsch brand. Randy Bachman was better known for his extensive collection of vintage Gretsch guitars, including many vintage 6120 examples, than he was for playing them. Pete Townsend used his 1960 model year 6120 (a gift from Joe Walsh) primarily in the studio, and although it was featured on classic albums like *Who's Next* and *Quadrophenia*, his fans did not really associate him with the guitar. Neil Young played a 6120 hollowbody in the Buffalo Springfield days, but was more recognized for his reliance on White Falcons since the 1970s. A few post-modern artists were known for using vintage Gretsch hollowbodies through the 1980s, including Martin Gore, Robert Smith, and Billy Duffy, but none of them embraced the 6120 model. There is a strong possibility that these purveyors of new music consciously elected to steer clear of the perceived squareness of the Chet Atkins and/or country western connection. So, at the end of the day, there remained one very obvious choice.

Brian Setzer and his Endorsement of Gretsch Guitars

Brian Setzer is a product of Long Island, New York, where, in the late 1970s, he bought his first Gretsch 6120 hollowbody guitar and began to craft his rockabilly sound with early bands—the Bloodless Pharaohs and the Tom Cats. The latter would become The Stray Cats in the summer of 1980, featuring Setzer (guitar/vocals), Lee Rocker (bass), and "Slim" Jim Phantom (drums). Finding little support for their music in the United States, the band relocated to the United Kingdom, where they had better luck and met artist/producer Dave Edmunds. After taking another unsuccessful stab at the United States' market, they returned to the United Kingdom. They signed with Arista Records there and released their self-titled debut album *Stray Cats* in February 1981.

The Stray Cat 6120

A later version of the Stray Cat 6120 (#33024) with different decals. By now the pickguard had been permanently removed. *Photo Courtesy of Kevin Winter/Time & Life Pictures/Getty Images.*

In the early days of the band, Brian Setzer relied on his legendary Gretsch 6120 (serial #33024), which has come to be known as the Stray Cat. He used it extensively from 1980 through the end of the decade. Setzer purchased the guitar, which was in pieces, for $100 in the late 1970s and modified it with Sperzel locking tuners, an altered zero fret, and infamous dice volume knobs. Unhappy with the tone options the mud switch offered, Setzer simply pushed it into the body of the guitar, and relocated the pickup selector switch to that less forward position.

Originally this guitar would have possessed a V-style Bigsby vibrato unit, but it seems to have acquired a replacement enamel-faced B6 plain bolt unit long ago, prompting the world to inadvertently designate it as a 1959 model year example. Interestingly, through all this customization, Setzer utilized the non-original space control bridge through much of his early career, which many players feel is not an optimal bridge for a vibrato-equipped guitar. Early photos also reveal the presence of a homemade translucent black pickguard, which was reportedly fashioned by Setzer and his friend Jess Oliver (vice president of Ampeg). In 1981, he replaced this with a more appropriate gold Lucite Chet Atkins signpost guard, which later was removed all together—a look that has become synonymous with Setzer's guitars. Other personal touches include the now famous record girl pinup decal, purchased at Ed's Lawnmower Repair in Long Island. Prior to this set up, Setzer had a black cat decal on the lower treble bout and a skull-and-crossbones sticker covering the inlaid horseshoe on the headstock.

The guitar has somehow survived serious damage caused by Setzer's over-exuberant showmanship, which resulted in the neck being detached from the body at a 1990 show in Tokyo. The guitar was later stolen after a 1996 Bryan Setzer Orchestra concert in Washington, DC, but was ultimately recovered and returned to Setzer almost two years later. Setzer officially retired the Stray Cat in 2003. Subsequently, he has purchased several other exceptional vintage examples of the single-cutaway 6120, including serial numbers #33718 and #34526.

Brian Setzer with the Stray Cat 6120 (#33024), complete with its early period decals. The guitar was outfitted with this gold Lucite signpost pickguard for a brief time. *Photo Courtesy of Michael Ochs Archive/Getty Images.*

Brian Setzer graced the cover of the May 1985 *Guitar World* magazine, accompanied by his trusty Gretsch model 6120 guitar.

Later that year The Stray Cats were vindicated with breakthrough hits, including "Rock This Town" and "Stray Cat Strut" in Europe, where they toured extensively. In the fall of 1981 the band finally made inroads into the home market with an ABC television appearance and an opportunity to open for The Rolling Stones' at the first few shows of their American tour (Fox Theater, Atlanta Georgia). It was not long until the band broke into the United States' market in 1982 and signed with EMI Records. This was followed by a successful tour of the United States that same summer, which propelled their debut album *Built for Speed* to number two on the United States' Billboard charts. The Stray Cats' timing was perfect to exploit the newest medium in music, the rock video, and the band's wild look was what is now referred to as MTV-friendly. As a result "Stray Cat Strut" and "Rock This Town" enjoyed heavy rotation on the fledgling network, driving each into the top 10 of the Billboard charts. This momentum was carried into the band's second album in the United States, *Rant*

'n Rave with the Stray Cats, which spawned a number five hit on the 1983 Billboard charts, "Sexy & 17." Rockabilly was suddenly alive and speaking to rebellious teens all across the United States.

In late 1984 the issues that commonly affect a band took their toll on the Stray Cats, and they disbanded for the first of what would become several break ups. A reunion was attempted in 1986, but the commercial window was closed by then. Setzer decided to pursue his solo career, producing the album *The Knife Feels Like Justice*, and doing side projects with a wide variety of established acts, including Bob Dylan, Robert Plant, and Stevie Nicks. Other Stray Cat reunions were attempted in 1989 (*Blast Off*), 1994 (*Choo Choo Hot Fish*), and 2003 (*Lonesome Tears*). Setzer's 1988 solo effort, *Live Nude Guitars*, did not get much notice. Then, in the few years following, he began to toy with the idea of forming a big band-style orchestra.

Brian Setzer with the Steve Miller 6120 (#33767). *Photo Courtesy of Annamaria DiSanto/WireImage/ Getty Images.*

The Steve Miller 6120

In August of 1983 Setzer met fellow guitarist and rock-star Steve Miller in Germany, an encounter that later resulted in Miller sending Setzer another 1960 model year 6120 (#33767). This was a stunning specimen with a heavily flamed maple top and a stock-equipped 1960 V-style Bigsby vibrato. This guitar was from the batch of 6120s produced just after the Stray Cat guitar, but the guitars from this #337xx batch of 6120s were a quarter of an inch shallower with a 2.5" body depth. A more mysterious feature, which is unique to this guitar, is a forth control knob, reportedly introduced prior to Miller's acquisition of the instrument. Setzer made his customary modifications, removing the pickguard and altering the zero fret. He began relying on this guitar more and more as time went on. Finally, in 1988, what has since been dubbed the Steve Miller guitar, officially replaced the road weary Stray Cat 6120 as Setzer's primary axe, going on to serve him well for the next 10 years.

In 1994, Setzer released *The Brian Setzer Orchestra* album featuring a 17-piece ensemble led by the driving Gretsch guitar of their heavily-tattooed leader. This effort was the beginning of something big. Their 1998 Grammy-winning album *The Dirty Boogie* was at ground zero of the emerging swing revival, and their cover version of "Jump, Jive, and Wail" was in heavy rotation on radio stations across the United States. Setzer had once again successfully reintroduced young music fans to a sound of prior generations. The Brian Setzer Orchestra (BSO) toured extensively and produced several more albums, which included more original material, swing standards, as well as some Stray Cats classics reworked to fit the orchestra environment. In recent years Setzer has continued to produce solo albums, while also touring in several smaller ensembles like the Brian Setzer Trio and Brian Setzer and the Nashvillians. A 2007 tour with the original Stray Cats lineup enabled him to get back to the roots that have made him such a recognized figure within American music.

Brian Setzer on the cover of the November 1998 *Guitar Player* magazine.

Brian Setzer making magic with his 1960 model year 6120 (#34580). *Photo Courtesy of Naoaki Toyofuku.*

By the mid-1990s, Setzer was relying on several Gretsch reissue 6120 models. He has been quoted as saying that the new guitars sound and play just as well as the vintage ones. This helped to prolong Setzer's stable of vintage 6120 examples, sparing them from the full load of touring wear and tear. Even so, by 1997 the trusty Steve Miller guitar was beginning to show its age. In 1998, Setzer, literally going back to his roots, located and purchased yet another vintage 1960 model year 6120 (#34580) in Long Island, New York. This guitar was produced two batches after the Steve Miller guitar. In preparation for this guitar to take over duty as Setzer's main instrument, he not only removed the pickguard and added his usual touches of Sperzel locking tuning machines and dice control knobs, but he actually had to replace the headstock because of the multiple holes previously introduced to accommodate several different sets of tuning machines. The surgery was completed flawlessly. A residual clue to this modification is the fact that there are no remnants of the zero fret that his other vintage 6120 guitars all display. This guitar took over as Setzer's number one instrument in 1999 and remains a workhorse today.

Brian Setzer Signature Nashville Model 6120 (1993)

Throughout his career, Brian Setzer has embodied the cool subculture of the rockabilly revival scene and unapologetically promoted his Gretsch 6120 model. By playing Chet Atkins 6120 hollowbody guitars, Setzer has also honored the memory of his hero Eddie Cochran. Setzer was rewarded for his reverence when he became the first artist to have a Gretsch signature 6120 model since Chet Atkins. In 1993 the Brian Setzer Signature Nashville model was born.

Acknowledged as an instrument with hybrid features, the Setzer Signature Nashville was largely inspired by the 1960 model year Filter'Tron-equipped 6120 guitars that Setzer has played throughout his career. The model included Setzer's now-famous modifications, including Sperzel locking tuners, strap locks, dice control knobs, and a graphite nut. The guitar's body accurately reflects the 15.75" width of vintage 6120 examples, even though Gretsch promotional materials list it as a 16" archtop. Perhaps that was part of the emulation, as the vintage model catalogs made that same inaccurate claim in the 1950s. Interestingly enough, however, the Setzer Signature Nashville's body had a 2.75" depth, which is more analogous to earlier vintage model year specifications. This feature, in addition to the enamel-faced B6 Bigsby, is forgiven, as they are each consistent with Setzer's original Stray Cat guitar. The modern, and more functional, Adjusto-Matic bridge was another deviation from vintage specs that most players were happy to rationalize. More importantly, these first generation Setzer Signature models still lacked an essential attribute of the vintage models that Setzer relied on—trestle bracing within the body.

The Brian Setzer Signature Nashville model was offered in a standard orange stain, but the optional emerald green is particularly striking. *Guitar Courtesy of Music Zoo. Photo by Tim Reynolds.*

Presumably, in tribute to the vintage Steve Miller guitar, the Setzer Signature Nashville model incorporated highly-figured tiger maple wood throughout, effectively separating it from the un-figured top on the standard, reissued 6120 model. Over-sized bound f-holes, neoclassic markers on an ebony fretboard, and 24k gold-plated hardware (including pickup covers, volume knobs, tone switch, and pickup selector switch) were standard features. The compulsory Gretsch orange stain finish was also standard, but these guitars were also offered in an emerald green option (G6120SSUGR). Perhaps this was an effort to rekindle the mojo of the Golden Era, when Gretsch had several hollowbody electric models in the line that were produced in distinct color alternatives. The orange-stained guitars were available with either a nitrocellulose lacquer (G6120SSL) or polyurethane (G6120SSU) overcoat. Most purists preferred the lacquer option, which came at a premium. The package was completed with a custom-engraved truss rod cover and gold signature pickguard, each displaying Setzer's autograph. In 2004 these models were upgraded with new TV Jones Classic Filter'Tron pickups, a pinned Adjusto-Matic bridge, and a thinner three-ply maple top. The all-important trestle-bracing feature was also finally introduced.

By the end of 1994, the Gretsch line of Nashville 6120 model options was up to ten and fell into three categories. The first consisted of the basic G6120, with four variations of that design: a left-handed version (G6120LH), the Western version (G6120W), a unique Blue Sunburst finish option (G6120BS), and a flamed tiger maple option (G6120TM). The second was the 1960 Nashville Reissue (G6120-1960) with a left-handed version of that same guitar (G6120-1960LH). The third and newest category offered the three variations of the Brian Setzer Signature Nashville.

Even the standard 6120 model was being pushed in new directions, as evidenced by this 1995 blue-burst-finished G6120BS example, the first of the Nashville lineup offered in something other than the traditional orange stain. *Photo Courtesy of Steve Wilson.*

A left-handed 1996 Nashville G6120LH. The "G" brand seems misplaced on what is an otherwise non-Western package. *Photo Courtesy of Southpaw Sanctum.*

Brian Setzer Signature Hot Rod Series 6120 (1999)

As Gretsch had hoped, the association with Brian Setzer was highly successful. Endeavoring to fully capitalize on this, and coinciding with Setzer's heightened popularity during the swing revival of the late 1990s, Gretsch designed yet another signature model inspired by Setzer's reputation for installing custom modifications to his vintage 6120 guitars. The model was dubbed the Brian Setzer Hot Rod, and Setzer debuted the guitar on the Tonight Show, just a few days before Christmas on Dec 21,1998. Taking full advantage of an unplanned marketing opportunity, Setzer had several prototype examples of different wild metallic colors in a rack on the set. Gretsch fans that stayed up for the performance were rewarded with a glimpse of what the company had yet to officially debut. The actual production of these guitars began soon after in January 1999.

Photo Courtesy of Steve Wilson.

Courtesy of The Gretsch Company.

This new signature model was purportedly a natural convergence of two of Setzer's favorite things, his love of hot rods and his trusty Gretsch guitar. This also provided the Gretsch designers an opportunity to once again experiment with the application of automotive-style finishes on guitars, an approach that harkened back to one of the brand's greatest legacies born 45 years earlier. The Hot Rod debut line offered metallic hues, including Tangerine, Regal Blue, Candy Apple Red, and Purple. Each of these colors corresponded to a different suffix on the base Hot Rod model designation (G6120SH). If a guitar came from the factory with the TV Jones Classic pickup option, the "TV" suffix was incorporated on the end. For instance, a Purple Hot Rod with TV Classic pickups would have a model designation of G6120SHPTV.

This first batch Regal Blue Hot Rod specimen from 1999 can be identified as a very early example by its standard Grover tuning machines (Sperzel locking tuning machines were used later), forward pickup selector switch location, and lack of flame motif on the silver pickguard. It also lacks trestle bracing. *Photo Courtesy of Steve Wilson.*

The Hot Rod concept was epitomized by its stripped down aesthetic. Stark and clean, these guitars lacked all unnecessary baggage, including tone and individual pickup volume controls. Also unique were the unbound over-sized f-holes and unbound headstock that initially employed standard Grover tuning machines. The chrome hardware consisted of a polished aluminum V-style Bigsby vibrato, adjustable floating bridge, pickup covers, single master volume "G" indent knob, and a three-way pickup selector switch located in the traditional location. Curiously these Setzer Signature models, unlike the others, were produced with a full 16" wide (by 2.5" deep) laminated maple archtop body. Standard features included an ebonized (dyed) rosewood fretboard with neoclassic markers and a silver Lucite pickguard with a simple Gretsch T-roof logo. A one-inch square, chrome headstock plaque identified the model with its stylized Brian Setzer Hot Rod insignia. These guitars debuted with a MSRP of $3025.

After the first few Hot Rod batches were produced, there was a change in hardware to Setzer-preferred, nickel-plated Sperzel locking tuners and a pinned Adjusto-Matic bridge. Also at that time, a subtle Hot Rod flame logo was added to the pickguard, coordinating with the similar graphic on the headstock plaque. It should be noted that the Hot Rod models share the unique 9.45" fretboard radius feature of all the Setzer-associated 6120 models.

The G6120SHBKTV (c.2008), in Flat-Black with TV Jones Classic Filter'Tron pickups. *Guitar Courtesy of Music Zoo. Photo by Tim Reynolds.*

The G6120SHLTV (c. 2004), in Lime Gold. *Photo Courtesy of Ellen Rugowski.*

In 2004 the stable of Setzer Hot Rod models not only boasted two new finish options—Flat Black and Lime Gold—they benefited from additional upgrades that better reflected Setzer's actual vintage 6120 stalwart guitars. Mike Lewis, then marketing manager for Gretsch, approved trestle bracing for all of the Setzer signature models, but only after running his own vintage 6120 hollowbody through a CAT scan machine to determine how the internal trestle bracing worked. With the new bracing the tops of these guitars could be made thinner, and TV Jones Classic pickups were offered as an option to the stock Hot Rod Filter'Trons. Another more subtle change was the relocation of the pickup selector switch to where the tone switch traditionally resided on the later vintage 6120 model. This detail emulates the wiring schematic that Setzer applied to his Stray Cat 6120 guitar. Interestingly enough, after all the fuss about trestle bracing, Setzer chose to use his pre-trestle, Hot Rod guitars on tour for the next few years. He also toured with guitars each finished in all-over silver and red sparkle, which are not standard Hot Rod finish options. As this model seems to represent a fertile platform to spawn periodic new finish introductions, there is every reason to assume more varieties will follow.

Photo Courtesy of Richard Osburn.

Influential Personality: Thomas "TV" Jones

Tom Jones founded TV Jones Inc. in 1993. Jones started out as a Fender set up technician and then honed his skills at a high-end instrument repair shop. In the early 1990s Jones worked on Brian Setzer's stable of instruments. This exposure led to Gretsch contracting Jones to design the Filter'Tron-style pickups destined for the pending Brian Setzer Hot Rod signature series guitars. Jones continued his relationship with Gretsch, working with the field guitar service program and interacting with the Gretsch endorsing artists to understand their various requirements. As history is prone to repeating itself, the introduction of Tom "TV" Jones' pickup technology to The Gretsch Company via Setzer was similar to Chet Atkins introducing the original Filter'Tron pickup's innovator, Ray Butts, to the company decades earlier.

Jones has made many contributions to the Gretsch product line, including his work on the Elliot Easton signature solidbody model and several guitars from the Electromatic line. At the Winter 2001 National Association of Music Merchants (NAMM) show, Gretsch introduced a series of solidbody guitars called Spectra Sonic, which were designed by Jones and Brian Setzer's guitar tech Rich Modica. Playing a role not unlike that of Jimmie Webster, Jones provides design improvements and has led workshops for Gretsch. He continues to contribute to the brand as an independent consultant, but also manages his own company and maintains an amazing list of high-profile artist clients.

Photo Courtesy of Richard Osburn.

In addition to, and as a result of, the success of the Brian Setzer Signature models, Gretsch endeavored to pursue new ways to promote the 6120 line. They did this by reaching back to the most notable 6120 model players of the Golden Era, as well as some other more contemporary musicians to create multiple signature 6120 models dedicated to the following guitarists:

Duane Eddy Signature 6120DE Model (1997)

One of the legends of instrumental pop guitar during the Golden Era, Duane Eddy was integral in developing the sound of twang with his 1957 model year Chet Atkins 6120 guitar. His signature model was introduced in September 1997 and was available in two finish options: the 6120DE Ebony Burst finish and 6120DEO standard Gretsch orange, each with a polyurethane overcoat. The guitar was reported to be the standard 16" wide by 3" deep, single-cutaway, laminated maple, archtop, but this reissue was true to its inspiration and was actuality closer to 15.75" wide. These models had two gold single-coil Dynasonic pickups, an aluminum enamel-faced Bigsby B6 vibrato with special flat bar handle, gold space control bridge, and gold "G" indent control knobs for volume and tone. Other features included an ebony fretboard with pearloid hump block markers and a brass nut on an inlaid horseshoe headstock. Finally, these guitars sported custom signature truss rod covers and gold signature pickguards. The original MSRP in 1997 was $3500.

The Duane Eddy model 6120DE came standard with a modern variation of the space control bridge, which this example does not depict.
Photo Courtesy of Mass Street Music.

The 6120KS signature model.
Photo Courtesy of James Dooms.

Keith Scott Signature 6120KS Model (1999)

Best known for his long-time collaboration with vocalist Bryan Adams, Keith Scott represented the unsung journeyman musician. His signature 6120KS model was officially introduced at the January 1999 NAMM show in Los Angeles. Constructed of laminated maple, its body dimensions are 16" wide and 2.75" deep. Possessing the standard 22 frets and 24.5" scale, this guitar's most striking feature is its flashy metallic gold-finished top, which contrasts with a dark mahogany-colored back and sides. The guitar also displays the familiar Gretsch pearloid hump block markers on an ebony fretboard, an inlaid horseshoe headstock, and bound over-sized f-holes. The hardware consists of a 24k gold-plated Gretsch V-style Bigsby vibrato; space control bridge; two, single coil Dynasonic pickups; master volume and two individual pickup volume knobs; and a tone knob. Final touches include a gold signature pickguard and custom signature truss rod cover.

Eddie Cochran-inspired G6120W-1957 Model (2001)

Eddie Cochran was an early rock hero associated with just one guitar during his all-too-short career—a 1955 Chet Atkins 6120. Not able to acquire the official license to use Cochran's name, Gretsch marketed this quasi-signature model in such a way as to make clear the affiliation. The guitar was first introduced at the Winter NAMM show in 2001. It was inexplicably designated as G6120W-1957, a curious model identifier considering the guitar reflected many of the typical specifications of a 1955 model year 6120, including the Western block inlays, steer's head headstock design, and a "G" brand on the lower bass bout. Unique features, which were associated with Cochran's original guitar, included a dog ear P-90 pickup in the neck position, a Dynasonic single coil pickup in the bridge position, and a transparent pickguard with Nashville signpost motif. Other features contributing to the aesthetic impact of this model were the gold-plated hardware (pickup selector, master volume knob, master tone knob, and two individual pickup volume knobs) and a polished aluminum enamel-faced swivel-handled Bigsby B6 vibrato with aluminum compensated bridge. The G6120W-1957 was the sole model featured on the cover of the 2001 Gretsch guitar catalog.

Reverend Horton Heat Signature G6120RHH Model (2005)

Considered an early influence on the pyschobilly (aka punkabilly) sub-genre of music, Jim Heath has been combining fast-paced, blistering guitar licks with clever lyrical content since the mid-1980s, when his brand of juiced-up rockabilly began to emerge. Introduced at the Winter NAMM in 2005, the G6120RHH guitar combines features from several vintage era 6120 formats. It has some typical 1955 model year appointments, including the "G"-branded body, steer's head headstock, and engraved Western motifs on wide block inlays, mixed with the more refined 1958-style Filter'Tron pickups (TV Jones Classics) and control arrangement including a mud switch for tone. The guitar's period-appropriate 15.5" wide by 2.75" deep body is of laminated maple construction with a nitrocellulose orange stain finish and ebony fretboard. This model came with a simple dowel sound post located under the bridge, presumably for added rigidity. The all-chrome hardware consisted of an aluminum enamel-faced B6 vibrato with a 1956-style handle, Adjusto-Matic bridge, gold pickup surrounds, Sperzel locking tuning machines, and the aforementioned humbucking pickup covers. Finally, a transparent Gretsch logo (only) pickguard and custom signature truss rod cover established this signature model's identity. The MSRP for this model upon its introduction was $4125

The G6120W-1957 model. *Guitar Courtesy of Dave Rogers. Photo by Tim Mullally.*

The G6120RHH signature model. *Guitar Courtesy of Dave Rogers. Photo by Tim Mullally.*

A Growing 6120 Family

When the 2001 Gretsch catalog of guitars came out, it showed that the venerable 6120 format had continued to expand in aesthetics, in artist collaborations, and even in its structural specifications. The basic G6120 Nashville remained available in Orange, Blue Sunburst, and Tiger Maple finishes, as well as the Western package. The G6120-1960 reissue was still in the line. However, the majority of the 6120 designs were now represented by the various signature models. This was the year that the Eddie Cochran-inspired model (G6120W-1957) was added to an already diverse group including the two Duane Eddy models (G6120DE), the Keith Scott model (G6120KS), and of course the flock of Brian Setzer signature models—his three original Nashville models (G6120SSU) and the four finish options for his Hot Rod series (G6120SH). Add to those the two left-handed 6120 versions and the total number of 6120 model options were 18, and Gretsch was not done yet.

6120JR

Pushing the envelope on structural mutations to the basic 6120 form, Gretsch introduced two smaller versions of the 6120 package. The G6120JR model combined a petite 14" wide by 2.25" deep laminated maple archtop body with most of the aesthetics and features of the G6120, except it displayed the newly reinstated neoclassic fretboard markers and a smaller B3-sized, gold-plated, V-style Bigsby. The 6120JR, which was released in 1996, had a single Filter'Tron pickup in its neck position, foregoing the need for a pickup selector switch. It employed the master volume knob on the cutaway and a tone knob on the lower treble bout, each with the classic "G" indent. In 1998 the 6120JR2 debuted with the more traditional dual-Filter'Tron pickup configuration and control knob layout. This version of the model looked a bit less stark compared to its single pickup brother and survived to become the sole example of the model by 1999. There is evidence that a double-cutaway version of the 6120JR2 was conceived, perhaps for the Japanese market. It is unknown if any production batches were created. This 6120 model downsizing experiment was discontinued in 2005.

The 6120JR2 epitomizes the expression, "Size isn't everything." *Photo Courtesy of Tony Baker.*

6120-6/12 Double-neck

As if the Gretsch designers were not feeling innovative enough, in 1997 the company produced what can only be described as the oddest looking 6120 of all time—the double-necked Nashville G6120-6/12. What must have been viewed as equally shocking to some, as it was functional to others, this instrument provided the player with the versatility of both a 6-string and a 12-string neck. To achieve this objective the Gretsch designers had to deviate from the standard 6120 guidelines. This guitar offered a 25.5" scale with a 17" wide by 2.75" deep body. The 12-string neck (top) joined at the 14th fret and the 6-string neck joined at the 17th fret. The body of the guitar was reminiscent of the Electrotone style with its sealed top and faux f-holes. The hardware was entirely 24k gold-plated and equipped much as a G6120 would be, times two. A "G" cutout tailpiece was placed on the 12-string area of the guitar. Visually the guitar was still all Gretsch, sporting the ubiquitous orange stained body and distinctive neoclassic markers on each of its two ebony fretboards. The controls were standard with "G" indent knobs for both tone and volume. However, in addition to a pickup selector switch, which was placed in its customary position, there was also a neck selector switch at the lower bout of the guitar.

Gretsch designers stretched the limits of the 6120 form with the 6120-6/12. *Photo Courtesy of Anthony Pupa.*

6120N New Nashville

Even with all the available permutations of the 6120 form, Gretsch apparently felt the need to produce yet another variation on the theme. In late 2001 the New Nashville model 6120N was introduced. It had the standard 6120 appointments, an orange stained 15.5" wide laminated maple body, gold hardware, V-style Bigsby with adjustable bridge, dual-Filter'Tron pickups, and volume and tone control knobs. Aesthetically this model was the first of the reissued 6120 guitars to reintroduce the hump block inlays onto its ebonized (dyed) rosewood fretboard. Curiously it omitted the horseshoe motif from its unusually dark headstock overlay, leaving the Gretsch T-roof logo in its customary position. The new structural adaptations to this guitar were significant, as it incorporated a sharp Florentine single-cutaway (a la Gibson ES-175) and an ultra-thin 1.75" body depth. In spite of these deviations from the classic Nashville form, the 6120N is easily recognizable as a member of the Gretsch 6120 family.

An ultra thin body and a razor sharp Florentine cutaway distinguish this 6120N model from the others. *Guitar Courtesy of Mark Sorenson. Photo by Joe Carducci.*

The Fender Musical Instrument Company and New Directions

...21% increase in guitars sales in 2003 in America, bringing the number of new electric guitars sold to over one million pieces there.

-The Gretsch House Telegram

Harkening back to the days of Lloyd Loar, each of the Custom Shop Nashvilles were hand signed by Stephen Stern, the master craftsman behind this 6120 WCST Custom Shop model. *Photo Courtesy of Warpdrive Music. Photos by John Sieger.*

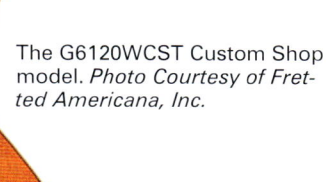

The G6120WCST Custom Shop model. *Photo Courtesy of Fretted Americana, Inc.*

The G6120DSW became the new Western-appointed option from the Professional Collection. *Guitar Courtesy of Dave Rogers. Photo by Tim Mullally.*

By 2003 the Fender Musical Instrument Company (FMIC) had taken over the development, marketing, manufacturing, and distribution of the Gretsch guitar brand, although Fred Gretsch remained the owner. One benefit of the Fender influence was quickly realized. The 2004 Gretsch guitar catalog promoted a Nashville model from a newly established Gretsch Custom Shop, located in Corona, California. The G6120WCST was a nitrocellulose-finished 15.5" wide by 2.75" deep, dual-Dynasonic-equipped guitar with all the Western motifs and features of a vintage 1955 model year example, including the classic gold fixed-arm, flat-handled, anodized aluminum B6 Bigsby vibrato (although an additional swivel-style Bigsby was included in the case as well). At an introductory MSRP of $8000, this price was quite a jump up from the similar Asian-made Professional Collection's new G6120DSW Nashville Western (MSRP $2975), which was an evolved Dynasonic-enabled version of the discontinued cowboy-styled G6120W. The G6120DSW also reached back to the earliest vintage style with arrow (only) control knobs, "G"-branded body, an enamel-faced B6 Bigsby with aluminum compensated bridge, and the steer's head inlaid headstock. In addition to this new Western-flavored model, Gretsch also offered the G6120DS Nashville, which is the same guitar without the "G" brand and the cows and cactus engravings on the block-style fretboard markers. It was also $100 cheaper.

Another 2003 release that was apparently executed under the radar was what appears to be a single batch of 6120TMSP Nashville models. These were standard specification 6120 guitars displaying intense flamed tiger maple through their orange stained finish. Much of the hardware was gold-plated with one exception being the enamel-faced B6 Bigsby and bar bridge. These guitars were equipped with dual-Filter'Tron pickups (alnico), neoclassic fretboard markers, and a Nashville signpost pickguard. Although it would be reasonable to surmise that these were simply special ("SP") examples of the 6120TM format, and in fact they are rumored to have been a short run produced for the large national retailer, The Guitar Center, they possess one other feature that at least suggests another possibility. In addition to having a dif-

ferent Bigsby unit from the standard 6120TM model's V-style vibrato, these "SP" examples also employed factory-installed Sperzel locking tuning machines. So, what this package essentially provided was a 6120SSU without dice control knobs and Brian Setzer's signature on the truss rod cover and pickguard. Based on serial numbers, the timing of this 6120TMSP batch appears to correspond to the period just before the upgrade package was applied to the Setzer signature lineup for 2004. A plausible scenario might be that these were the last of the non-tresle braced, thicker topped, 6120SSU bodies.

The 2005 limited run 6120LSB guitars were never listed in a catalog, but their highly figured sunburst bodies made them a welcome alternative to the sea of Western orange within the Gretsch 6120 lineup. Only several hundred of the 6120LSB were rumored to have been made. *Photos Courtesy of Craig Witty.*

A 2008 example of the G6120AM finish package, complete with its wonderfully figured grain top and newly reinstated Chet Atkins signpost pickguard. *Guitar Courtesy of Dave Rogers. Photo by Tim Mullally.*

The 2004 Nashville family continued to include the basic G6120 Nashville, but by then a version with black finish (G6120BK) and a stunning natural finish called Tiger Maple Amber (G6120AM) had been added. The veteran G6120-1960 was still around, as was the Eddie Cochran-inspired G6120W-1957. A refreshingly new Nashville was also added in 2004 that commemorated the 50th anniversary of the 6120 format—the aptly designated G6120GA, the Golden Anniversary Nashville (MSRP $3675). This stunning guitar displayed an all-over metallic gold finish and gold-plated hardware, including the dual-TV Jones Classic pickups, and black enamel-faced B6 vibrato with bar bridge. It also possessed a 9.45" fretboard radius on its neck, making it more akin to the Setzer model 6120 guitars in that regard, as the standard specification for the Nashville line was a 12" radius fretboard. The G6120GA debuted with an appropriately bold aesthetic statement, just like the original 6120 Chet Atkins hollowbody coming off the production line in late 1954.

Celebrating 50 years of the 6120 model, the G6120GA is a striking site with its all-over gold aesthetic. *Guitar Courtesy of Tim Harman. Photo by Robert McCarty.*

Another interesting 2004 addition was the G6120DC or double-cutaway Nashville (MSRP $3900). Some may find this somewhat ironic, as it seems that many vintage Gretsch purists consider the demise of the single-cutaway hollowbody 6120 as the end of the story. This model, however, was reportedly used by John Lennon during the Paperback Writer sessions in 1966 and thousands were sold in the 1960s and early 1970s. The fact that FMIC/Gretsch reissued this format suggests that they felt there were enough people out there who preferred this thinner double-cutaway sealed body and all its gadgetry to project some degree of positive sales performance. This guitar was modeled after the post-1962 configuration with painted on f-holes, gold-plated Filter'Tron pickups, tone switch, zero fret, and cast aluminum V-style Bigsby and bar bridge. It also displays some of the Jimmie Webster influences, such as a flip-up mute (lever) system and a snap-on back pad.

During 2004 FMIC/Gretsch produced a limited edition Nashville that was a very accurate reproduction of the classic 1959 model year guitar, the 6120SLTV. The run was reported to be limited to no more than 50 guitars (MSRP $4600) and it did not appear in the catalog for that year. Features included a 1959 vintage correct 15.75" wide by 2.75" deep body with trestle bracing, zero fret, tone switch, neoclassic markers, and a nitrocellulose lacquer finish. It was outfitted with two TV Jones Classic Filter'Tron pickups and the standard gold Nashville signpost pickguard. Interestingly this guitar also possessed an enamel-faced B6 Bigsby vibrato, which was in fact the correct vibrato unit for the 1959 model year, a detail the company lost track of on its later 1959 model year 6120 reissue.

This interesting 2005 Nashville variant (G6120DCBK) deviates in both its unusual black finish, as well as its 1962 model year-like dial-up mute control knob. This knob is merely aesthetic and the mechanism still operates like the lever style. *Photo Courtesy of Sharp Guitars Online.*

This 2008 model G6120DSV was clearly inspired by the aesthetics of the 1957 model year 6120. *Guitar Courtesy of Dave Rogers. Photo by Tim Mullally.*

As far as the Setzer Signature line went, the 2004 catalog featured the three usual Nashville models now outfitted with 1959-style trestle bracing, TV Jones Classic pickups, and a pinned bridge along with another new addition to the Setzer series, the Vintage Orange Lacquer (G6120SSLVO) model. The Hot Rod clan consisted of six (mostly metallic) finish options.

The 2005 model year brought the introduction of yet another Dynasonic-equipped Nashville model, the 1957-inspired G6120DSV. An obvious effort was made to produce this model with a darker amber colored stain, helping to distinguish it from others in the line, but also to better emulate the vintage examples from the period just after the Western decorations began to disappear. This guitar, which had a B6 Bigsby with a 1956-style handle and a rocking bar bridge, brought back the familiar hump block fretboard inlays so identified with the classic 1957 model year 6120 examples.

First in 2004, then again in 2005, FMIC/Gretsch began using the semi-annual NAMM event to feature unique 6120 specimens that were never intended for mass production, but were instead more of an artistic statement, or what might be considered the ultimate in 6120 personalization. Pop-culture artist Sara Ray used the basic 6120 format as her canvas to produce the "Victory Guitar" followed by the "Red Baron Guitar." These highly stylized instruments reflected World War II and World War I themes respectively, each bearing images in tribute to the icons of those periods. The guitars themselves were a unique conglomeration of features not all associated with the conventional 6120 form, but artistic license prevailed to create each themed package. These instruments, which were assembled by Chris Fleming at the Gretsch Custom Shop, were used as promotional devices at the NAMM shows and then sold. Subsequently for the 2009 Winter NAMM event, a third Sara Ray-conceived 6120 guitar was displayed called "The Jolly Roger," which presented a nautical theme. Its listed MSRP was $14,000.

The Brian Setzer Signature 6120SSLVO model with vintage lacquer finish. *Guitar Courtesy of Dave Rogers. Photo by Tim Mullally.*

The Sara Ray guitars are examples of one-off designs that were never intended to be anything more than a marketing device. It seemed, however, that FMIC/Gretsch was experimenting with the concept of limited-edition guitar production, when at the 2006 NAMM show they displayed the G6120FTW Filter'Tron Western. This design was rumored to have been a prototype for the Reverend Horton Heat signature model released the previous year. Evidence that may corroborate this claim includes the fact that the serial numbers on the G6120FTW guitars disclose that they were produced in September of 2004. These guitars possessed all the features and attributes of the G6120RHH, with the exception of a bar-style bridge instead of the Adjusto-Matic, a more standard gold signpost pickguard, trestle bracing, and gold-plated hardware. Supposedly only 48 total units of this model were made and their introductory MSRP was $4125.

An even more boutique approach was taken with the G6120WTV guitars, of which only 12 guitars were supposedly produced. This model was also dubbed the Nashville Firebird, no doubt as a reference to its more-red-than-orange finish. This too represented a montage of features based on a basic 1955 era design, but this guitar also employed TV Jones Filter'Tron pickups. The serial numbers from these indicate that they were produced in August of 2006. Sharing so many similarities with the G6120RHH and the G6120FTW, and considering its miniscule production run, this was a surprisingly affordable guitar with a MSRP of just $3262.

A lacquer-finished 2006 example of the G6120-1959LTV-LH in the left-handed format with TV Jones Classic Filter'Tron pickups. *Photo Courtesy of Southpaw Sanctum.*

This 2008 example of the G6120-1959 reflects much of the mojo that the lauded 1959 model year vintage specimens exploited. *Guitar Courtesy of Dave Rogers. Photo by Tim Mullally.*

In 2006 Gretsch went back to another classic 1950s design inspiration with the debut of the G6120-1959 Nashville. This model's orange body was 15.75" wide by 2.75" deep. The 1959 model year was the last model year with this depth. Gretsch literature suggested that this guitar also varied from the standard reissue specification with a 9.45" fretboard radius. It had the zero fret, neoclassic fretboard markers, and gold-plated "G" indent knobs and tone switch, which were all indicative of this vintage. One obvious oversight, however, is the inclusion of the aluminum V-style Bigsby vibrato, which is a signature feature of the 1960 model year 6120. Modern advantages this reissue model benefited from included its CTS/Switchcraft electronic harness, two gold-plated High Sensitive Filter'Tron pickups, and a urethane finish. A second version, the G6120-1959LTV, came with a more traditional lacquer finish, sonically accurate TV Jones Classic Filter'Tron pickups, and a 12" fretboard radius. This upgraded package also existed in a left-handed format (G6120-1959LTV-LH). The introduction of this 1959 model year-inspired guitar seemed to have also signaled the demise of the long running reissue model, the 6120-1960.

During the first couple of years that FMIC steered the Gretsch brand, they also enjoyed the success of their Fender-branded relic line of solidbody guitars. Controversial since the concept's inception, components were purposefully battered and factory-aged to simulate differing degrees of wear. Using their expertise in this process, FMIC set out to recreate several celebrity-inspired limited edition Fender models. These guitars were intended to emulate, in exacting detail, the features, modifications, age, and wear characteristics of legendary guitars used by artists like Stevie Ray Vaughn and Jeff Beck. It seemed only a matter of time before this industry trend was applied to the Gretsch line, and more specifically, Brian Setzer's legendary 6120 hollowbody.

Limited Edition Brian Setzer G6120SSC-Tribute Model (2006)

In 2006 Stephen Stern of the Gretsch Custom Shop designed The Brian Setzer 6120 Tribute model, which was for all intents and purposes a relic-style signature model. This was an attempt to capture and religiously reproduce every nuance of the famous Stray Cat 6120 guitar that Setzer used between 1980 and 1992—from the lovingly scarred 15.75" body right down to the missing tone switch and bent output jack. The guitar's features and aesthetics reflect a very early stage of the instrument's life with Setzer, verified by the dark plexi pickguard and decal collection. The label inside displays a model number of "G6120SSC Tribute" and serial number "33024", which matches Setzer's original. Setzer owns the first Tribute example, which features the word "prototype" handwritten next to the serial number. Only 59 of these limited edition guitars were produced with a sobering MSRP of $29,000. In subsequent years these guitars were being traded for less than half that figure.

The Setzer Tribute package was comprised of the guitar, a jeweled strap, reproductions of the several decals that Brian used, backstage pass reproductions from the Stray Cats days, and an OK card signed by Setzer himself. Further accessories included a white leather cowboy case and a DVD with Gretsch Custom Shop footage and an interview with Setzer. In an innovative marketing move, Gretsch assembled a traveling trade show-style booth, which displayed many examples of the company's electric archtop guitar lineup, highlighted by the presence of a Setzer Tribute guitar. This display traveled with the Brian Setzer Orchestra on their 2006 Christmas tour, exposing thousands of Setzer fans to the offering.

Reconnecting with Chet Atkins (2007)

The 2007 reinstatement of the Chet Atkins name through his estate resulted in the ability to remarket the entire series of Gretsch Professional Collection guitars, which fell into four categories. There were five models of the Chet Atkins Country Gentleman, two models of the Chet Atkins solidbody, four models of the Chet Atkins Tennessee Rose, and most notably 13 models of the Chet Atkins hollowbody in the traditional 6120 format.

As far as feature changes there were not many, except for the obvious addition of the familiar Chet Atkins signpost insignia on all the pickguards within these groups. The basic orange stained G6120 remained with each of its variations (Blue-Burst, Black, Tiger Maple, and Amber Tiger Maple). Also part of the Chet Atkins lineup were several reissues, the G6120W-1957, the G6120WCST-1955, and the G6120-1959 with its lacquer and left-handed options. Others that were still in the stable included the G6120DSV and the G6120DSW. The plain version (G6120-DS) was discontinued the previous year.

The final member of the new Chet Atkins-attributed 6120 stable of guitars was the Nashville double-cutaway model G6120DC. At its original inception in 1962, the development of this Electrotone-bodied manifestation of the 6120 was originally motivated by none other than Atkins himself. It was his big opportunity to do many of the things he had always wanted to do with the earlier 6120 designs. That said if FMIC/Gretsch intended to use this new arrangement with Atkins' estate to honor the spirit of his contributions to the Gretsch brand, it seems mandatory that this reissue be included in the series. As it was in 1962, the signpost motif on the gold Lucite pickguard was replaced by Atkins' autograph hovering over the Gretsch T-roof logo.

They say imitation is the highest form of flattery, so it seems poetic that Brian Setzer's original Stray Cat guitar was cloned 59 times in this limited Tribute edition. *Guitar Courtesy of Dave Rogers. Photo by Tim Mullally.*

State of the Gretsch Brand and 6120 Model

Today the Gretsch brand is capably managed by FMIC, which is producing what may be the highest quality electric archtops in its history. The 6120 model remains the flagship format of their Professional Collection of guitars. However, as has always been the case, its survival depends on the next generation of consumers accepting its highly evolved form. In a strategic decision, and risking the erosion of their existing product line, FMIC/Gretsch began producing a lower-end line of 16" single-cutaway, deep body electric archtops branded with the old "Electromatic" name (and headstock design) in 2004. This product line has since grown to consist of multiple models with different pickup styles and color finish options. In 2006 the G5120 model was released in an all-over orange stain with chrome hardware version that sported dual-humbucking-style pickups, neoclassic fretboard inlays, and an aluminum B6-style Bigsby vibrato, essentially constituting a poor man's Nashville. At an MSRP of $1100, about a third of the retail cost of the Professional Collection 6120 archtops, these budget models were an effort to provide a new generation of players an affordable entry into the Gretsch hollowbody experience. This will be a critical market segment for the Gretsch brand to infiltrate as the Baby Boomer demographic, which served to subsidize the rebirth of the Gretsch brand begins to shrink.

Photo Courtesy of Steve Wilson.

A reproduction Chet Atkins signpost pickguard was added to this orange-stained Electromatic archtop step-child, which brings out more of the family resemblance to the grand old 6120 model flagship. *Photo Courtesy of Steve Wilson.*

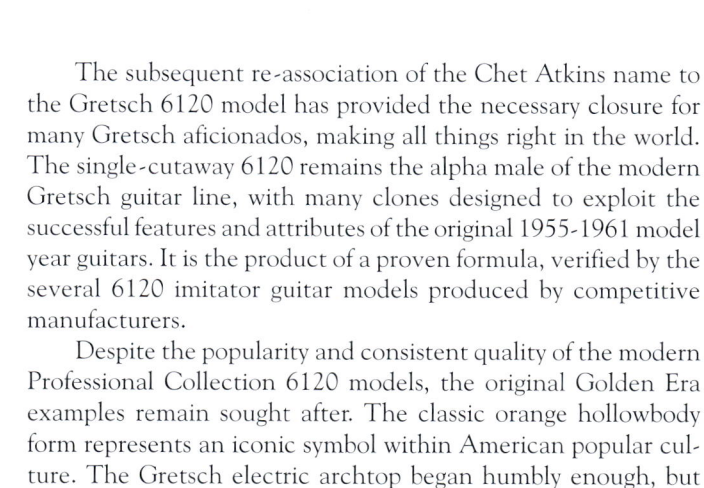

The subsequent re-association of the Chet Atkins name to the Gretsch 6120 model has provided the necessary closure for many Gretsch aficionados, making all things right in the world. The single-cutaway 6120 remains the alpha male of the modern Gretsch guitar line, with many clones designed to exploit the successful features and attributes of the original 1955-1961 model year guitars. It is the product of a proven formula, verified by the several 6120 imitator guitar models produced by competitive manufacturers.

Despite the popularity and consistent quality of the modern Professional Collection 6120 models, the original Golden Era examples remain sought after. The classic orange hollowbody form represents an iconic symbol within American popular culture. The Gretsch electric archtop began humbly enough, but as a result of environmental changes within the marketplace, including significant cultural modernization and technological advancements, descent with modification served to shed away the extraneous traits and features and emphasized the advantageous ones. The 1950s were an incubator for these changes and several generations of electric archtop guitars were produced in relatively rapid succession, manifesting a classic, albeit accelerated, example of natural selection.

This gorgeous 1960 model year Chet Atkins 6120 (batch #337xx) is the epitome of the form. Its distinctive tone is matched only by its bold aesthetic. It is an American classic. *Guitar Courtesy of Chris Guido. Photo by Rick Burda.*

Photo Courtesy of Steve Wilson.

As was the case in the 1950s, FMIC/Gretsch will have to continue to devise ways to maintain the 6120 model's relevance as the world around it changes. Today, however, the current market, musical environment, manufacturing excellence, and expansive product offering have led many to postulate that now is, in fact, the new Golden Era for the Gretsch brand. It will be incumbent on the leadership of FMIC/Gretsch to learn from the past and to avoid becoming complacent in a dynamic environment. Even the most perfect of species can be impacted by change, made less relevant, or influenced to mutate into less successful forms. Awareness and anticipation of new cultural drivers, artistic tastes, and technological enablers will be as critical to the success of the brand tomorrow as it was in 1955. But for now, and as long as cool remains in vogue, and people seek to communicate through high volume sonic expression, the Gretsch electric archtop will survive. And sitting at the top of that particular family tree, will no doubt be the King of the Jungle, the legendary Gretsch 6120 hollowbody model.

A limited edition 6120 model crafted by the Gretsch Custom Shop and master builder Stephen Stern to commemorate the 125th Anniversary of The Gretsch Company was introduced at the 2008 Winter NAMM in Anaheim, California. It was finished with a transparent orange stain over actual gold leaf to produce a unique visual appearance. All the hardware is gold-plated, including the two TV Jones Classic Filter'Tron pickups. The guitar has vintage appointments including a V-style Bigsby vibrato, neoclassic fretboard markers, trestle bracing, and a 2.75" deep body. Gretsch only made 25 of these G6120-125 guitars, which came with a special Gretsch 125th Anniversary tooled leather strap and belt buckle. The introductory MSRP was $12,500.

Guitar Courtesy of Music Zoo. Photo by Tim Reynolds.

In the summer of 2008 FMIC/Gretsch released yet another limited edition 6120 model. Introduced with great fanfare, the G6120-CGP Chet Atkins Stereo guitar was unveiled at the 24th annual Chet Atkins Appreciation Society (CAAS) convention in Nashville, Tennessee. Atkins' close friend and collaborator Paul Yandell made the official announcement. Yandell also played a significant role in the design of this new model, of which only 75 first-production run units were created. The guitar's concept was inspired by, and fashioned after, the famous 1955 red sealed-top prototype that Atkins frequently used to record with in the 1950s. Features that reflect that vintage prototype include the simulated f-holes, mismatched B6 base with Chet Atkins handle, and the plain block fretboard markers that the original prototype displayed after its neck was replaced in 1957. The big technical advancement of the original 1955 sealed-top guitar was its Ray Butts designed prototypical Filter'Tron pickups, represented with aesthetic authenticity on the 6120-CGP by white bobbin dual-coil units made specifically for this model by Tom TV Jones. The guitar featured a flip switch to engage the stereo mode, isolating the low E, A, and D strings to a separate output jack from the G, B, and E strings. The limited nature of this first edition G6120-CGP made it a very popular release at its MSRP of $3850.

Guitar Courtesy of Fred Stucky.

Bibliography

Atkins, Chet. *Chet Atkins, Me and My Guitars*, (Milwaukee. Wisconsin: Hal Leonard Corporation, 2003).

Bacon, Tony. *The Ultimate Guitar Book*. (London, England: Dorling Kindersley Limited, 1991).

Bacon, Tony. *Fifty Years of Gretsch Electrics*. (San Francisco, California: Backbeat Books, 2005).

Brookes, Tim. *Guitar: An American Life*. (New York, New York: Grove Press, 2005).

Brooks, Michael. "Pete Townshend Interview." *Guitar Player* magazine (May-June 1972).

Duffy, Dan. *Inside the Gretsch Guitar Factory*. (Victoria, British Columbia: Trafford Publishing, 2005).

Duffy, Dan. Online comments. (The Gretsch Pages: http://gretschpages.com, 2006-2007).

Gagliano, Greg. "The Decline of the Guitar Industry: Then and Now." *20ᵗʰ Century Guitar* magazine (November 1999).

Gregory, Hugh. *1000 Great Guitarists*. (San Francisco, California: Miller Freeman Books/GPI Books, 1994).

Gruhn, George, and Walter Carter. *Electric Guitars and Basses, A Photographic History*. (San Francisco, California: Miller Freeman Books/GPI Books, 1994).

Kyle, Dave. "An Interview With Ray Butts." *Vintage Guitar Magazine,* (November 1994).

Landers, Rick. "Fred Gretsch Interview." *Modern Guitars Magazine* (September 2007)

Sallis, James. *The Guitar Players*. (Lincoln, Nebraska: University of Nebraska Press/Bison Books, 1982).

Scott, Jay. *The Guitars of the Fred Gretsch Company*. (Fullerton, California: Centerstream Publishing, 1992).

Soros, Bianca. "Gretsch Synchromatics and the Steamline Style."*Vintage Gallery* magazine (April 1995).

Webster, Jimmie. *The Touch System for Electric and Amplified Spanish Guitar*. (New York, New York: Wm. J. Smith Music Company, 1952).

Wheeler, Tom. *American Guitars, An Illustrated History*. (New York, New York: HarperCollins Publishers, 1992).

Appraisal Guide (average retail values with range for condition)

Model Year	Model	Batch	Notes	Appraisal Range
1939-1941	no #	all	Electromatic Spanish, first Gretsch electric archtop (Kay made)	$750-1200
1949-1953	6185	all	Electromatic, single pickup, non-cutaway	$1000-1500
1951-1953	6187-8	all	Electro II, dual-pickup, non-cutaway	$1200-1700
1951-1953	6192-3	all	Electro II, 17", dual-pickup, single cutaway	$1700-2500
1953-1958	6192	all	Country Club, sunburst	$1700-2500
1953-1958	6193	all	Country Club, natural	$1900-2750
1953-1958	6196	all	Country Club, Cadillac Green	$2800-4000
1959-1965	6192	all	Country Club, sunburst	$1700-2500
1959-1965	6193	all	Country Club, natural	$1700-2500
1959-1965	6196	all	Country Club, Cadillac Green	$2200-3200
1953-1956	6182	all	Corvette, single pickup, sunburst	$900-1500
1953-1956	6183	all	Corvette, single pickup, natural	$1000-1700
1953-1956	6184	all	Corvette, single pickup, Jaguar Tan	$1200-2000
1953	6190-1	all	Pre-Streamliner Electromatic, single pickup, single cutaway	$1000-1500
1954-1958	6190	all	Streamliner, sunburst	$1200-1800
1954-1958	6191	all	Streamliner, natural	$1500-2300
1954	6189	all	Streamliner, Jaguar Tan	$1800-2800
1955-1958	6189	all	Streamliner, Bamboo Ivory/Copper Mist	$1500-2300
1955	6120	16450-16550	Chet Atkins hollowbody, Western, inaugural batch	$10K-13K
1955	6120	169xx	Chet Atkins hollowbody, Western, Eddie Cochran batch	$10K-13K
1955	6120	173xx	Chet Atkins hollowbody, Western	$10K-13K
1955	6121	all	Chet Atkins solidbody	$11K-15K
1956	6120	182xx	Chet Atkins hollowbody, Western, large truss rod cover, enamel Bigsby	$9K-12K
1956	6120	185xx	Chet Atkins hollowbody, Western	$9K-12K
1956	6120	189xx	Chet Atkins hollowbody, Western, breakaway Bigsby	$10K-13K
1956	6120	200xx	Chet Atkins hollowbody, Western, breakaway Bigsby	$10K-13K
1956	6120	208xx	Chet Atkins hollowbody, Western	$9K-12K
1956	6121	all	Chet Atkins solidbody	$11K-15K
1957	6120	216xx	Chet Atkins hollowbody, no G-brand, hump block markers	$9K-12K
1957	6120	220xx	Chet Atkins hollowbody	$9K-12K
1957	6120	224xx	Chet Atkins hollowbody	TBD
1957	6120	232xx	Chet Atkins hollowbody	$9K-12K
1957	6120	234xx	Chet Atkins hollowbody, small batch (50)	$9K-12K
1957	6120	250xx	Chet Atkins hollowbody	$9K-12K
1957	6120	253xx	Chet Atkins hollowbody	$9K-12K
1957	6120	258xx	Chet Atkins hollowbody, Duane Eddy batch (70)	$10K-13K
1957	6121	all	Chet Atkins solidbody	$11K-15K
1958	6120	258xx	Chet Atkins hollowbody, neoclassic markers, trestle bracing, small group (30)	$9K-12K
1958	6120	265xx	Chet Atkins hollowbody, Filter'Tron pickups	$9K-12K
1958	6120	269xx	Chet Atkins hollowbody	$9K-12K
1958	6120	276xx	Chet Atkins hollowbody	$9K-12K
1958	6120	284xx	Chet Atkins hollowbody	$9K-12K

1958	6121	all	Chet Atkins solidbody	$11K-15K
1959	6120	293xx	Chet Atkins hollowbody, zero fret	$10K-13K
1959	6120	299xx	Chet Atkins hollowbody	$10K-13K
1959	6120	307xx	Chet Atkins hollowbody	$10K-13K
1959	6120	312xx	Chet Atkins hollowbody, light bracing	$11K-15K
1959	6120	316xx	Chet Atkins hollowbody	$11K-15K
1959	6120	322xx	Chet Atkins hollowbody, small batch (50)	$11K-15K
1959	6120	325xx	Chet Atkins hollowbody, small batch (50)	$11K-15K
1959	6121	all	Chet Atkins solidbody	$11K-15K
1960	6120	330xx	Chet Atkins hollowbody, V-style Bigsby, Brian Setzer batch	$13K-17K
1960	6120	337xx	Chet Atkins hollowbody, 2.5" body, Brian Setzer batch	$13K-17K
1960	6120	341xx	Chet Atkins hollowbody, small batch (50)	$9K-12K
1960	6120	345xx	Chet Atkins hollowbody, Brian Setzer batch	$11K-15K
1960	6120	354xx	Chet Atkins hollowbody	$9K-12K
1960	6120	359xx	Chet Atkins hollowbody, Entwistle batch, flame grain	$12K-16K
1960	6120	367xx	Chet Atkins hollowbody	$9K-12K
1960	6120	376xx	Chet Atkins hollowbody	$9K-12K
1960	6120	388xx	Chet Atkins hollowbody	$9K-12K
1960	6120	394xx	Chet Atkins hollowbody	$9K-12K
1960	6121	all	Chet Atkins solidbody	$11K-15K
1961	6120	395xx	Chet Atkins hollowbody, 2.25" body, small batch (50)	$7K-10K
1961	6120	398xx	Chet Atkins hollowbody	$7K-10K
1961	6120	407xx	Chet Atkins hollowbody	$7K-10K
1961	6120	413xx	Chet Atkins hollowbody	$7K-10K
1961	6120	423xx	Chet Atkins hollowbody	$7K-10K
1961	6120	428xx	Chet Atkins hollowbody	$7K-10K
1961	6120	431xx	Chet Atkins hollowbody, standby switch	$7K-10K
1961	6120	446xx	Chet Atkins hollowbody, small batch (50)	$7K-10K
1961	6121	all	Chet Atkins solidbody	$11K-15K
1962	6120	all	Chet Atkins hollowbody, Electrotone body, dial-up mute	$3000-4500
1962	6121	all	Chet Atkins solidbody, double cutaway	$11K-15K
1963-1965	6120	all	Chet Atkins hollowbody, red felt mute lever	$2000-3500
1966-1972	6120	all	Nashville, black felt mute lever, headstock plaque	$2000-3500
1972-1980	7660	all	Nashville, maroon finish, open f-holes, Burns gearbox	$1500-2300

Index

References to images and photographs are printed in boldface type.